Augustine, Martyrdom, and Classical Rhetoric

Augustine, Martyrdom, and Classical Rhetoric

ADAM PLOYD

Wesley House, Cambridge

OXFORD
UNIVERSITY PRESS

Oxford University Press is a department of the University of Oxford. It furthers
the University's objective of excellence in research, scholarship, and education
by publishing worldwide. Oxford is a registered trade mark of Oxford University
Press in the UK and certain other countries.

Published in the United States of America by Oxford University Press
198 Madison Avenue, New York, NY 10016, United States of America.

© Oxford University Press 2023

All rights reserved. No part of this publication may be reproduced, stored in
a retrieval system, or transmitted, in any form or by any means, without the
prior permission in writing of Oxford University Press, or as expressly permitted
by law, by license, or under terms agreed with the appropriate reproduction
rights organization. Inquiries concerning reproduction outside the scope of the
above should be sent to the Rights Department, Oxford University Press, at the
address above.

You must not circulate this work in any other form
and you must impose this same condition on any acquirer.

Library of Congress Cataloging-in-Publication Data
Names: Ployd, Adam, author.
Title: Augustine, martyrdom, and classical rhetoric / Adam Ployd.
Description: New York, NY : Oxford University Press, 2023. |
Includes bibliographical references and index.
Identifiers: LCCN 2022061051 (print) | LCCN 2022061052 (ebook) |
ISBN 9780190914141 (hardback) | ISBN 9780190914165 (epub) |
ISBN 9780190914158 | ISBN 9780190914172
Subjects: LCSH: Augustine, of Hippo, Saint, 354–430. |
Martyrdom—Christianity. | Martyrs—Cult. | Rhetoric, Ancient.
Classification: LCC BR65.A9 P56 2023 (print) | LCC BR65.A9 (ebook) |
DDC 270.2092—dc23/eng/20230119
LC record available at https://lccn.loc.gov/2022061051
LC ebook record available at https://lccn.loc.gov/2022061052

DOI: 10.1093/oso/9780190914141.001.0001

Printed by Integrated Books International, United States of America

*In loving memory of Christopher Riddle Ployd,
whose memory provides examples of many virtues
and just the right number of vices*

Contents

Acknowledgments — ix
Abbreviations — xi

Introduction — 1

1. The Context of the Martyrs — 8
   Introduction — 8
   The Cult of the Martyrs in North Africa — 9
   The Cult of the Martyrs in Augustine — 14
   Martyrs and Manichaeanism — 20
   Martyrs and Pelagianism — 24
   Conclusion — 31

2. The Example of the Martyrs — 33
   Introduction — 33
   Exempla in Classical Rhetoric — 35
   Exemplum exemplorum: Christ as Model Martyr — 39
   Exempla martyrum — 42
   Exempla contra cultum — 45
   Ἐτυμολογία and *Adnominatio* — 49
   Exempla and Ἐτυμολογία — 54
   Conclusion — 59

3. The Time of the Martyrs — 61
   Introduction — 61
   Rhetoric, Historiography, and *Exempla* of Virtue — 62
   A Trans-Historical Enemy — 69
   Antithetical Beauty — 73
   The Martyrs within Antithetical History — 78
   Conclusion — 81

4. The Court of the Martyrs — 83
   Introduction — 83
   Non poena sed causa — 84
   For Their Own Good — 95
   Conclusion — 107

5. The Rhetoric of the Martyrs — 109
   Introduction — 109
   Classical Ideals — 110
   Augustinian Transformations — 118
   The Martyrs as Ideal Christian Rhetor-Statesmen — 124
   Conclusion — 134

Conclusion — 135

Bibliography — 143
Subject Index — 155
Writings Index — 161

Acknowledgments

This book began as a short communication at the International Patristics Conference at Oxford in 2015. Since that brief paper, this project has been supported by a host of colleagues, students, and friends. My memory is too feeble to remember them all. But I would be remiss not to name those who do come to mind, with sincerest apologies to those I neglect.

First and foremost, I give thanks for the loving support of my wife, Diane Kenaston, and for the inspiration of our son, Isaac, who came into this world midway through completion of this project. Both have provided the laughter and encouragement needed to keep going on a book that all too often seemed like it would never materialize.

At the top of the list of the many patristics and early Christianity scholars who have strengthened this work, I must name my doktorvater, Lewis Ayres, who repeatedly advised me not to let go of what he assured me was a promising project. Many other colleagues offered advice, read drafts, or otherwise served as conversation partners along the way. These include, in no particular order, Diane Fruchtman, Emily Cain, Anthony Dupont, J. Patout Burns, Elizabeth Castelli, David Hunter, Ian McFarland, Brian Gronewoller, Michael Cameron, Rafał Toczko, and so many more.

This work arose within particular institutional contexts, without whose support it would not have been completed. I therefore express my fulsome gratitude to the faculty, staff, and students of Eden Theological Seminary in St. Louis and of Wesley House, Cambridge.

Portions of chapters 1 and 4 previously appeared as "*Non poena sed causa*: Augustine's Anti-Donatist Rhetoric of Martyrdom," *Augustinian Studies* 49 (2018): 25–44 and "For Their Own Good: Augustine and the Rhetoric of Beneficial Persecution," in *Heirs of Roman Persecution: Studies on a Christian and Para-Christian Discourse in Late Antiquity*, edited by Eric Fournier (London: Routledge, 2019), 95–111. Part of chapter 3 previously appeared as "Augustine, Martyrdom, and the Exemplary Rhetoric of History," *Journal of Early Christian Studies* 28 (2020): 423–41. An earlier version of chapter 5 previously appeared as "Augustine's Martyrs as Ideal Christian Rhetors," *Augustiniana* 71 (2021): 27–43. I am grateful to the respective publishers for permission to include revised versions of these texts in this book.

Abbreviations

CCSL	*Corpus Christianorum. Series Latina*
Chadwick	Henry Chadwick, trans., *Confessions*
CSEL	*Corpus Scriptorum Ecclesiasticorum Latinorum*
LCL	Loeb Classical Library
MA	*Miscellanea Agostiniana*
O'Donnell	J. J. O'Donnell, ed., *Augustine: Confessions*
OOSA	*Sancti Ambrosii Mediolanensis Episcopi Opera Omnia*
PL	*Patrologiae Cursus Completus, Series Latina*
PLS	Supplement to the *Patrologiae Cursus Completus, Series Latina*
RB	*Revue Bénédictine*
SE	*Sacris Erudiri*
SPM	*Stromata Patristica et Mediaevalia*
WSA	The Works of Saint Augustine

For titles of specific works of Augustine and others, see the bibliography.

Introduction

"The blood of the martyrs is the seed of the church." Tertullian never said that. He did say, "The blood of Christians is seed." But this common misquotation is not far off from what he meant. Tertullian had in mind the ironically persuasive effect that persecution supposedly had on Christianity's numerical increase:

> Whenever we are mown down by you, we grow even more numerous. The blood of Christians is seed! Many of your own people encourage enduring pain and death, like Cicero in the Tusculans, or Seneca in his Chances, or Diogenes, or Pyrrhus, or Callinicus; and yet their words do not find as many disciples as the deeds of Christians do. That obstinacy itself, which you condemn, is the teacher. For who, contemplating it, is not roused to investigate what lies at the heart of it? Who, when he has investigated, does not assent [to Christianity]? And when he has assented, who does not long to suffer that he might obtain the full grace of God, that he might procure from God complete forgiveness, by the compensation of his blood?[1]

Martyrdom performs a rhetorical function for Tertullian. Just as treasured "pagan" authors seek to persuade their readers to brave endurance with words—that is, with literary rhetoric—so the actions of the martyrs accomplish the same thing, exhorting others, by the eloquence of their endurance unto death, to examine what could inspire such heroic commitment. Having responded to martyrdom's wooing, as it were, the explorer themself becomes an adherent to the doctrines of the church to the extent that they too might give their blood to share in God's forgiving grace.

While Tertullian depicts the martyrs and their martyrdoms as rhetorically efficacious, it is Tertullian himself who is doing the rhetorical work, at least

---

[1] Tertullian, *apol.* 50 (CCSL 1:171). Unless otherwise noted, all translations are my own. Blake Leyerle has placed the famous phrase, "the blood of Christians is seed," within the context of Jewish ritual understandings of blood, an appreciation that further expands the rhetorical scope of this image. See Leyerle, "Blood Is Seed," *Journal of Religion* 81 (2001): 26–48.

from an historical perspective. He is the one who constructs the martyrs as persuasive. Whether or not he accurately represents the growth of the church vis-à-vis persecution, the argument questions not only the legitimacy of persecution but also its efficacy. The martyrs are his rhetorical tools whose significance he can craft with skill. In this case, they become, in their persuasive power, agents of God's providence, subverting the powers of this world for the building up of God's church. In a theological sense, then, God is the rhetor, "speaking" the martyrs' deaths for the sake of persuasion, conversion, and, by these means, salvation.

At one level, in this book I argue that Augustine does the same thing that Tertullian does. For both of them, the martyrs are rhetorical, both in the sense that the martyrs are the subject of rhetorical skill and in the sense that the martyrs are themselves depicted as persuasive. Further, both Tertullian and Augustine do so for particular theological ends.

But that level of analysis is only the starting place for this study. The heart of my argument lies in how Augustine accomplishes this goal and what his particular theological ends are, especially in a postpersecution context.

To allude once more to Tertullian,[2] martyrs are not born; they are constructed and, when necessary, reconstructed. Martyrs and martyrdom are not static categories or events, but culturally powerful artifacts and tools of communal memory and social persuasion. Over the last few decades, scholars of early Christian martyrdom have come to emphasize the way in which martyr accounts reflect efforts to shape identity and ideology within and between Christian communities.[3] By now it is de rigueur to describe early Christian martyr discourse as "rhetorical," signaling that texts and (for some) their authors are doing more than merely reporting facts; they are interpreting facts, sometimes creating them, and always deploying them to accomplish some persuasive end.

This rhetorical turn in martyr studies, though firmly established, still leaves much work to be done in understanding the mechanics and significance of martyr rhetoric in late antique Christianity. Much (though not

---

[2] Tertullian, *apol.* 18: "Christians are made, not born."
[3] E.g., Candida Moss, *The Myth of Persecution: How Early Christians Invented a Story of Martyrdom* (New York: HarperCollins, 2013); Moss, *The Other Christs: Imitating Jesus in Ancient Christian Ideologies of Martyrdom* (New York: Oxford University Press, 2010); Elizabeth Castelli, *Martyrdom and Memory: Early Christian Culture Making* (New York: Columbia University Press, 2004); Lucy Grig, *Making Martyrs in Late Antiquity* (London: Bristol Classical Press, 2004). On theorizing the concept of "martyrdom" from an interdisciplinary perspective, see Michaela DeSoucey, Jo-Ellen Pozner, Corey Fields, Kerry Dobransky, and Gary Alan Fine, "Memory and Sacrifice: An Embodied Theory of Martyrdom," *Cultural Sociology* 2 (2008): 99–121.

all[4]) of the rhetorical analysis provided so far uses categories derived from modern theorists, and fruitfully so. But, having identified the rhetorical nature of these texts and of the larger discourse on martyrdom, more analysis is also needed that draws upon the rhetorical theory and practice of the late antique world if we are to perceive how the cultural tools available to early Christian authors are actively deployed for various ends. Moreover, there is need for theologians to engage more robustly with these historiographical developments.

In this study, I seek to fill these lacunae by examining the work of Augustine.[5] Augustine is an appropriate source for at least two reasons. First, his treatises, letters, and especially sermons are filled with discussions of martyrs and martyrdom. Whether he is preaching on a particular saint's feast day or reflecting on his mother's practices within the cult of the martyrs, Augustine has the martyrs ever on the tips of both his tongue and his pen. Because martyrdom is a perennial theme for the bishop of Hippo, he provides a rich well from which to draw on the subject.[6]

---

[4] See, e.g., the discussion of ἔκφρασις in Diane Fruchtman, "Living in a Martyrial World: Living Martyrs and the Creation of Martyrial Consciousness in the Late Antique Latin West" (PhD diss., Indiana University, 2014); and the analysis of encomium and panegyric in Pauline Allen et al., *"Let Us Die That We May Live": Greek Homilies on Christian Martyrs from Asia Minor, Palestine and Syria* (c. AD 350–AD 450) (London: Routledge, 2003).

[5] For the *status quaestionis* on martyrdom in Augustine, see Anthony Dupont, "Augustine's Homiletic Definition of Martyrdom: The Centrality of the Martyr's Grace in His Anti-Donatist and Anti-Pelagian *Sermones ad Populum*," in *Christian Martyrdom in Late Antiquity (300–450 AD): History and Discourse, Tradition and Religious Identity*, ed. Peter Gemeinhardt and Johan Leemans (Berlin: DeGruyter, 2012), 155–78, esp. 155–61.

[6] Oddly, this book is the first monograph on Augustine and martyrdom in English. This is not to say that the topic has gone unexamined. Numerous shorter studies exist, as suggested above. In addition to Dupont, "Augustine's Homiletic Definition of Martyrdom," see Dupont, *Preacher of Grace: A Critical Reappraisal of Augustine's Doctrine of Grace in His Sermones ad Populum on Liturgical Feasts and during the Donatist Controversy* (Leiden: Brill, 2014), 137–59; Collin Garbarino, "Augustine, Donatists, and Martyrdom," in *An Age of Saints? Power, Conflict, and Dissent in Early Medieval Christianity*, ed. Peeter Sarris, Matthew Dal Santo, and Phil Booth (Leiden: Brill, 2011), 49–61; Dupont, "*Imitatio Christi, Imitatio Stephani*: Augustine's Thinking on Martyrdom Based on His *Sermones* on the Protomartyr Stephen," *Augustiniana* 56 (2006): 29–61; Tarcisius van Bavel, "The Cult of Martyrs in St. Augustine: Theology versus Popular Religion?," in *Martyrium in Multidisciplinary Perspective*, ed. Mathijs Lamberigts and Peter van Deun (Leuven: Peeters, 1995), 351–56; Jan den Boeft, "'*Martyres sunt, sed homines fuerunt*': Augustine on Martyrdom," in *Fructus Centesimus: Mélanges offerts à Gereard J. M. Bartelink à l'occasion de son soixante-cinquième anniversaire*, ed. A. A. R. Bastiaensen, A. Hilhorst, and C. H. Kneepkens (Turnhout: Brepols, 1989), 115–24; C. P. Mayer, "'*Attende Stephanum conservum tuum*' (*Serm.* 317, 2, 3). Sinn und Wert der Märtyrerverehrung nach den Stephanuspredigten Augustins," in Fructus Centesimus, 217–37; A. A. R. Bastiaensen, "Quelques observations sur la terminologie du martyre chez saint Augustin," in *Signum Pietatis: Festgabe für Cornelius Petrus Mayer OSA zum 60. Geburtstag*, ed. Adolar Zumkeller (Würzburg: Augustinus-Verlag, 1989), 201–16; M. Pellegrino, "Chiesa e martirio in Sant'Agostino," in *Richerche Patristiche* 1 (Torino, 1982), 507–633; M. Pellegrino, "Christo e il martire nel pensiero di Sant'Agostino," in *Richerche Patristiche* 1, 633–68; A.-M. La Bonnardière, "Les Enarrationes in Psalmos prêchées par saint Augustin à l'occasion de fêtes de martyrs," *Recherches Augustiniennes et Patristiques* 7 (1971): 73–104; Cyrille Lambot, "Les sermons de saint Augustin pour les fêtes de

4 INTRODUCTION

Second, Augustine, prior to his conversion to Catholic Christianity, was a professional rhetor, selling his skill to student and emperor alike. Later he deployed the full range of his craft not only in preaching but also in his literary output. He wrestled with the morality of rhetoric and created an influential Christian vision of the art. Few late antique Christian figures would be as fruitful a source for investigating what it means to call martyr discourse rhetorical. Indeed, my argument draws on a newer way of reading Augustine's rhetoric, for only now are scholars beginning to take notice of the argumentative aspects of his rhetoric, and not just the stylistic.[7]

I argue that Augustine's martyr discourse may be considered rhetorical in three ways. First, Augustine develops and deploys his understanding of

---

martyrs," *Analecta Bollandiana* 67 (1949): 249–66. The closest thing we have to a monograph study in English is Elena Martin, "*Sanctae Famulae Dei*: Towards a Reading of Augustine's Female Martyrs" (PhD thesis, Durham University, 2009). Even outside of English, monographic treatments are hard to come by. See esp. Guy Lapointe, *La celebration des martyrs en Afrique d'après les sermons de saint Augustin* (Montreal, 1972). For a more specific focus, see Wojciech Lazewski, "La Sentenza Agostiniana Martyrem Facit Non Poena Sed Causa" (PhD diss., Pontificia Universitas Lateranensis, 1987). One oft-repeated theme in the literature that I will not engage, but which is worth acknowledging here, is the periodization of Augustine's martyr texts. I accept the traditional threefold delineation: 309–401 (in which he battled cultic excesses), 401–15 (a period defined by Donatist concerns and therefore more constructive engagement with martyrdom), and 415–30 (a more enthusiastic period of martyr promotion following the discovery of the relics of the proto-martyr Stephen). On this periodization, see Victor Saxer, *Morts, martyrs, reliques en Afrique chrétienne aux premiers siècles. Les témoignages de Tertullien, Cyprien et Augusttine à l'archéologie africaine.* Theologie historique 55 (Paris: Beauchesne, 1980), 124; van Bavel, "The Cult of the Martyrs," 351–61; and Dupont, "Augustine's Homiletic Definition of Martyrdom," 157 n.7. My lack of discussion of this periodization comes from my agreement with van Bavel, "The Cult of the Martyrs," 361: "The conclusion of this paper is that after his conversion Augustine never repudiated the cult of the martyrs, but that new facts and experiences were at the origin of some changes, while his theological insights remained essentially the same. What he always refuted were the—in his eyes—theologically wrong interpretations of the cult of the martyrs."

[7] See esp. Rafał Toczko, Crimen Obicere: *Forensic Rhetoric and Augustine's Anti-Donatist Correspondence*. Forschungen zur Kirchen- und Dogmengeschichte 120 (Göttingen: Vandenhoeck & Ruprecht Verlag, 2020). Although Henri-Irenée Marrou, *Saint Augustin et la fin de la culture antique*, 4th ed. (Paris: Éditions E. de Boccard, 1958) remains important for Augustine's engagement with late antique grammatical and rhetorical culture, several recent works have rehabilitated our appreciation for the way these liberal arts shaped Augustine's scriptural interpretation and theology. See esp. Michael Cameron, *Christ Meets Me Everywhere: Augustine's Early Figurative Exegesis* (New York: Oxford, 2012); Robert Dodaro, "Language Matters: Augustine's Use of Literary Decorum in Theological Argument," *Augustinian Studies* 45, no. 1 (2014): 1–28; Lewis Ayres, "Into the Poem of the Universe: *Exempla*, Conversion, and Church in Augustine's *Confessiones*," *Zeitschrift für antikes Christentum* 13 (2009): 263–81; Dodaro, "Literary Decorum in Scriptural Exegesis: Augustine of Hippo, *Epistula* 138," in *L'esegi di Padri Latini, Dalle origini a Gregorio Magno* (Rome: Institutum Patristicum Augustinianum, 2000), 1:159–74; Dodaro, "*Quid deceat videre* (Cicero, *Orator* 70): Literary Propriety and Doctrinal Orthodoxy in Augustine of Hippo," in *Orthodoxie, christianisme, histoire*, ed. Susanna Elm et al. (Rome: École Française de Rome, 2000), 57–81; Dodaro, "The Theologian as Grammarian: Literary Decorum in Augustine's Defense of Orthodox Discourse," *Studia Patristica* 38 (2001): 70–83.

martyrdom within particular rhetorical contexts. This is the weakest and most general sense of "rhetorical" that will appear in this study, falling short of, yet providing the necessary context for, the more technical analyses that make up the heart of the book. Chapter 1 establishes these cultural contexts, emphasizing the development of martyr discourse within North Africa up to and including the Donatist controversy and Augustine's personal encounter with the practices associated with the cult. This chapter further looks at two polemical contexts—the Manichaean and Pelagian controversies—that are not typically associated with martyrdom. By highlighting these unusual polemical contexts, I emphasize the ubiquity of martyr rhetoric within Augustine's larger theological oeuvre.

The second way in which Augustine's martyr discourse may be considered rhetorical is that he uses techniques of classical rhetorical argumentation to construct his martyrs and to create their theological significance. Here I am not primarily referring to techniques of ornamentation or style, although these will occasionally appear. Rather, I mean those techniques more associated with the category of *inventio* and to some degree *dispositio*. To this end, Chapter 2 takes up the tool of *exempla* to elucidate Augustine's most common use of martyrs, that is, as models for spiritual imitation. This theme is accentuated by examining a particular construction of *exempla*, a method I call "nominal etymology" whereby the names of the martyrs become the keys to their exemplary significance.

Chapter 3 remains in the realm of *exempla*, now understood within the context of Roman historiography. Here I demonstrate that Augustine's use of the martyrs as exemplary Christians serves to construct a Christian historiography that rejects the Roman penchant for narratives of decline. The chapter concludes with Augustine's depiction of the martyrs as beautiful, despite, or indeed because of, their grotesque sufferings. His use of rhetorical antithesis not only highlights the contrast between the martyrs and the beauty of this world but also reflects his understanding of God's providential ordering of history in which the martyrs take part.

Chapter 4 turns to the field of forensic rhetoric and Augustine's conflict with the Donatists. Here I argue that Augustine's famous slogan, that it is the cause not the punishment that makes a martyr, is best understood within the realm of legal issue theory as an issue of definition. The second half of this chapter turns from the issue of definition to an issue of quality. Taken together, these two issues point to the ever-present legal context within which the Donatist controversy took place, all parties jockeying for imperial favor or legitimacy, often with claims to martyrdom at the center of such contestation.

The third and final way in which I claim Augustine's martyr discourse may be considered rhetorical is that, in his depiction, the martyrs themselves are ideal Christian rhetors. I tackle this claim in Chapter 5, tracing the Greco-Roman tradition of the ideal rhetor alongside Augustine's Christianization of the theme to show how his martyrs embody it. As ideal rhetors, however, Augustine's martyrs play another significant role, that is, as the ideal Christian statesmen. While it is well known that martyrs would reign with Christ after their deaths, as ideal rhetor-statesmen Augustine's martyrs, though not holding temporal power, operate as agents of Christ working to establish the city of God within this world. Thus, Augustine imbues the martyrs with their own rhetorical power, or, rather, he identifies the way in which they are Christ's rhetors, exhorting all to leave behind the things of this world and cling to those of heaven, to become citizens of the city of God whose virtues they model. On the one hand, this approach is merely an extension of Augustine's own rhetorical agency. On the other, it suggests a deeper meaning for a bishop who believed his own oratorical skill to be in the service of salvific, divine persuasion.

My argument does not rest only in the rhetorical world. There is also a theological angle to this study. The central theme that will soon become apparent is the way in which Augustine uses the martyrs to reorient the spiritual vision of his readers and hearers. Or, we may more accurately say, it is the way in which Augustine believes that Christ uses the martyrs to direct the vision of all Christians toward the things of true value. At the most basic level, this means leading the faithful to concern themselves with heavenly goods instead of earthly, just as the martyrs are depicted as having done. But delving deeper, we see that the martyrs are more than mere moral exemplars. They are also key figures within the history of the city of God. Inasmuch as they are moral exemplars, they inspire faithful vigilance in a time of perceived peace, reminding the faithful that any period of history is ripe for spiritual persecution. Thus, the martyrs hold a key place within the economy of salvation as they both reveal the divine ordering of history and bridge the divide between the epoch-defining sacrifice of Christ and the seemingly triumphant period of Christian empire. It is in this last context, that of Augustine himself, that Christ uses the martyrs as ideal rhetors and statesmen of the city of God. Within this ultimate role, Augustine's martyrs bring us back around to their original role, as exemplars and exhorters, promoting true piety as the true good of the divine city. But in the end, we will see that this exemplary role is part of Christ's larger work of salvation in history. Indeed, for Augustine, the rhetorical tools that he deploys to construct the meaning of martyrdom are only echoes of the divine work of persuasion that God performs through the martyrs' words, deeds, and memories.

Let us begin, then, by defining the contexts within which these rhetorical and theological moves occur.

1
The Context of the Martyrs

Introduction

Augustine's rhetoric of martyrdom does not arise in a void. He is not constructing a theory of martyrdom removed from the contexts of his polemics and ministry. Rather than an abstract vision of martyrdom, Augustine's rhetoric is grounded in the reality of conflicts within and without his Christian community. To appreciate the more technical aspects of his rhetoric, then, we must first analyze the rhetorical contexts for his efforts. Such is the goal of this chapter.

By "rhetorical contexts" I refer to a more general understanding of rhetoric than I will use for the rest of the book. I consider a rhetorical context to be any context in which the ideas or practices associated with martyrs carry cultural power, making martyrdom the object or means of contestation or construction. I do not mean by the phrase that the contexts are themselves rhetorically constructed—though of course many of them are. Nor do I mean that classical rhetoric is necessarily deployed within those contexts—though of course it often is. My use of the phrase "rhetorical context" represents a simpler, more basic understanding of sociocultural or intellectual contexts in which the meaning of martyrdom or the figures of the martyrs are constructed and contested and, for our purposes, in which Augustine is engaged.

I pursue these rhetorical contexts in four phases. First, I examine the most practical context for martyr discourse: the cult of the martyrs in North Africa. Beginning in the late second century, I trace the significance of martyrdom up to Augustine, concluding with his own engagement with the cult as depicted in the *Confessions*. Next, I examine the most trenchant context for Augustine's martyr rhetoric, that is, the Donatist controversy, a conflict originating in Diocletian's persecution and manifesting in contestation over which communion can claim to be the "church of the martyrs." The final two phases look to Augustine's polemics against the Manichaeans and the Pelagians at the beginning and end of his career, respectively, two contexts that do not deal extensively with martyrdom but which both illustrate the ubiquity of its discursive presence.

The Cult of the Martyrs in North Africa

Although cults of the martyrs were widely observed in one form or another throughout the late antique Christian world, the African church has a strong claim to a unique proclivity.[1] Augustine's rhetoric of martyrdom grows in discursive soil fertilized by over two centuries of persecution memory and hero veneration. Although martyrs and martyrdom appear within Augustine's brief Italian context, as I will discuss later in this chapter, we must begin in North Africa in order to understand the quotidian concern for the topic that shaped his earliest experience of Christianity along with his later ministerial context.

The earliest text we have preserved from Christian North Africa is a martyrdom account, the *Acts of the Scillitan Martyrs*. The text purports to recount the trial of twelve Numidian Christians. They explicitly reject the empire of this world in favor of allegiance to God, proudly and defiantly proclaiming, "I am a Christian." After their death sentence is passed, they offer thanks to God. The author then explains that they were "crowned with martyrdom" and "reign" with the Trinity forever, imagery that will become standard in future martyr discourse.[2] The Scillitan martyrs were still honored with feast days in Augustine's time.[3]

Similar language is used to describe the deaths of Perpetua, Felicitas, and their fellow Christians a generation later. In the *Passion of Perpetua and Felicitas*, a first-hand account from the former woman that is edited with an introduction and conclusion by another hand, we find the same unbending affirmation of Christian identity.[4] Perpetua points to a pitcher, asks if it can be called anything else, and, upon being told "no," proclaims, "Neither can I be called anything other than a Christian."[5] In dreams, Perpetua envisions

---

[1] See Candida Moss, "Martyr Veneration in Late Antique North Africa," in *The Donatist Controversy and Contexts*, ed. Richard Miles (Liverpool: Liverpool University Press, 2016), 54–69.
[2] *Scil.* 13–17; Fabio Ruggiero, ed., *Atti Dei Martiri Scilitani: Introduzione, Testo, Traduzione, Testimonianze e Commento* (Roma: Atti Della Accademia Nazionale Dei Lincei, 1991), 73–74.
[3] See esp. *s.* 299D–F.
[4] See Joyce E. Salisbury, *Perpetua's Passion: The Death and Memory of a Young Roman Woman* (New York: Routledge, 1997).
[5] *Perp.* 3; L. Stephanie Cobb, ed., *The Passion of Perpetua and Felicitas in Late Antiquity* (Oakland: University of California Press, 2021), 22–24.

martyrdom as climbing a ladder to heaven by crushing the serpent under her foot and demonstrates the power of confessors and martyrs to intercede for the dead.[6] Most important for the present study, the editor of the text describes this account as containing "examples for the edification of the people" and evincing "other virtues of the Spirit."[7] I will have much to say later about the significance of examples and virtue. For now, it is enough to note that Perpetua and Felicitas also continue to receive veneration in Augustine's day.[8]

Perpetua's contemporary, Tertullian, allows the historian and theologian to move beyond *Acta* and *Passiones* to encounter explicit reflection on and polemics about martyrs and martyrdom.[9] Tertullian discusses the nature and significance of martyrdom repeatedly in his works, even changing his mind regarding the legitimacy of flight during persecution.[10] A representative text is his *Antidote to the Scorpion's Sting*, written against the Valentinian accusation that martyrdom was contrary to the will of the true God. Tertullian argues that martyrdom is in fact a good commanded by God: "The goodness of the very thing, that is, of martyrdom, will prove that God wills it because nothing can be good unless the good one wills it. I contend that martyrdom is good to the very same God by whom idolatry is forbidden and punished. For martyrdom struggles against and is contrary to idolatry. And it is not possible for something to struggle against and be contrary to evil unless it is good."[11] And, most famously, he declares that "the blood of Christians is seed,"[12] often glossed as "the blood of the martyrs is the seed of the church." Tertullian thus represents the beginning of explicit theological reflection on martyrs and martyrdom, its ubiquity in his writings representing the theme's early role within North African Christian self-understanding.

As significant as Tertullian is as a witness to North African theologies of martyrdom, on this topic and in this region no figure looms so large as that of Cyprian of Carthage.[13] As bishop, Cyprian struggled to guide his flock

---

[6] *Perp.* 4, 7–8.
[7] *Perp.* 1; Cobb, *The Passion of Perpetua*, 22.
[8] See *s.* 280–82.
[9] See Saxer, *Morts, martyrs, reliques*, 73–83.
[10] Compare his position in the early texts *pat.* 13.6 and *ux.* 1.3.4 with that of the later *fug.* 4. See Ruth Sutcliffe, "To Flee or Not to Flee: Matthew 10:23 and Third-Century Flight in Persecution," *Scrinium* 14 (2018): 133–60.
[11] Tertullian, *scorp.* 5.3 (CCSL 2:1077).
[12] Tertullian, *apol.* 50 (CCSL 1:171).
[13] The most important work on Cyprian remains J. Patout Burns, *Cyprian the Bishop*, Routledge Early Church Monographs (New York: Routledge, 2002). See also, Saxer, *Morts, martyrs, reliques*, 104–8.

through the Decian and Valerian persecutions of the 250s. Cyprian himself would lose his head under Valerius and become the paradigmatic martyr-bishop of the African church, but before he earned his crown, he wrestled with the vexing practical problems that arise when the spiritual authority of martyrs meets the reality of human frailty. What was to be done with those Christians who lapsed during the persecution, failing to confess Christ in one way or another while their coreligionists suffered exile, torture, and even death? Could such apostasy be forgiven by the church, or must the lapsed remain penitential outside of the church until their death?[14] This question is complicated when confessors, bearing the authority of soon-to-be martyrs, promise to secure the forgiveness of Christ for those who have lapsed. As the church divided into laxist and rigorist factions, Cyprian roped the martyrs into his rhetorical defense of the unity of the church.

Cyprian had to curb the practice of appealing to the authority of the confessors and recent martyrs while not seeming to undermine the honor due to them. His *On the Fallen* walks this rhetorical tightrope by playing upon the pious virtue martyrs necessarily possessed:

> Let no one, most beloved brothers, defame the dignity of the martyrs. Let no one demolish their glories and their crowns. Let the strength of their uncorrupted faith remain unharmed. The one whose faith and hope and strength and glory are all in Christ cannot say or do anything against Christ. Therefore, these [martyrs] who have done the commands of God are not able to be the authorities by which bishops act against the commands of God.[15]

Instead of openly contesting the martyrs' authority to absolve apostates of their sins, Cyprian suggests that laxist bishops who appeal to such martyrial authority in reconciling apostates without a period of penance are acting in a way inconsistent with the faith and righteousness of the martyrs. Similarly, Cyprian appeals to Matt 10:32–33 where Christ affirms that he will not only confess to the Father on behalf of those who confess him but also deny those who deny him. Cyprian uses the North African church's commitment to the first half of this verse—the reward promised to confessors and martyrs—to uphold what he sees as the necessary consequence of the second half, that

---

[14] See esp. the exchange preserved in Cyprian, *ep.* 55.
[15] Cyprian, *laps.* 20 (CCSL 3:232–33).

those who denied Christ cannot be readmitted to the church without performing penance.[16] Cyprian thus appeals to his community's reverence for martyrs in order to undermine what he fears are practical abuses of that reverence in the administration of ecclesial boundaries.

In his other major treatise, *On the Unity of the Church*, Cyprian further circumscribes the authority of martyrdom, this time in the context of schism and competing ecclesial communions associated with Felicissimus in Carthage and Novatian in Rome, the former representing a laxist approach to readmission of the fallen and the latter a rigorist one.[17] In order to deny the legitimacy of their communions, Cyprian must also deny their claim to have true martyrs:

> Such persons [who gather not in Cyprian's church but in the competing communions of Novatian or Felicissimus] will not have this stain washed away by blood, even if they were killed for confessing the name [of Christ]. The crime of discord is serious and inexpiable, and it is not cleansed by suffering. It is not possible for one who is not in the church to be a martyr.[18]

As Augustine does over a century later, Cyprian is working to delimit the scope of martyrdom by denying his opponents' claim to the title. The identity of the North African church is so tied to the martyrs that Cyprian cannot allow a competing communion to claim any of them. Cyprian, therefore, represents the practical significance of martyrdom within North African Christianity as well as the rhetorical power that the martyrs carried. Indeed, Cyprian himself will become the martyr whose authority both Augustine and his opponents will claim as support for their ecclesiological positions.

Cyprian's conflicts represent clear precedents for Augustine's struggles with the Donatists.[19] Not only did Cyprian's own legacy serve as contested

---

[16] Cyprian, *laps.* 20.

[17] On the two versions of *unit. eccl.* and the contexts for each, see Karl Shuve, "Cyprian of Carthage's Writings from the Rebaptism Controversy: Two Revisionary Proposals Reconsidered," *Journal of Theological Studies* 61 (2010): 627–43; Burns, *Cyprian the Bishop*, 93–95. The portion quoted is identical in both versions.

[18] Cyprian, *unit. eccl.* 14 (CCSL 3:259). On the significance of this position, see Allen Brent, "Cyprian's Reconstruction of the Martyr Tradition," *Journal of Ecclesiastical History* 53, no. 2 (2002): 251–63.

[19] On the role of martyrdom in the Donatist conflict, see Brent Shaw, *Sacred Violence: African Christians and Sectarian Hatred in the Age of Augustine* (Cambridge: Cambridge University Press, 2011); Maureen Tilley, *Donatist Martyr Stories: The Church in Conflict in Roman North Africa* (Liverpool: Liverpool University Press, 1996); Anthony Dupont, "Augustine's Homiletic Definition of Martyrdom: The Centrality of the Martyr's Grace in his Anti-Donatist and Anti-Pelagian Sermones ad Populum," in *Christian Martyrdom in Late Antiquity (300–450 AD): History and Discourse,*

ground for the competing communions,[20] but also his struggle to define the limits of a martyr's legitimacy and authority anticipate the way the Donatists will paint themselves as the church of the martyrs and the way Augustine will work to subvert that claim. Augustine himself preserves some of the Donatists' own discourse on martyrdom. For instance, the Donatist bishop Petilian turns the accusation of rebaptism into a discussion of Donatist suffering at the hands of the Catholics: "Blush! Blush, persecutors! You make martyrs who are like Christ; after the true baptism of water, a baptism of blood bathes them."[21] This is the same bishop who declares at the Conference of Carthage in 411, "With us is found the true Catholic Church, that which suffers persecution, not that which inflicts it."[22]

The Donatists even cultivated their own martyr traditions in an effort to shape their particular ecclesial identity. While some of these martyr stories are set during the Diocletianic persecutions or earlier (including a Donatist version of Cyprian's own passion), others take place in more recent contexts, most notably during the repressions carried out under the imperial notary Macarius from 346 to 348.[23] In the *Passion of Isaac and Maximian*, the author identifies the devil as the agent of the Macarian decrees, who "again ordered an agreement of sacrilegious unity established by torture to be celebrated."[24] In the same account, when Isaac is brought before the proconsul, he heroically exclaims, "*Traditores*, come! Preserve your mad unity!"[25] Here we see

---

Tradition and Religious Identity, ed. Peter Gemeinhardt and Johan Leemans (Berlin: DeGruyter, 2012), 161–66; Collin Garbarino, "Augustine, Donatists, and Martyrdom," in *An Age of Saints? Power, Conflict, and Dissent in Early Medieval Christianity*, ed. Peter Sarris, Matthew Dal Santo, and Phil Booth (Leiden: Brill, 2011), 49–61; Alan Dearn, "Donatist Martyrs, Stories, and Attitudes," in *The Donatist Schism*, ed. Richard Miles, 70–100.

[20] On Cyprian's legacy in the Donatist controversy, see Matthew Alan Gaumer, *Augustine's Cyprian: Authority in Roman Africa* (Leiden: Brill, 2016); Gaumer, "Dealing with the Donatist Church: Augustine of Hippo's Nuanced Claim to the Authority of Cyprian of Carthage," in *Cyprian of Carthage: Studies in His Life, Language, and Thought*, ed. Henk Bakker, Paul van Geest, and Hans van Loon (Leuven: Peeters, 2010), 181–202; J. Patout Burns, "Appropriating Augustine Appropriating Cyprian," *Augustinian Studies* 36, no. 1 (2005): 113–37.

[21] Quoted in *c. litt. Pet.* 2.23.51 (CSEL 52:50).

[22] *conl. Carth.* 3.22 (CCSL 149A:184).

[23] In 347, in an effort to establish ecclesial peace in North Africa, the emperor Constans dispatched Macarius, aided by another representative, Paul, to bring the Donatists into Catholic unity. When Donatists protested the efforts, several of them, including a bishop, were imprisoned, were tortured, and either died in prison or were executed. For recent discussions of these events, see Noel Lenski, "Imperial Legislation and the Donatist Controversy: From Constantine to Honorius," in *The Donatist Schism*, ed. Richard Miles, 176–77; and Shaw, *Sacred Violence*, 162–71.

[24] *pass. Isaac* 3 (TU 134:261–62). For more on *pass. Isaac* and its context, see Alan Dearn, "Donatist Martyrs, Stories, and Attitudes," in *The Donatist Schism*, ed. Richard Miles, 80–86; and Tilley, *Donatist Martyr Stories*, 61–62.

[25] *pass. Isaac* 6 (TU 134:165).

the rhetorical power of martyrdom. For all the lofty talk of the good of unity on the Catholic side, the portrayal of heroic martyrdom within these texts turns such unity into demonic blasphemy. The author further heightens this contrast: A large group amasses to honor the titular martyrs. The proconsul has them drowned in the sea. But the sea itself gathers the dead bodies "into one" and washes them all upon the shore, where the living members "rejoiced at the arrival of the temples of Christ."[26] True ecclesial unity, the text suggests, is unity with the martyrs, not a false unity with those who create martyrs through the use of imperial coercion. God uses the sea to create this true martyrial unity between the living and the dead; the devil works through the so-called Catholics and their imperial power to establish a sacrilegious imitation.

It is within this context of entrenched martyr veneration and intercommunal contestation that Augustine was born, was raised, and served as priest and bishop. But what did Augustine himself make of this aspect of North African Christianity? While future chapters will offer more nuanced answers to this question, I turn now to Augustine's discussion of the cult of the martyrs in the *Confessions* and in his early letters.

The Cult of the Martyrs in Augustine

Confessions 6.2.2

Augustine's most famous account of the cult of the martyrs involves his mother, Monica. In *Confessions* 6, he recounts how, having followed him to Milan, she began to practice her piety in the way to which she was accustomed.[27] Allow me to quote the relevant passage at length:

> In accordance with my mother's custom in Africa, she had taken to the memorial shrines of the saints cakes and bread and wine, and was forbidden by the janitor. When she knew that the bishop [Ambrose] was responsible for the prohibition, she accepted it in so devout and docile a manner that

---

[26] *pass. Isaac* 15–16 (TU 134: 273–74).
[27] On Augustine's relationship to the cult of the martyrs, see the classic study by Johannes Quasten, "Die Reform des Martyrerkultes durch Augustinus," *Theologie und Glaube* 25 (1933): 318–31. See also Saxer, *Morts, martyrs, reliques*, 170–280; Tarcisius van Bavel, "The Cult of the Martyrs in St. Augustine: Theology Versus Popular Religion?," in *Martyrium in Multidisciplinary Perspective*, ed. Mathijs Lamberigts and Peter Van Deun (Leuven: Peeters, 1995), 351–61.

I myself was amazed how easy it was for her to find fault with her own custom rather than to dispute this ban. Her spirit was not obsessed by excessive drinking, and no love of wine stimulated her into opposing the truth. . . . After bringing her basket of ceremonial food which she would first taste and then share round the company, she used to present not more than one tiny glass of wine diluted to suit her very sober palate. She would take a sip as an act of respect. If there were many memorial shrines of the dead which were to be honored in that way, it was one and the same cup which she carried about and presented at each place. The wine was not merely drenched with water but also quite tepid; the share she gave to those present was only small sips. Her quest was for devotion, not pleasure. When she learned that the famous preacher and religious leader had ordered that no such offerings were to be made, even by those who acted soberly, to avert any pretext for intoxication being given to drinkers and because the ceremonies were like meals to propitiate the departed spirits and similar to heather superstition, she happily abstained. Instead of a basket full of the fruits of the earth, she learned to bring a heart full of purer vows to the memorials of the martyrs. She would give what she could to the needy; and then the communion of the Lord body was celebrated at the shrines of the martyrs who in imitation of the Lord's passion were sacrificed and crowned.[28]

An entire monograph could be written on this single passage. I will limit myself to a brief series of observations. First, Augustine's description of his mother's behavior and that of Christians like her gives us a picture of the practices associated with the cult of the martyrs. Central to these practices is the celebration of feasts with the martyrs at their shrines. These feasts included cakes and wine, and Augustine suggests the dangers of excess in his insistence upon his mother's moderation as well as in Ambrose's concern to avoid opportunity for inebriation. His mother's moderation also alludes to the reality of excessive indulgence among other participants.

[28] *conf.* 6.2.2 (O'Donnell, 58–59; trans. Chadwick, 91–92). For summaries of these meals and their significance, see Paula Rose, "*Refrigerium*," in *Augustinus-Lexikon* 4, ed. C. P. Mayer (Basel: Schwabe, 2018), 1104–7; Robin Jensen, "Dining with the Dead: From *Mensa* to the Altar in Christian Late Antiquity," in *Commemorating the Dead: Texts and Artifacts in Context: Studies of Roman, Jewish, and Christian Burials*, ed. Laurie Brink and Deborah Green (Berlin: DeGruyter, 2008), 107–43. For the development of Augustine's thoughts on these *refrigeria*, see Rose, "Augustine's Reassessment of the Commemoration Meal: *Quod quidem a christianis melioribus non fit*," in *Rituals in Early Christianity: New Perspectives on Tradition and Transformation*, ed. Nienke M. Vos and Albert C. Geljon (Leiden: Brill, 2021).

Second, Augustine's emphasis on his mother's willingness to submit to Ambrose's prohibition precisely because it was Ambrose implies the relative intransigence of the participants of the martyr cults in North Africa (again, as Augustine is depicting them). If it takes a bishop as preeminent as Ambrose to make Augustine's saintly mother refrain from such a beloved form of piety, what must we think of those she had left back home? Of course, we can confidently speculate that Augustine's purpose in this passage is not just to relate a story about his mother but to promote her as the ideal participant in the cult of the martyrs. When she does celebrate meals at the martyr shrines, she is a model of moderation and temperance. And when she is prevented from doing so by a bishop, she readily obeys, perhaps as Augustine wishes others would when their bishop tries to govern the practices of commemoration that attend to the Christian heroes.

Finally, in Monica's postchastisement behavior, we have an example of what Augustine may want commemoration of the martyrs to look like. The memorial feasts are replaced by the ecclesially controlled eucharist. Instead of giving to the dead, Monica gives to the poor, a practice Augustine urges in other texts seeking to reform martyr devotion.[29] And her offerings to the martyrs become offerings of solemn vows. Augustine also suggests one reason this alternative might have been so important for him: celebrating meals with the martyrs resembles too closely "pagan" rituals of honoring the dead. Ambrose, in Augustine's voice, may be thinking of the *parentalia* in which families brought offerings of food and wine to the ancestral tombs.[30] Thus, the question of such practices is a question of drawing a clear dividing line between Christian and "pagan," of cultivating a Christian identity delineated by its ritual practices.

ep. 22

Before he wrote the *Confessions*, however, Augustine was already expressing similar concerns about the cult of the martyrs. Sometime between 391 and 393, while still a priest, he writes to Aurelius, bishop of Carthage, urging him to curb the excesses of the cultic practices. The themes we saw in brief in

---

[29] See *ep.* 22.1.6.
[30] On *parentalia*, see Mary Beard et al., *Religions of Rome: A History* (Cambridge: Cambridge University Press, 1998), 50.

Augustine's account of his mother we now see elaborated and expanded, providing a fuller picture of cultic practices and of Augustine's objections.

Augustine laments that, of the three pairs of vices referenced in Rom 13:13–14 (feasting and drunkenness, fornication and impurity, and strife and jealousy), the church seems concerned only with the second set. Indeed, they are "considered so great a crime that no one is thought worthy, not only of ecclesiastical ministry but even of the communion of the sacraments."[31] The first pair, however, seems not just tolerated but encouraged "not only on the solemn days in honor of the blessed martyrs, but even daily."[32] Augustine thus suggests that the commemoration of the martyrs is a routine event, not limited by the establishment of a liturgical calendar but guided, presumably, by the devotional desires of the laity. Augustine expresses his disgust for these practices:

> Who, seeing not with carnal eyes, does not see that this is something to be grieved? This vileness, were it only shameful and not also sacrilegious, we might consider something to be endured with whatever strength of tolerance we have. . . . At least let this disgrace be kept away from the tombs of the saints' bodies, from the places for the sacraments, from houses of prayer. For who dares prohibit in private what is often named the honor of the martyrs in holy places.[33]

The rhetorical context begins to take shape. The shrines, the relics, and the churches dedicated to the martyrs are not merely the physical location of veneration; they are spaces of contestation, places, both conceptual and physical, in which the power of the bishops comes into conflict with the practices of popular piety.

Augustine next proposes a way forward: "The pestilence of this evil is such that it cannot, so it seems to me, be utterly healed without the authority of a council."[34] Here we have the purpose of Augustine's letter. His concern about the excesses of the martyr feasts leads him to request a full-scale council, something that Aurelius as bishop of Carthage can call. Yet this is not the only avenue Augustine considers: "If the treatment must begin from one church, just as it seems audacious to try to change what the church of Carthage holds,

---

[31] *ep.* 22.3 (CCSL 31:53).
[32] *ep.* 22.3 (CCSL 31:53).
[33] *ep.* 22.3 (CCSL 31:53–54).
[34] *ep.* 22.4 (CCSL 31:54).

so it is of great impudence to wish to keep what the church of Carthage has corrected. Yet for this matter what other bishop should be desired than he who as a deacon cursed these things."[35] Augustine appeals to the authority not only of Aurelius but also of the church of Carthage itself as the flagship church of all North Africa. He is attempting to bring to bear all practical ecclesial power upon practices he deems impious.

And yet, Augustine qualifies these efforts by explaining that persuasion, not force, should be the method for eradicating the problem. "What was to be grieved then now must be gotten rid of, not harshly, but, as scripture says, in a spirit of gentleness and kindness.... Therefore, these practices are destroyed, it seems to me, not with harshness, nor with strength, nor with power, but by teaching rather than ordering, by warning rather than threatening."[36] Augustine makes a rhetorical turn here. Yes, the authority of a council or of the Carthaginian see is necessary, but to have an effect they must be promoted not through the application of strict penalties but through persuasion. Cult participants are not to be dragged along; they are to be drawn, to be wooed.

Augustine's Promotion of the Cult

We should not, however, take from these testimonies the impression that Augustine was adamantly opposed to the cult of the martyrs per se. Rather, as we will see throughout this book, he is less interested in abolishing it than he is in reforming it. He does not find devotion to the martyrs at their shrines and with their relics to be superstitious; on the contrary, he views connection to the martyrs as a powerful spiritual gift to the faithful. In fact, we have several examples of Augustine actively promoting devotional adoration of the martyrs.[37]

Most famously, in *Confessions* 9, Augustine recounts the providential discovery of two martyrs' bodies. Again, I quote from that work at length:

> This was the time when through a vision you revealed to the bishop already mentioned the place where lay hidden the bodies of the martyrs Protasius

---

[35] *ep.* 22.4 (CCSL 31:54).
[36] *ep.* 22.5 (CCSL 31:54).
[37] Of course, Augustine's most common engagement with the cult came through the sermons on feast days. On the liturgical setting and the sermons themselves, see Guy Lapointe, *La célébration des martyrs en Afrique d'après les sermons de saint Augustin* (Montreal: s.n., 1972), remains indispensable.

and Gervasius. For many years you had kept them from corruption, hidden away in your secret treasury, out of which at the right moment you produced them to restrain the fury of a woman, indeed a lady of the royal family. When they had been produced and dug out, they were transferred with due honour to Ambrose's basilica, and some people vexed by impure spirits were healed, the very demons themselves making public confession. Moreover, a citizen who had been blind many years and was well known in the city, heard the people in a state of tumultuous jubilation and asked the reason for it. On learning the answer he leapt up and asked his guide to lead him there. When he arrived, he begged admission so that he might touch with his cloth the bier on which lay your saints whose death is precious in your sight. When he did this and applied the cloth to his eyes, immediately they were opened. From that point the news spread fast, praises of you were fervent and radiant, and the mind of that hostile woman, though not converted to sound faith, was nevertheless checked in its anger.[38]

"That hostile woman" is Justina, an "Arian" and the wife of Valentinian. In 386, Ambrose resisted her efforts to promote Gothic Arianism by forcing Catholic churches to be opened for Arian worship. The revelation of the bodies of Protasius and Gervasius itself reveals the rhetorical power of the martyrs to rally the Catholic faithful and force Justina to back down in the face of such popular resistance. Further, it says much about Augustine's attitude toward martyrdom that he betrays no cynicism at the convenience of the martyrs discovery. Instead, he affirms God's providential work, suggesting that the martyrs are part of how God operates within the world, a manifestation of divine grace bestowed upon what he sees as the one true faith. Moreover, Augustine also affirms the miraculous nature of the martyr's relics, which are able to mediate God's grace and healing power. Augustine, therefore, asserts the spiritual power of the martyrs and their relics and affirms the tumultuous celebration of them in Milan.

We see similar affirmation in Augustine's discussion regarding the translation of relics of the proto-martyr Stephen to North Africa.[39] After the

---

[38] *Conf.* 9.7.16 (O'Donnell, 109; trans. Chadwick, 165).
[39] See Anthony Dupont, "*Imitatio Christi, Imitatio Stephani*: Augustine's Thinking on Martyrdom Based on His *Sermones* on the Protomartyr Stephen," *Augustiniana* 56 (2006): 29–61; C. P. Mayer, "'*Attende Stephanum conservum tuum*' (SErm. 317, 2, 3). Sinn und Wert der Martyrerverehrung nach den Stephanuspredigten Augustins," in Fructus Centesimus: *Mélanges offerts à Gerard J. M. Bartelink à l'occaion de son soixante-cinquième anniversaire*, ed. A. A. R. Bastiaensen, A. Hilhorst, and C. H. Kneepkens (Turnhout: Brepols, 1989), 217–37.

discovery of Stephen's body in 415, some parts found their way to Hippo. The new cult was quite popular, with Augustine even testifying to the healing powers of the relics near the end of *City of God*.[40] He preached at least ten sermons on the martyr,[41] and as we will see, Stephen became emblematic for imitation of Christ and winning the martyr's crown.

Finally, Augustine does not relent in supporting the cult associated with North Africa's celebrated martyr-bishop Cyprian, though he does, as we will see later, try to tame what he sees as its excesses. He preaches no less than twelve sermons on Cyprian, but more significant, perhaps, is the central role that Cyprian plays in the Donatist controversy as Augustine seeks to wrestle the bishop's legacy from the clenches of his Donatist opponents.

Martyrs and Manichaeanism

In the final two sections of this chapter, I want to highlight two lesser polemical contexts, lesser, that is, in their use of martyrdom as a locus of contestation. The Manichaean and Pelagian controversies bookend Augustine's theological life, but in neither of them do the combatants deploy martyr rhetoric extensively. Yet, what martyr material they do have is worth examining to demonstrate how even these conflicts are unable to ignore the ubiquitous rhetorical power of martyrdom altogether. Moreover, while the anti-Manichaean sources will illustrate some perennial themes in Augustine's martyr theology, the anti-Pelagian will demonstrate how the martyr discourse is able to draw precise philosophical distinctions into its orbit.

The rhetoric of martyrdom plays only a small role in Augustine's conflict with the Manichees. In fact, aside from two brief mentions in *The Catholic Way of Life*, martyrs do not show up in Augustine's anti-Manichaean works until the relatively late *Against Faustus* (398–400). In this work we see the power of martyr discourse in Augustine's vehement defense of its cultic practices. Beyond the fact that Augustine rehearses themes that are central to his martyr theology that we will examine in more depth in future chapters, we can conclude that the rhetoric of martyrdom possesses little significance in Augustine's anti-Manichaean work.

---

[40] *ciu.* 22.5.
[41] *s.* 314–21, 323–24.

Martyrs show up twice in Augustine's *The Catholic Way of Life*, an early work from 387–389. First, in describing "the road that God has constructed for us," Augustine names "the blood of the martyrs" in a list that includes, inter alia, "the bonds of the law," "the sacrament of the man assumed [by God]," and "the conversion of the nations."[42] The significance of this passage will be made clear when I discuss the relationship between historiography and rhetoric in chapter 3. For now, I note that the reference is made in passing and the inclusion of martyrs appears, at least for the sake of the argument at hand, to be incidental.

The same may be said for the second appearance of martyrdom in *The Catholic Way of Life*. Here, Augustine seeks to prove that Ps 44:22, as quoted by Paul at Rom 8:36, is not only an original part of the text but also an accurate reflection of the life of the true Christian. The argument culminates by daring his opponents to say, "It ought not be believed that the apostles and martyrs are said to have been afflicted with grave sufferings for the sake of Christ, or that they were considered as sheep for the slaughter by their persecutors."[43] Augustine takes for granted the authority of the martyrs as having suffered for their faith. To deny the legitimacy and even holiness of their suffering is tantamount to losing the argument. In this passage, then, though martyrdom still appears only in passing, it does so with a demonstration of its rhetorical power.

Over ten years pass before Augustine once again takes up the topic of martyrs in an anti-Manichaean context. In *Against Faustus*, martyrdom makes four appearances, but only one of these deserves extensive exposition as the most expansive discussion of martyrdom in Augustine's anti-Manichaean corpus. Nevertheless, it is worth rehearsing the other instances. First, Augustine challenges Faustus to a martyr contest in order to prove whose religion has the most and the most celebrated martyrs.[44] We will see similar rhetorical contestations when I turn to the forensic rhetoric of the Donatist conflict in chapter 4. Next, we have a brief reference to martyrs in a passage discussing the glory that accompanies Christ's conquering of death.[45] Third, Augustine quotes Faustus's use of Deut 21:23, that all who hang upon a tree are cursed, to show that Christians ought not revere the Old Testament not only because of Christ's death but also because of those of his

---

[42] *mor.* 1.7.12 (CSEL 90:14–15).
[43] *mor.* 1.9.15 (CSEL 90:18).
[44] *c. Faust.* 5.8.
[45] *c. Faust.* 12.28.

martyrs.[46] Here we see that the Manichaean approach to martyrdom might be a bit more nuanced than Augustine assumed in his arguments from *The Catholic Way of Life*.

But the most significant discussion of martyrdom in *Against Faustus* comes in book 20, in which Faustus critiques the Catholics for appropriating "pagan" practices:

> Truly you transformed their [gentiles'] sacrifices into agapes and their idols into martyrs whom you worship with similar prayer. You placate the shades of the dead with wine and sacrificial feasts; you celebrate the solemn days of the gentiles with them, like the kalends and the solstices. You have really changed nothing from their way of life.[47]

In this anti-martyr rhetoric, which would appear quite at home in some modern analyses of early Christian cultic practices, Faustus attempts to dismiss Catholic Christianity as a mere appropriation of gentile religion and culture, perhaps playing on some of the intra-Christian concerns noted earlier in my discussion of cultic practice. If nothing else, this passage represents significant anti-martyr rhetoric that demonstrates the prominence of martyrdom in outside perceptions of Catholic Christianity.

More important, though, is Augustine's response to these allegations, in which he marshals many of the elements of his martyr theology that will become standard in the following chapters. After mocking Faustus for his supposed doctrinal inconsistency in speaking of "shades of the dead," Augustine proffers his own positive description of Catholic approaches to martyr veneration. First, "the Christian people celebrate the memorials of the martyrs with religious solemnity both to inspire imitation and to be joined together through their merits and aided by their prayers."[48] We see here an explanation of the purpose of martyr veneration: imitation, to which I will return repeatedly, and intercession. Augustine proposes a true cultic benefit from the veneration of the martyrs, that is, that the participants might benefit from the martyrs' prayers but also that they might be inspired by them.

Second, though, Augustine makes clear that the martyrs are not the ultimate objects of worship:

---

[46] *c. Faust.* 14.1.
[47] *c. Faust.* 20.4 (CSEL 25:538).
[48] *c. Faust.* 20.21 (CSEL 25:562).

> We do not erect altars to the martyrs but to the God of the martyrs, though we do so at the memorials of the martyrs. For what bishop, standing at the altar in the places of the holy bodies, ever said, "We make offering to you, Peter or Paul or Cyprian"? No, what is offered is offered to the God who crowned the martyrs, crowning them at their own memorials, so that by the remembrance at those places a greater feeling might arise to increase love both of those whom we are able to imitate and of him by whose help we are able to do so.[49]

This distinction between worshipping the martyrs and worshipping God is one of the most prominent themes in Augustine's preaching on the martyrs, suggesting that for all his emphasis here, the actual cultic practices of everyday Christians in Hippo might have been more ambiguous. Nevertheless, in the present passage Augustine takes pains to defend the practice of martyr veneration by distinguishing that worship which is due only to God. Moreover, we again see the emphasis on imitation of the martyrs that will become a repeated theme throughout this study.

Finally, Augustine denounces "those who get drunk at the memorials of the martyrs." His further explanation suggests the bishop's difficulties in controlling the martyr cult:

> But what we teach is one thing; what we tolerate is another. What we are commanded to instruct is one thing; what we are instructed to correct is another. And so long as we correct, we are compelled to tolerate. The discipline of Christians is one thing; the extravagance of the drunken and the error of the infirm are another. And in this manner the sins of the drunken and those of the sacrilegious are very far apart from one another. Obviously, it is a much lesser sin to return drunk from the martyrs than to make a sacrifice of fasting to the martyrs.[50]

Again, we see parallels between Faustus's accusation and Augustine's own frustrations with his flock. But Augustine is careful here to distinguish such practice, even when drunken, from pagan sacrifice. Even the holiest of practices in the truest of religions, he seems to suggest, can be disgraced by unruly behavior and yet not therefore be deemed pagan. So long as the

---

[49] *c. Faust.* 20.21 (CSEL 25:562).
[50] *c. Faust.* 20.21 (CSEL 25:563–64).

drunken reveler is directing their veneration toward the true God and not toward the martyr, then they remain more pious than the sober celebrant who offers their gifts to the martyrs themselves in a truly pagan manner.

Thus, in Augustine's anti-Manichaean works, we may find few references to the martyrs, but what we do find, especially in *Against Faustus* 20, provides a dense summary of some of Augustine's most important martyrial themes. Worship is to be directed only to God, not to the martyrs themselves. Veneration of the martyrs is, first and foremost, for the sake of imitation. And drunkenness and other forms of celebratory excess are to be condemned, even if they must temporarily be tolerated.

Martyrs and Pelagianism

If the anti-Manichaean texts represent typical Augustinian discourse upon the martyrs, the anti-Pelagian works provide a more idiosyncratic example, one more conditioned by Augustine's dispute with Julian of Eclanum. In addition to competing over the authority of the martyrs, Augustine and his Pelagian opponents also bring the martyrs to bear upon a particular point of disagreement: Is death a punishment for Adam's sin, and therefore always an evil? Or can it be construed as a gift, even a good?[51] Both sides claim that the quasi-mythic period of the martyrs supports their position on death. It is a universal polemical truth in early Christianity that whoever can claim to have the martyrs on their side automatically carries an increased level of authority. Thus, it should come as no surprise that both sides in the Pelagian controversy sought to recruit long-dead martyrs, either specific ones or the general category, to their cause.

Augustine, as in the Donatist controversy, appeals to the authority of Cyprian. It is well known that Augustine claims that the Carthaginian bishop taught a version of original sin,[52] but it should also be observed that Augustine is intentional about stressing Cyprian's status not just as a

---

[51] For further analysis on the role of martyrdom in the anti-Pelagian conflict around the nature of death, this time focusing on *s.* 299 and 335B, see Dupont, "Augustine's Homiletic Definition of Martyrdom," 166–77; Anthony Dupont, "Augustine's Anti-Pelagian Interpretation of Two Martyr Sermons. Sermones 299 and 335B on the Unnaturalness of Human Death," in *Martyrdom and Persecution in Late Antique Christianity (100–700 ad). Essays in Honour of Boudewijn Dehandschutter on the Occasion of His Retirement as Professor of Greek and Oriental Patrology at the Faculty of Theology of the K.U. Leuven*, ed. Johann Leemans (Leuven: Peeters, 2010), 87–102.

[52] See Anthony Dupont, "Original Sin in Tertullian and Cyprian: Conceptual Presence and Pre-Augustinian Content?," *Revue d'études augustiniennes et patristique* 63 (2017): 1–29.

bishop but as a martyr. For example, in his *Incomplete Work against Julian*, Augustine quotes Cyprian's *Letter* 64 and then comments, "Behold, I used the words of the Punic bishop, Cyprian. You bark against him, even though he was a martyr, when you assault the most firm faith of the church on behalf of which he shed [his] blood."[53] Cyprian's martyrdom adds an extra layer of significance to his use as an authority.

Similarly, earlier in the same work, Augustine connects his cause not only to Cyprian the martyr but also to all the martyrs that Cyprian represents. Julian had rebuked what he took to be Augustine's unjust God, saying:

> He is not [the God] in whom the patriarchs, the prophets, and the apostles believed, nor is he the one in whom the church of the first [Christians], which was enlisted in the heavens, hoped and [still] hopes. He is not the one whom the rational creature believes to be its judge and whom the Holy Spirit announces will judge justly. No one with prudence would ever have shed their blood for such a lord, for he would not merit the ardor of our love so that he could impose the obligation of suffering for him.[54]

Without using the word, Julian has appealed to the legacy of the martyrs, those heroes of the church who were so devoted to the true (and just) God that they were willing to suffer and die. How could Augustine's cruel deity inspire such devotion?

Of course, Augustine will have none of this. He responds by pointing to Cyprian in a way that invokes all of the martyrs: "But how can you say that no wise persons shed their blood for the Lord whom we worship, since the most glorious Cyprian worshiped him and shed his blood for him. . . . Do you not see that you are rather the criminal when you blaspheme against the God of the holy martyrs?"

While these general uses of martyr rhetoric illustrate the continued discursive power of the theme for Augustine beyond the Donatist controversy, they demonstrate only minimal theological significance. Everyone wants the martyrs on their side, and, for Augustine, Cyprian is the martyr-bishop par excellence precisely because he can appeal to him as a theological predecessor. But martyrs play a larger role in the theological dispute than mere

---

[53] Augustine, *c. Iul. imp.* 1.106 (CSEL 85.1:125).
[54] Augustine, *c. Iul. imp.* 1.50 (CSEL 85.1:42).

authorities. They serve as illustrations at the heart of a dispute regarding the nature of death.

Death and the Martyrs: Julian's Position

In this section I want to look at two passages that Augustine relates from Julian of Eclanum that outline the latter's theology of death. Only one of these passages explicitly mentions martyrdom, but we need both if we are to understand the scope of the argument and Augustine's response to it.

First, in his *Answer to the Two Letters of the Pelagians*—the letters being from Julian—Augustine reports that "they" proclaim that every soul comes into existence without the "stain of sin." He continues:

> On account of this, they also say that from Adam no evil has passed on to the rest except death, which, they say, is not always an evil, since it is also the cause of the martyrs' reward, and [they also say] it is not the dissolution of the body, which will be raised up in every kind of human being, that makes death to be called either good or evil, but the diversity of merits which arises from human freedom.[55]

This is the clearest explanation of Julian's position on death and the martyrs, although there are other allusions to it, normally in Augustine's refutation of an unspecified claim. But I will come to that below. For now, I want to unpack what Augustine has cited here from Julian's letter.

First, I note that Julian does claim that death has passed on to humanity from Adam, but it was the only inheritance. That is to say, sin and guilt are not congenitally transmitted. We do not all sin in Adam. Moreover, death is not always evil; that is to say, it is not even always a punishment that we suffer. It may in fact be a good. Whether death is good or evil depends not on death itself but on the merits of the one who suffers it.

Consider also Julian's reading of Gen 3:19 as reported in the *Incomplete Work against Julian*: "Until you return to the earth from which you were taken, for you are earth and you will return to the earth." This passage proves for Julian that death comes not as a punishment but as a gift, a relief: "It comforts the man with the promise of an end. After all, since it had previously

---

[55] *c. ep. Pel.* 4.2.2 (CSEL 60:521).

mentioned the pains, labor, and sweat, which nature had experienced and which the person experienced in a greater amount, the indication of an end mitigates the suffering so that this would not seem to go on forever." Moreover, the "earth to earth" portion also supports Julian's claim that "it was undoubtedly not because of sin, but because of his mortal nature that he who was not eternal would face the dissolution of the body."[56]

I argue that we should read Julian's position on death as an expression of a Stoic ethic of indifference. For him, the value of death, whether it is to be seen as a good or as an evil, depends upon the use of it. This fits well with the Stoic view of goods and evils as presented, for example, in Diogenes Laertius. According to him, the Stoics affirmed that the only true goods were the virtues and the only true evils were their opposites, the vices. Everything else in this life is indifferent, neither good nor bad, except according to their use. Among these things are both life and death, the former a "preferred" indifferent, the latter a "nonpreferred" indifferent. All things considered, it is better to be alive than dead, but both can be used virtuously and therefore death cannot be called evil simpliciter. As Diogenes Laertius reports, "They say that that is not good of which both good and bad use can be made; but of wealth and health both good and bad use can be made; therefore, wealth and health are not good."[57] And neither are they evils, as the argument can be inverted to show that nothing is evil if good and bad use can be made of it.

This understanding of indifferents fits Julian's depiction of death. He insists that because death can be used well, either through the glory of martyrdom or as a respite from the suffering of this life, it cannot be considered a true evil. Its value depends on its use. Augustine's response to this argument will look quite similar, turning as it does upon how death is used, but he will reach a different conclusion through the application of a rhetorical, instead of a philosophical, frame to the issue.

Death and the Martyrs: Augustine's Response

Augustine does not respond directly to the quotation from Julian's letter in *Answer to the Two Letters of the Pelagians*. To see how he argues against Julian, then, we must turn to later texts, his *Against Julian* and the *Incomplete*

---

[56] Augustine, *c. Iul. imp.* 6.27 (CSEL 85.2:396).
[57] Diogenes Laertius, 7.103 (Greek original and English translation, LCL 208–9).

Work against Julian. In the former and earlier of the two, Augustine explains, "Though death is the punishment of the sinner, it becomes the martyr's source of merit when that evil is used well."[58] At first glance Augustine may seem to be repeating what Julian himself said. Yes, both men agree that death can look very different depending on how one approaches it. But for Augustine, unlike Julian, the nature of death does not change. Death is always an evil, always part of the punishment that all humans suffer as a consequence for our sin in Adam. The virtuous work of a martyr does not make of death a good. Rather, he has merely used an evil thing well.

This argument is related to Augustine's view of providence, itself so important to the Pelagian controversy. We see this connection with providence at work in an earlier passage from the same text, where Augustine explains how God fashioned the goods of marriage and intercourse out of the evil of concupiscence. Martyrdom should be understood likewise. "Even from the persecutions which he permitted the devil to bring about, he knew how to produce crowns for the martyrs, making good use of every kind of evil for the benefit of the good."[59]

I argue that, while Julian's depiction of death as made good by good use depends on a Stoic notion of indifferents, Augustine's assertion that death, even when used well, is still an evil depends on a rhetorical understanding of arrangement, economy, or, to use the preferred Latin term, *dispositio*. *Dispositio* is the second part of rhetoric following *inventio*. The *Rhetoric to Herennius* describes it as "the order and distribution of the matter, which demonstrates what ought to be located at which place."[60] Cicero's definition amounts to the same thing, but he also offers this description of how to arrange difficult material in a legal speech:

> One should also be careful not to insert a narrative when it might be harmful [to one's case].... A narrative can be harmful when the exposition of the events by themselves causes great offence, which it will be necessary to soften by arguing and pleading the case. When this occurs, one ought to disperse the parts [of the narrative] piecemeal throughout the speech and apply (*accommodare*) an explanation right away so that the medicine at hand may heal the wound and the defense may immediately mitigate the anger.[61]

---

[58] *c. Iul.* 6.55 (PL 44:855).
[59] *c. Iul.* 4.38 (PL 44:757–58).
[60] *rhet. Her.* 1.2.3 (LCL 403:6).
[61] Cicero, *inv.* 1.21.30 (LCL 386:60).

CONTEXT OF THE MARTYRS   29

A key element of *dispositio*, then, is the proper ordering of material so that negative elements of a speech are integrated into a positive whole. See also Quintilian's description of the Homeric method of arrangement:

> The question is also asked, whether the most powerful arguments should be put at the beginning so as to take possession of the judge's mind, or at the end, so as to leave a final impression on him, or be divided between the beginning and the end, in any case following Homer's tactics of putting the weakest in the center and, as it were, giving them more courage?[62]

Again, we see a concern in *dispositio* to incorporate weaker elements into the larger arrangement of the whole speech. The whole becomes strong—even, one might say, good—by this arrangement, but the individual elements are still weak or problematic on their own.

This understanding of *dispositio* is present from Augustine's earliest writings to his latest. For instance, in *On Music* he offers an extended depiction of God's arrangement of the cosmos, culminating in the following:

> So, God ordered the sinning human as filthy, but not filthily. For, he [the human] was made filthy by [his own] will, by losing altogether that which he possessed [so long as] he complied with the precepts of God. And he ordered in a part so that he who did not wish to pursue the law was pursued by the law.[63]

Augustine wants to depict God's arrangement of the world as unthwartable. No bad thing, such as sin or the foul will of a human, can disrupt the beauty of God's order. God's divine *dispositio* knows how to make good use even of sin, but the sin remains evil.

God's divine disposition remains a constant theme in Augustine's theology as witnessed by a passage from book 11 of the *City of God*:

> Just as God is the supreme Creator of good natures, so also is he the most just orderer (*ordinatur*) of evil wills. And so, just as those who use good natures wickedly, so God uses even wicked wills well. Thus, he made it so

---

[62] Quintilian, *inst.* 5.12.14 (Latin original and English translation LCL 125:462).
[63] Augustine, *mus.* 6.11.30 (CSEL 102:215).

that the devil, good by God's creation but wicked by his own will, was ordered among the lower things, becoming the sport of his angels: i.e., God caused the temptations [of the devil] to bring good to the saints whom the devil wishes to harm by them.[64]

Note that God is defined as the "orderer" of evil wills, a term associated with *dispositio*. In the same way, he orders the devil's wickedness by using it well, for the glory of the saints who, through God's grace and the help of the angels, contribute to a good whole. But no matter how good the whole may be, it is clear that the devil, according to his will, remains wicked.

So, we see the rhetorical and theological frame for Augustine's response to Julian. Yes, death can be used well, but that does not make it a good. Julian's Stoic ethical approach mistakes the good of the arranged whole for the good of the element arranged. The martyr's death is not, in and of itself, good. It is only the glorious use that God makes of it that is good.

Augustine's comments on death against Julian are not always as obviously set within this frame. Nevertheless, I believe that they can still be read as consistent with it. For example, in the *Incomplete Work against Julian*, Augustine opines, "Yet why are the martyrs preached with such glory because they died for justice, unless it is because it is a greater virtue to spurn death than to spurn labor?"[65] Here Augustine takes direct aim at Julian's contention that death is a gift to relieve us from a life of toil. But more virtue is needed to face death than to face hard work. A little later Augustine comments, "For, just as death is contrary to life, so punishment is contrary to reward. And since the holy martyrs have struggled and conquered through this punishment, that is, through the death of the body, their death in which they now sleep is precious in the sight of the Lord, not by reason of its nature but by reason of his gift."[66]

Both of these citations fit within the rhetorical frame of divine *dispositio*. In the first, we see what it means for the martyrs to use an evil well. They face it with virtue despite the natural desire to avoid it. Such courage and fidelity make the martyrs partners in the divine work of *dispositio*, arranging even the evils of this world into a glorious whole. Similarly, the second quotation demonstrates that the reward of the martyrs is not a sign that death is made

---

[64] Augustine, *ciu.* 11.17 (CCSL 48:336–37).
[65] Augustine, *c. Iul. imp.* 6.27.11 (CSEL 85.2:401).
[66] Augustine, *c. Iul. imp.* 6.36.5 (CSEL 85.2:440).

good but that death is indeed quite evil. It is only God's grace that makes such an evil to be used well, and God views it as precious from the perspective of the whole.

Conclusion

The point of this chapter is simple: martyrs were a big deal in Augustine's North African (and Milanese) context. The zeal of the North African martyr cult is difficult to overstate. In the midst of the popular participation in the memory of these Christian heroes, theological commitments as well as contentions arose. No conflict is more emblematic of this than the Donatist schism. While the schisms of Cyprian's time that preceded it also highlighted the polemical and pastoral power of martyrdom, all involved still shared a common enemy in the persecuting empire. For the Donatists, who styled themselves as "the church of the martyrs," their opponents were not just disrespecting the martyrs; they were persecuting them all over again, including persecuting new victims.

Despite the prominence of the Donatist controversy for Augustine's rhetorical and polemical use of martyrdom, martyrs play an important role in other controversies, including in his bookending conflicts with the Manichaeans and the Pelagians. In his defense of the cult of the martyrs against Faustus, Augustine expresses many of the themes that will become commonplace in his later preaching on martyrdom, especially the emphases upon imitation of their virtues, the priority of divine worship and not that of the martyrs themselves, and the need for propriety in practices of veneration. With Julian of Eclanum, Augustine not only appeals to the authority of the martyrs, especially of Cyprian, to support his position but also engages Julian in a dispute about the meaning of martyrdom for a theology of death. If the martyrs gain glory through their death, does that mean that death, at least sometimes, can be considered a good? For Julian, drawing upon a Stoic ethical frame, the answer is yes, because death, like life and health, is an indifferent whose moral value depends upon its use. Augustine disagrees; death, for him, is always an evil, a punishment for our sin. But, keeping with the rhetorical nature of martyr discourse, he frames this in terms of divine *dispositio*. It is true that death can be used well, but like an incriminating element in a speech, its arrangement into the beautiful whole does not change its individual value as an evil.

Even beyond these polemical concerns, however, Augustine had a flourishing martyr cult within his own church to deal with. While he approved of martyr veneration, he was wary of some aspects of it. And so he worked hard to, we might say, domesticate or tame the cult to conform more to his vision of true Christian faith. With that in mind, then, let us turn to Augustine's construction of the example of the martyrs.

2
The Example of the Martyrs

Introduction

On November 15, 408, Augustine joined his flock to celebrate the feast day of the Twenty Martyrs.[1] He opened by praying for the assistance of the martyrs that he might speak appropriately about them. Having thus paid the necessary homage to the subjects of the day's feast, Augustine turns to chastise his audience for the way they have failed to honor the martyrs appropriately in their celebrations:

> First, let us not think we are conferring anything upon the martyrs because we celebrate their most solemn feast days. They have no need of our feasts because they rejoice in heaven with the angels; nevertheless, they rejoice together with us, not if we honor them, but if we imitate them. But to honor and not to imitate is nothing other than to fawn falsely. For this reason, therefore, these feasts have been established in the church of Christ: so that through them the congregation of Christ's members might be admonished to imitate Christ's martyrs. This is the only utility of this feast; there is none other.[2]

In this paragraph, Augustine clarifies the direction of effectiveness in the dead martyr/living Christian relationship. It is not we who act upon them but they who act upon us. The martyrs do not benefit from the cultic practices offered to them by their devotees. They receive nothing from the drinking and feasting that occur at their shrines. While it is good to honor and revere

---

[1] For the dating of this and other sermons, see Roger Gryson, *Répertoire general des auteurs ecclésiastiques Latins de l'antiquité et du haut moyen âge* (Freiberg: Herder, 2007), 1:231–69. Cf. the charts in Éric Rebillard, "*Sermones*," in *Augustine through the Ages: An Encyclopedia*, ed. Allan Fitzgerald (Grand Rapids, MI: Eerdmans, 1999), 774–89; and WSA 3.1:138–63. These in turn depend on H. J. Frede, *Kirchenschriftsteller Verzeichnis und Sigel. 4. Aktualisierte Auflage*, Vetus Latina 1/1 (Freiburg: Herder, 1995); and Pierre-Patrick Verbraken, *Études critiques sur les Sermons authentiques de St. Augustin*, Instrumenta Patristica 12 (Steenbrugge, 1976).

[2] *s.* 325.1 (PL 38:1447).

these heroes of the faith, true honor comes from something else: imitation. What does it matter, Augustine suggests, if we praise the martyrs but do not emulate them in our own lives?

In reframing martyr veneration as oriented toward imitation and emulation, Augustine draws upon the rhetorical tool of *exempla*.[3] *Exempla* are rhetorically constructed models drawn from history—real or fictional—and presented to one's audience as positive or negative examples that inspire imitation or its opposite. *Exempla* will be a recurring theme throughout the rest of this book, and therefore this chapter is in some ways a propaedeutic for later discussions. Thus, I begin my argument here with an overview of the nature and role of *exempla* within classical rhetorical theory and practice.

With this particular chapter, however, I want to show how Augustine uses *exempla* to contest and reconstruct the significance of the martyrs for North African Christianity.[4] Both in his episcopal home of Hippo and in Carthage, Augustine preaches numerous sermons on feast days, alluding to the cult practices that attend such celebrations, as mentioned in the previous chapter. In these sermons, he seeks to domesticate these practices (or at least their excesses) by challenging his congregation to move from mere celebration of the martyrs, especially from raucous indulgence, and toward emulation of the virtues the martyrs illustrated in their martyrdom. Of course, this approach has the benefit of allowing Augustine himself to define just what those virtues are. Therefore, after establishing what rhetorical *exempla* are, I will show how Augustine uses them to cultivate a vision of Christian virtue and to redefine what it means to venerate the martyrs faithfully. Finally, to underscore the significance of martyrial *exempla* in Augustine's martyr discourse, I analyze

---

[3] For a treatment of Augustine and *exempla*, see Lewis Ayres, "Into the Poem of the Universe: *Exempla*, Conversion, and Church in Augustine's *Confessiones*," *Zeitschrift für antikes Christentum* 13 (2009): 163–81.

[4] The idea that, for Augustine, true martyrial veneration means imitation is well attested in secondary literature. In this chapter, I build upon this established knowledge by framing it in terms of the rhetorical technique of *exempla*, which is often left implicit in other studies, as well as the technique of etymology, mentioned only in passing by other authors. For appreciation of imitation in Augustine's martyr discourse, see Candida Moss, *The Other Christs: Imitating Jesus in Ancient Christian Ideologies of Martyrdom* (New York: Oxford University Press, 2010), 166–69; Anthony Dupont, "*Imitatio Christi, Imitatio Stephani*: Augustine's Thinking on Martyrdom Based on his *Sermones* on the Protomartyr Stephen," *Augustiniana* 56 (2006): 29–61; M. Pellegrino, "Cristo e il martire nel pensiero di Sant'Agostino," in *Richerche Patristiche* (Torino, 1982), 633–68; Guy Lapointe, *La celebration des martyrs en Afrique d'après les sermons de saint Augustin* (Montreal, 1972), 174–80. On martyrdom and exemplarity more broadly, see James Petitfils, *Mos Christianorum: The Roman Discourse of Exemplarity and the Jewish and Christian Language of Leadership* (Tübingen: Mohr Siebeck, 2016), 224–42.

Augustine's use of nominal etymology, a practice whereby he interprets the very names of the martyrs as indicative of their exemplarity.

Exempla in Classical Rhetoric

The most extensive discussion of *exempla* appears in Quintilian.[5] A brief summation of his description will set the rhetorical stage for our understanding of Augustine's martyrial performance. Quintilian depicts an *exemplum* as a type of inductive proof and defines it more precisely as "the reference to a [past] event or something treated like an event to make that which you intend more persuasive."[6] The "historic" nature of the examples is significant, as will be explored more in chapter 3. For now, its importance lies in the established nature of the *exemplum*. That is to say, its power derives from its authority, and authority takes time to develop. While one may use a current event or figure to illustrate a point, its social value is transitory, subject to change over time. Only the historical, be it actual *res gestae* or poetic accounts drawn from historically established sources like the Aeneid, can serve the persuasive purpose of *exempla* because the rhetor must be able to assume that their audience will share a common evaluation of the event narrated.

Within judicial speeches, these examples play on different degrees of similarity as the basis for judgment. For instance, Quintilian cites the following as an example of an *exemplum* argument of similarity: "Saturninus was justly killed, just as the Gracchi."[7] Here, the question is whether or not Lucius Appuleius Saturninus was justly killed in 100 BCE. Saturninus and his

---

[5] For a concise summary of the nature and purpose of *exempla* as well as more evidence from Cicero and the anonymous *rhet. Her.*, see Roger Blockley, "Ammianus Marcellinus's Use of *Exempla*," *Florilegium* 13 (1994): 53–64. Blockley is particularly helpful in highlighting that, no matter the specific genre in which *exempla* are deployed, they always seek to persuade to some ethical standard: "In distinction from educators and philosophers, Roman lawyers often made use of *exempla* more neutrally, as precedents to support or undermine arguments. Oratorical theory, therefore, as represented in Cicero and the *ad Herennium*, is concerned primarily with the marshalling of *exempla* for proof and persuasion. Nevertheless, oratorical theory does recognize the ethical content of *exempla* in all three categories of usage—ornamentation, clarification, and proof—, all of which have the ultimate goal of persuading the listeners.... Even when the *exemplum* is cited as a precedent, the material chosen usually has an ethical force" (53). See also K. Alewell, "Über das rhetorische Paradeigma. Theorie, Beispelsammlungen, Verwendung in der römischen Literatur der Kaiserzeit" (PhD diss., University of Leipzig, 1913); H. Kornhardt, "Exemplum. Eine bedeutungsgeschichtliche Studie" (PhD diss., University of Göttingen, 1936).

[6] Quintilian 5.11.6 (LCL 125:432).

[7] Quintilian 5.11.6 (LCL 125:432).

cotribune, Gaius Servilius Glaucia, were both killed in response to their populist reforms, military manipulation, and fatal political tactics. By appealing to the killing of the Gracchi, earlier populist leaders deemed dangerous for their demagoguery, the imaginary rhetor can advocate for the legitimacy of Saturninus's killing by playing on the similarities between his situation and that of the already vilified Gracchi. That is to say, it is already assumed that the audience will agree that the Gracchi were justly killed, and by associating Saturninus with those villains, his own death is justified.

If such similarity represents the basic mode of *exemplum*, several deviations from this norm allow for more nuanced uses of this rhetorical technique. These include the "dissimilar": "Brutus killed his sons who were plotting betrayal; Manlius punished his son's virtue with death."[8] Here the same action is distinguished by different motives or *causae*. Both men kill their sons, but one is punishing wickedness while the other is punishing goodness. The former father is justified while the latter is blameworthy, despite the similarity of the actions. More distinct are "contrary" *exempla*: "Marcellus restored ornaments to the Syracusans when they were our enemies; Verres removed the same from them when they were our allies."[9] Here the actions under consideration are exact opposites and the righteousness of one determines the injustice of the other. The *exemplum* is of someone doing bad to those who are good; the present case is of someone doing good to those who are bad. While the bad/good contrast in the former represents the virtue of the actors (helping even enemies), the good/bad contrast in the latter indicates villainy (harming even friends). The contrariety accentuates the villainy of the present case in the light of the virtue of the *exemplum*.

To these degrees of similarity and dissimilarity should be added exemplary arguments "from the greater to the lesser" and "from the lesser to the greater."[10] These take an established example and make a comparative argument for the present issue: if X (the *exemplum*) is the case, how much more so/less so should Y be the case? In all of these instances, the *exemplum* is used to demonstrate the justice or injustice of a present issue by some correspondence. While the *exempla* carry authority in themselves, the job of the rhetor is to draw out that correspondence, be it through similarity, dissimilarity, or any variant in between.

---

[8] Quintilian 5.11.7 (LCL 125:432).
[9] Quintilian 5.11.7 (LCL 125:432).
[10] Quintilian 5.11.9 (LCL 125:434).

While Quintilian describes *exempla* primarily in terms of judicial rhetoric, he also refers to their significance in the other rhetorical modes: "Confirmation of approval and blame by examples takes the same three forms [that is, similarity, difference, and contrariety]. A reminder of parallels will be useful also when speaking about the future; for example, anyone saying that Dionysius was asking for a personal bodyguard in order to seize absolute power with their help could adduce as an example the fact that Pisistratus attained power in the same way."[11] Here the *exemplum* provides precedent for suspecting pretenses to tyranny due to a common action—requesting a bodyguard.

Both demonstrative and deliberative speeches, then, can make use of *exempla*. In the former, the epideictic use of *exemplum* would draw a correspondence between the subject of the speech and an historical figure or event. Such correspondence may be either positive or negative depending on the rhetor's purpose and on the common assessment of the *exemplum* used. For a modern example, we can consider someone lionizing a US president by comparing them to Abraham Lincoln or condemning a UK prime minister by associating them with Neville Chamberlain. Similarly, the deliberative speech may deploy *exempla* to provide precedent for an action. The Pisistratus example above uses a positive precedent to inspire pursuing a similar course. However, we can also imagine a negative use meant to dissuade one from choosing some option because it parallels a previous disaster. For instance, one might appeal to the story of the Trojan horse to caution against accepting what seems to be a gift from one's enemies.

In addition to these uses of *exempla*, there is a more basic role that they play in classical culture: as moral models in education. Quintilian, describing the early education of a would-be rhetor, highlights the exemplary role that reading material should play:

> These tender minds, which will be dragged down to the depths by whatever takes possession of them while they are still rough and entirely ignorant, should study not only eloquent works but, more importantly, those that are morally upright. . . . [L]et the mind rise by the sublimity of heroic songs

---

[11] Quintilian 5.11.7–8 (Latin original and English translation, LCL 125:432–35).

and, considering the greatness of their meanings, let it be filled with the highest principles.... With boys, what nourishes the mind and augments the character ought to be read first.[12]

There is a noticeable slippage in my use of the term *exemplum* here. In this passage, Quintilian is concerned not with oration itself but with the effect that literature has on the young man in his early education. The exemplary role of literature is about character formation, about instilling not only linguistic virtues but also moral ones. Even here, though, we are concerned with matters of persuasion, and it is this pedagogical role of rhetoric that will characterize most of Augustine's use of martyrs as *exempla*. As we will see in chapter 5, this concern for the moral character of the orator influences how Augustine depicts the martyr herself. For this chapter, however, my concern is to highlight that there is a protreptic role to the idea of *exempla* that lies at the very root of rhetorical education. This approach to the literary education of the young student assumes and ingrains the importance of culturally valued narratives as authoritative sources of ethical standards and evaluation. Indeed, the care that Quintilian (and Augustine[13]) takes to delineate between morally helpful and morally problematic texts only serves to reinforce the power of the exemplary, indeed, the rhetorical, effect upon the reader or auditor. Given this educational background, therefore, we can see how all rhetorical uses of *exempla* preserve their moral valence, be it implicit or explicit, and even if, as in deliberative speeches, that virtue is reduced to matters of utility.

And so we come to Augustine, a man trained by *exempla* and in their use. In what follows, I explore how Augustine merges different aspects of *exempla* to redefine the meaning of martyrdom and challenge what he sees as the more excessive practices among the cult of the martyrs. What we will find is that Augustine preaches and writes at a crucial moment in the life of an *exemplum*. He is not merely deploying the martyrs as established *exempla*; he is constructing them as such. Their cultural power is established, but their theological meaning is still malleable.

---

[12] Quintilian 1.8.4–8 (LCL 124:200–2). For the association of this concern for ethics in reading material and the concept of *exempla*, see Lausberg, §§ 24, 29.
[13] See *conf.* 1.16.25–26.

Exemplum exemplorum: Christ as Model Martyr

Augustine opens a sermon from 396 on the feast day of Fructuosus, Augurius, and Eulogius with what may serve as a programmatic statement on martyrial *exempla*: "The Lord Jesus not only instructed his martyrs by precept, but he also strengthened them by his example, so that when they suffered they would have something to follow. First, he suffered for them; he demonstrated the journey and then he made the way."[14] Though, as we will see below, Augustine more often depicts the martyrs as *exempla*, here he strengthens the significance of martyrial *exempla* by establishing Christ himself as the *exemplum exemplorum*.[15] The martyrs themselves require an *exemplum* to inspire, move, and strengthen them in their sufferings and deaths.

Nowhere do we see Christ's role as the martyrs' *exemplum* more explicitly than in Augustine's depiction of the proto-martyr Stephen. The stoned young man is not only the first to imitate Christ in dying; he also imitates Christ's disposition in death:

> What did Stephen do? What? First, attend to the one whom this good friend was imitating. The Lord Jesus Christ, when he was hanging on the cross, said, "Father, into your hands I commend my spirit" (Lk 23:46).... He [Christ] said "Father"; Stephen said, "Lord Jesus." What else did he also say? "Receive my spirit" (Acts 7:58).... That he prayed on his own account; something else came into his mind, whence he might imitate his Lord. Recall the words of the one hanging on the cross and note the words of the one who was stoned for confessing him. What did the former say? "Father, forgive them, because they do not know what they are doing" (Lk 23:34)....

---

[14] *s.* 273.1 (PL 38:1247).

[15] On the relationship between Christ and the martyrs, see Hans von Campenhausen's classic study, "Christus und de Märtyrer," chap. 3 in *Die Idee des Martyriums in der alten Kirche* (Göttingen: Vandenhoeck & Ruprecht, 1936), 56–105. This martyrial *imitatio Christi* is the focus of Candida Moss, *The Other Christs*. In a section on Augustine, Moss highlights the bishop's concern to distinguish worship of Christ from veneration of the saints, suggesting that Augustine "was combating practices and belief that did not distinguish between the two. It is all too tempting to conclude that popular believe in North Africa maintained that Christ and the martyrs were ontologically identical and hierarchically equal. There is, however, no concrete evidence for this. While it is a possibility, it is just as likely that Augustine's audience simply did not distinguish—ritually or theologically—between the martyrs and Christ" (168). The latter option is certainly more likely, though I am inclined to emphasize ritual confusion over the explicitly theological, inasmuch as those can be distinguished.

Imitating his Lord in this very thing, so that he might be his friend, he too said, "Lord, do not hold this sin against them" (Acts 7:59).[16]

In chapter 5 I will consider the effect of Stephen's own words, the extent to which he himself can be considered a rhetor and not just an *exemplum*. For now, though, if Christ is the ideal martyr *exemplum*, Stephen represents the ideal imitator, the model response to Christ's *exemplum*. Christ may set the mold for all martyrs who take up their cross and follow him as literally as possible to their own demise, but his crucifixion provides more to emulate than death. Here Stephen picks up on two deeper themes of Christ's exemplary martyrdom: trust in God/Christ and forgiveness for his persecutors. Augustine describes these as two kinds of prayers: one for himself, one for others. Christ has literally given Stephen the words to say to make his death cruciform.

Yet not every martyr can follow Christ so closely, in such lockstep as Stephen does. Nevertheless, in looking to Christ as the martyrial *exemplum*, they learn not just *to* die but *how* to die; they learn what sort of virtue should accompany their suffering and death. We get a glimpse of this in a sermon preached in 397 on the feast of the Scillitan martyrs. Augustine paints a picture of Christ before his persecutor, Pilate. As Pilate gloats about the power he has over Jesus, Christ could, Augustine notes, have said:

> "You do not have power over me, but I rather have power over you." If the Lord had said that, he would have spoken the truth, but he would not have provided us an example.... So what did he say? "You would have no power over me, unless it had been given to you from above." ... He taught the martyr that he ought to submit, not to a human, but to God; he taught the martyr, when she suffered anything at the hand of a human, to fear, not the human, but the one who permits the human to do the thing, the one who gives the human authority.[17]

Christ thus models a type of humility in the presence of one's persecutor. Though Christ had power over his persecutor, the martyrs do not over theirs, at least not of their own accord. Augustine goes on to quote 1 Pt 2:13 to

---

[16] *s.* 316.3 (PL 38:1433–34). See Dupont, "*Imitatio Christi, Imitatio Stephani*," 46–48; C. P. Mayer, "'*Attende Stephanum conservum tuum*' (*Serm.* 317, 2, 3). Sinn und Wert der Märtyrerverehrung nach den Stephanuspredigten Augustins," in Fructus Centesimus, 217–37.

[17] *s.* 299E.2 (MA 1:552–53).

support obedience even to evil worldly powers. But the ultimate reason for humility is not obedience for the sake of obedience but an awareness that all power comes from God and that it works, eventually, for God's purposes. The martyrs did not fight against their fate but humbly submitted to it out of trust in God. Nor did they believe it was their authority that was shown in their suffering but, again, only that of God.

Augustine even uses Christ as a martyrial *exemplum* in a judicial mode. In a sermon from 410 on the martyrdom of Cyprian, Augustine takes up two related questions: (1) was Cyprian justified in abandoning his post to avoid martyrdom and (2) are Donatists justified in (allegedly) committing suicide for the sake of martyrdom? The legitimacy of these claims aside, they provide a joint opportunity for deploying Christ as the ideal *exemplum* of martyrdom. The key moment comes as Christ heads for the Mount of Olives:

> Therefore, while he had come so that the Father might hand him over to the impious in order to redeem us, and that he might hand himself over to the impious in order to redeem us, all the same, after the supper, he withdrew to the Mount, he fled from the eyes of the persecutors. He wished them to come to him; he did not hand himself over voluntarily.[18]

For the case of Cyprian, this reading represents an *exemplum* of similarity. Just as Jesus retreated from his persecutors but did not resist them when they came, so did Cyprian. Therefore, if Jesus is to be judged righteous in this action, so should Cyprian. On the other hand, the alleged Donatist cliff divers fail to emulate Christ's *exemplum*, and their dissimilarity condemns them just as it exonerates Cyprian.

If Christ is such a powerful *exemplum* for martyrdom, why is there a need for anyone else? Why preach on the martyrs and not just on Christ's own passion? Part of the answer lies in the previous two chapters as we saw the rhetorical power of the martyrs, power that Augustine did not create and which he could not eliminate had he wanted to do so. The memory of the martyrs was going to do *something*; Augustine needed to shape what that something was. But another part of the answer lies in Augustine's own understanding—or construction—of the martyrs' particular significance vis-à-vis the model of Christ: "Who among us can do what the divine Christ can do? Someone says to himself, 'Christ prayed for his enemies because he's Christ, he's God,

---

[18] *s.* 313E.5 (MA 1:540).

he's the Only Son; so who am I to do this thing?'" Who indeed? It is difficult to have a "what would Jesus do" morality when Jesus has been definitively established as fully divine. With this difficulty, however, Augustine is able to move from the *exemplum* of Christ to the *exemplum* of the martyrs themselves:

> If your Lord is too much for you, do you not know that Stephen is your fellow servant? God has taught you a lesson through Stephen whose life had not yet drained away. If you see that these things happened before in the gospel, my brothers, no one should say in her heart "Who can do that?" Behold, Stephen did it. By himself? Of his own power? Yet if he did it by the gift of God, surely he did not enter only to shut the door against you.[19]

Here we see the exemplary power of the martyrs. If they have followed Christ, then we can follow them. They are mediatory *exempla*, bringing to the human level the divine works of Christ so that we who are too aware of our human limitations might find inspiration from other humans like us. This, then, brings us to the martyrs themselves and to the way that Augustine deploys them as *exempla* for his audience.

Exempla martyrum

In a brief sermon on the passion of St. Vincent—the significance of whose name I will discuss below—Augustine transitions from praising Christ as the "king of the martyrs" to instructing how one should emulate the martyrs. It is from Christ that Vincent received the faith for which he suffered and the strength that allowed him to endure.

> Vincent the deacon had received them both, he had received them, and he had them. For unless he had received them, how would he have had them? He had faithfulness in his speech; he had endurance in his suffering. So let no one presume in their heart when speaking. Let no one be confident in their own strength when suffering torments; because the wisdom by which we say good things prudently is from him, and from him is our endurance.[20]

---

[19] *s.* 315.8 (PL 38:1430).
[20] *s.* 276.1 (PL 38:1256).

Here we see the transitive relationship between Christ, the martyrs, and Augustine's contemporary Christians. The martyrs depend upon the grace of Christ for their victory and so should living Christians. The martyr is an *exemplum* of humility and dependence upon Christ. Augustine explicitly connects his account of the martyr to his audience's need to emulate them in a "from the greater to the lesser" form of the *exemplum*. If even someone we all acknowledge to be as great as Vincent only achieved what he did because of the grace of Christ, how much more so ought we to depend on the same grace in our lives? Though not all martyrial *exempla* will connect to Christ in this way, this use of Vincent represents the paradigm for martyr *exempla*: the life and death of the martyrs serve a protreptic purpose similar to the role of literary *exempla* in a rhetor's education. In this passage, then, Augustine makes Vincent's exemplary function explicit, but in doing so he also allows us to see all other descriptions of the martyrs' virtues as functional *exempla*, moral models that his audience is intended to emulate.

This theme of the martyrs' need for God's grace appears frequently in Augustine's sermons.[21] We see this dependency illustrated in an early sermon on the martyrdom of Castus and Aemilius. The pair provide ideal models for this virtue because they failed the test of martyrdom the first time. During the Decian persecutions, they gave in to torture and apostatized. Soon after, they earned their reconciliation through a baptism of blood. In their story, Augustine says, we can see the need to trust not in ourselves but in Christ:

> Perhaps at first they presumed upon their own power, and therefore they fell. [The Lord] showed them who they themselves were, as compared to who he was. He checked them in their presuming, he called them in their believing; he aided them as they fought, he crowned them when they won.... Let us desire to imitate not when they were defeated but when they were conquered. This is why the fall of great men has not been hidden, so that they might fear who presume upon their own power.[22]

Below I will discuss what I take to be the most interesting aspect of this line of argumentation, that is, Augustine's attempts to domesticate the cult of the

---

[21] See Dupont, "*Imitatio Christi, Imitatio Stephani*," 44–46; Jan den Boeft, "'*Martyres sunt, sed homines fuerunt*': Augustine on Martyrdom," in Fructus Centesimus: *Mélanges offerts à Gereard J. M. Bartelink à l'occasion de son soixante-cinquième anniversaire*, ed. A. A. R. Bastiaensen, A. Hilhorst, and C. H. Kneepkens (Turnhout: Brepols, 1989), 120.

[22] *s.* 285.4 (SE 56:84–85).

martyrs by enervating them of any self-sufficient heroism. For now, though, I want to highlight the way in which this passage points beyond the martyrs to Augustine's audience. As with St. Vincent, here the implication is that any Christian, especially those who have committed sin, must rely upon the grace of God to restore them.

One other perennial theme in martyr *exempla* is the proper valuation of the things of this world in contrast to those of heaven.[23] For example, returning to *s.* 273 on the martyrdoms of Fructuosus, Augurius, and Eulogius, we see Augustine turning the martyr celebration to this theme:

> The blessed saints, in whose memory we celebrate this day of their passion, have received, in exchange for temporal well-being, an eternal crown and immortality without end; in these solemnities they have left instruction for us. When we hear how the martyrs suffered, we rejoice and glorify God through them; and we do not grieve because they died. For even if they had not died for Christ, would they have lived until today? Why should confession not do what disease is going to do?[24]

No reader will be surprised by Augustine's spiritual turn here. What could those who gave their lives for Christ exemplify better than a contempt (or at least a relativized love) for this world? Augustine contrasts the mortal life of temporal well-being to the reward of immortality. Why should the martyrs have feared to die? They were going to do so either way. They chose to die by confessing Christ so that they might live eternally with Christ. The intended parallel is clear. We, like the martyrs, are mortal, enjoying the created, temporal goods of this ephemeral life. But our faith calls us to something more, something unfading. But inasmuch as we want to cling to the things of this world, we ought never do so at the expense of our faith. While the martyrs were willing to give up their lives, what are we willing to give up for the sake of Christ? Here we have an implicit "from the greater to the lesser" *exemplum*: "The martyrs were able to give up earthly life itself; surely you can give up X."

We see versions of this type of martyrial *exemplum* repeated *ad nauseam* in Augustine's sermons. In a sermon on St. Vincent, Augustine takes care to dispel the idea that the martyrs despised their bodies; but he is

---

[23] On this theme in Augustine's theology of martyrdom, see den Boeft, "*Martyres sunt*," 120.
[24] *s.* 273.2 (PL 38:1248–49).

also clear that they had their priorities straight: "[The martyrs] were looking out for [the body] when they seemed to be neglecting it; when persisting in it faithfully, they endured temporary torments, they acquire eternal glory even for the flesh itself."[25] Or in a sermon on the Scillitan martyrs: "The blessed saints spoke the truth and were killed. So what? If no one had killed them, would they have lived until now? How much better that witnessing to the truth should do what a fever was going to do soon enough! Spare this life and lose true life. Spare the transient things and lose the eternal ones."[26] Or in a sermon on St. Lawrence where Augustine more explicitly draws the connection between the martyrs and his exhortation to devalue this life: "From love of this temporal life, approach, if you are able, to loving the eternal life which the martyrs loved, who despised these temporal things. I beg, I beseech, I implore not only you, but you and us, let us cherish eternal life."[27]

Sentiments like these, of course, can be found throughout Augustine's writings. As with many early Christian writers, the relative valuing of earthly and heavenly lives is a leitmotif in his work. But this is exactly the point: in these sermons, Augustine deploys the rhetorical tool of *exempla* to shape the martyrs into models for his most cherished theological and pastoral assumptions. Of course, the martyrs encourage Christians to forsake things of this life for things of the next. How could Augustine's martyrs not do this? What else could someone like Augustine possibly use them for if not for this?

Exempla contra cultum

As significant as these virtuous *exempla* are, they risk standing in a vacuum. Augustine thinks his audience needs to cultivate humility and spiritual perspective, and the martyrs provide a prime source for such examples. More important, I believe, are his contextualized uses of the martyrial *exempla*. He is preaching about the martyrs (usually) not on a random day but on their feast days. He is preaching in the context of the larger cult of the martyrs and all the observances that accompany it. His preaching is not indifferent to this fact. It is clear that he has an agenda: to domesticate what he sees as the excesses of the celebrations by redefining what it means to honor the

---

[25] s. 277.3 (PL 38:1259).
[26] s. 299F.3 (PLS 2:790–91).
[27] s. 302.2 (SPM 1:101).

martyrs.[28] True honor means imitation, and Augustine is in the right position to define just what the imitation should look like, mapping the virtues of the Christian life as he sees it upon the powerful cultural memory of the martyrs. This maneuver is the heart of his use of martyrs as *exempla*.

We can unpack this use of martyr *exempla* against the traditional celebration of the cult in four ways. First, Augustine repeatedly contrasts imitation of the martyrs with mere veneration. Celebration is good, but imitation is better: "May the holy martyrs pray for us that we might not only celebrate their solemnities but also imitate their virtues."[29] Again, "This festival of all the glorious martyrs has been instituted in the church so that those who did not see them suffering might be led by faith to imitation and may be reminded of them by the festival.... [L]et us prepare our hearts for their feast in such a way that we do not cut ourselves off from their imitation."[30] This emphasis sets up every martyrial *exemplum* Augustine offers, both those we have seen above and those we will see below. It is the foundational move that seeks to redefine the very nature of martyr veneration itself. Here we see, then, Augustine negotiating with the power of the martyr cults and beginning to turn them to his pastoral ends.

Second, Augustine uses this emphasis on imitation in the midst of celebration to summon his audience to emulate many of the same (or similar) virtues that we saw above. Augustine comments on the feast day of Cyprian:

> But the celebration of the feast of the martyrs ought to be the imitation of their virtue. It is easy to celebrate a martyr's honor; the great thing is to imitate the martyr's faith and patience. Thus, let us do the former so that we choose to do the latter. Let us so celebrate [the feast] that we might love to imitate [the virtues]. What do we praise in the faith of a martyr? That she fought to the death for the truth, and in this she conquered. She scorned the flattery of the world; she did not fall to its savagery.[31]

The reader hears an echo of themes we have already explored. Not only should the celebration of the martyrs lead to imitation of the martyrs, but also imitation ought to focus on, among other things, sharing the martyrs'

---

[28] Johannes Quasten, "Die Reform des Martyrerkultes durch Augustinus," *Theologie und Glaube* 25 (1933): 318–31.
[29] *s.* 299F.4 (PLS 2:791).
[30] *s.* 305A.1 (MA 1:56).
[31] *s.* 311.1 (PL 38:1414).

faith, especially that faith which despises the things of this world. Augustine, therefore, turns Cyprian's feast into an occasion to instruct his audience on what a proper spiritual disposition should look like, with the honored martyr-bishop as a powerful *exemplum*.

Third, Augustine not only adds imitation of virtue to the celebration but also uses the *exempla* of the martyrs to critique the excesses he sees within the cult of the martyrs itself. In the same sermon on Cyprian, Augustine warns his audience against behavior that he sees as all too worldly:

> How in this place, while psalms are to be sung, ought anyone to dance? Not so many years ago, even this place was invaded by the wantonness of dancers. A place so holy, where the body of so holy a martyr lies, even this holy place.... This place, I repeat, so holy a place had been invaded by the pestilence and wantonness of dancers. Throughout the whole night impious things were sung, and there was dancing to the singing.[32]

This passage suggests that, prior to a prohibition of such behavior, celebrations on the feast day of Cyprian included dancing that Augustine considered disruptive and disrespectful. Similarly, Augustine concludes a sermon on an unnamed group of martyrs by exhorting his audience, "So this is what it means to love the martyrs, this is what celebrating the feast day of the martyrs with devotion and piety really means—not drowning yourself in wine, but imitating their faith and endurance."[33] Excessive drinking represents not a past but a present concern for Augustine, likely referring to the practice of *refrigeria* that could easily, he suggests, get out of hand.

While the above passages describe Augustine's concerns about the dangers of martyr veneration practices, he also brings the *exempla* of the martyrs to bear upon this concern, recruiting the saints to shame such behavior. Preaching on the deaths of Marianus and James, he describes their own imbibing:

> From here [from God], from here our martyrs drank; from here they were made so drunk, that they did not recognize their relations. For how many holy martyrs, as their passions drew near, were tempted by the coaxing of their relations who were trying to call them back to this temporal, empty,

---

[32] *s.* 311.5 (PL 38:1415).
[33] *s.* 328.8 (RB 51).

and fleeting sweetness? But they who in their thirst had drunk from the fountain which is with God, and were drunk; in confessing, they belched Christ, ignoring their carnal relations who were drunk on the wine of error.[34]

The intoxication of the martyrs stands in stark contrast to that of Augustine's parishioners—or at least to how he portrays them to themselves. The intoxication of revelers at martyr shrines—again, as depicted by Augustine—is too worldly, too tied to the pleasures of the flesh. Truly honoring the martyrs, truly celebrating them, means imitating their virtue, striving to be like them as much as possible even if literal martyrdom itself is not an option. And emulating the *exempla* of the martyrs means celebrating them without drunken excess. Instead, Augustine proposes, become drunk in the Lord, not in the flesh.

Finally, in what is Augustine's most consistent and vehement use of the martyr *exempla* in response to the cult practices, he reminds his audience to worship not the martyrs but the one whom the martyrs worshipped.[35] Returning to Augustine's sermon on Fructuosus, Augurius, and Eulogius, we see just how adamant he is on this point. He describes one of the latter two, both deacons, being asked whether they worship the bishop Fructuosus, who may have been martyred prior to them. The deacon's response: "'I do not worship Fructuosus, but I worship God, whom Fructuosus also worships.' In this way he admonished us that we should honor the martyrs and with the martyrs worship God. For we ought not to be the kind of people the pagans are, whom we grieve. And indeed, they do worship dead human beings. . . . But the only true God ought to have a temple, and to the only true God sacrifice should be offered."[36] We may use that early sermon from 396 as a bookend with a sermon from 425 on the enshrining of relics of the proto-martyr Stephen: "Therefore both this place and this day are commended to your love; both are to be celebrated to the honor of God, whom Stephen confessed. For we have not built an altar in this place to Stephen, but an altar to God from Stephen's relics."[37] Combining this last quotation with Augustine's urging to imitate the martyrs on their feast day and the *exemplum* of the martyrs themselves pointing toward God and away from themselves, we can see that

---

[34] *s.* 284.2 (PL 38:1288–89).
[35] Campenhausen, *Die Idee des Martyriums in der alten Kirche*, 101–6.
[36] *s.* 273.3–4 (PL 38:1249).
[37] *s.* 318.1 (PL 38:1438).

throughout his career as bishop Augustine has a concern to reorient the veneration of the martyrs toward worship of God. We know that Augustine and others were concerned that the cult of the martyrs might appear to be too "pagan," too akin to the worship of deified humans that might either distract from the worship of God or even lead to heretical polytheism, at least in practice if not in doctrine. Indeed, all of Augustine's use of martyrial *exempla* can be conceived as pointing toward proper worship of God. The virtues that his audience are to imitate go hand in hand with honoring God, not humans. They require a proper perspective upon the limitations of the things of this world, including human heroes, and a true trust in the grace of the true God.

Ἐτυμολογία and *Adnominatio*

From the perspective of the historian, the exemplary power of the martyrs is a social and rhetorical construction, not original to Augustine, but masterfully deployed by him. Yet for Augustine himself, the martyrs are inherently exemplary. He, thus, unearths the providential work of God that occurs in and through the martyrs, a theme I will explore in more depth in chapters 3 and 5. We can gain a glimpse of this theme, though, by linking the practice of *exempla* to another rhetorical (and grammatical) technique, namely, the use of etymology. Augustine helps define the exemplary significance of the martyrs by using etymological analyses of their names. After surveying the importance of etymology in grammatical and rhetorical discourse, I will discuss Augustine's use of nominal etymology in general and, specifically, with the proto-martyr Stephen, Perpetua and Felicitas, and the martyr-bishop Cyprian. Augustine finds the not-so-hidden purposes of God revealed in the names of the martyrs.

"This day," Augustine tells his audience, "occurring annually, recalls to our memory, and in some way represents, the day on which the holy slaves of God, Perpetua and Felicity, decorated with the crowns of martyrdom, flowered into perpetual felicity, clinging to the name of Christ in the fight (*praelio*), and at the same time also finding their own names in the reward (*praemio*)."[38] In this opening passage to a sermon on the feast of the famous North African martyrs Perpetua and Felicity,[39] Augustine plays upon the

---

[38] s. 280.1 (PL 38:1281). For the significance of this rhyming construction, see chapter 3.
[39] On Augustine's treatment of Perpetua and Felicitas, see Elena Martin, "*Sanctae Famulae Dei*: Towards a Reading of Augustine's Female Martyrs" (PhD thesis, Durham University, 2009).

meaning of their names to highlight the goal to which all Christians should aspire, namely, the eternal happiness of life with God. But is this mere "play"? That is to say, is Augustine providing a rhetorical flourish to ornament his real argument, or is this commentary on the meaning of their names central to the argument itself? To put it in rhetorical terms, is this a matter of mere *adnominatio/paronomasia*, a figure meant to adorn one's speech, or is it etymology, here considered as part of *inventio* and therefore essential to the argument?

Den Boeft has argued that this very passage is an example of the former, that it is not central to the argument but merely an ornament, a "word-play," as it were.[40] He also distinguishes between the technical and the topical use of etymology, the former pertaining to the work of the grammarian (though rooted in the philosophical tradition that goes back through the Stoics to Plato's *Cratylus*), and the latter pertaining to the work of the rhetor who uses them to support her arguments. In what follows, I challenge den Boeft's reading in two ways. First, Augustine's explication of the meaning of names fits within the technical tradition that den Boeft references, and understanding Augustine's method and assumptions will require us to connect them to the *Cratylus* and the Stoic-influenced work of Varro. Second, building on this tradition, Augustine's use of what I call "nominal etymology" is in fact central to his argument in these sermons if we understand, as I believe I have shown we should, that their argument is an exhortation to emulation. Thus, while I will note important places where Augustine's technique may fall short of some etymological strictures, it is nevertheless closer to the work of etymology than it is to the wordplay of *adnominatio*.

Den Boeft describes the relationship of *adnominatio* to etymology this way:

> In spite of some similarities *adnominatio* fundamentally differs from etymology in its rhetorical use in that the latter . . . belongs to the domain of the *loci* and thus to that of *inventio*, whereas *adnominatio* is treated in the department of *elocutio*. Its main function is not to provide arguments to prove a point, but as one of the *figurae verborum*, to add *ornatus* to a text. . . . *Adnominatio* is a stylistic technique, *etymologia* has an argumentative force.[41]

---

[40] Jan den Boeft, "Etymologies in Augustine's *De Civitate Dei* X," *Vigiliae Christianae* 33 (1979): 242–59, see esp. 246.
[41] Den Boeft, "Some Etymologies," 245.

EXAMPLE OF THE MARTYRS 51

Further, he quotes Mohrmann as elucidating the nature of *adnominatio* thus: "One might define word-play as the establishing of an etymological, or seemingly etymological, connection between two words (*paronomasia*)."[42] Two things are significant about these distinctions. First, both Mohrmann and den Boeft treat *adnominatio* and ἐτυμολογία as linked, the former perhaps even depending upon an etymological move. Second, den Boeft delineates the two based upon their function. While *adnominatio* may be etymological, it is not etymology in the full rhetorical sense unless it is used for argumentative purposes rather than ornamental. The first point, I will show, does not align with the depiction of *adnominatio* in the Latin sources, especially in the *Rhetoric to Herennius*. To the second point, I will show that Augustine's etymology of the martyrs' names is in fact central to his exemplary argument.

I turn first to the description of *adnominatio* in the *Rhetoric to Herennius*. The anonymous author offers several ways in which the figure might be accomplished. "*Adnominatio* is when an alteration of tone or of letters is added to a verb or noun so that similar words are accommodated to different meanings."[43] This definition does not describe the use of etymologically related words. It describes, essentially, a pun. The copious examples the author provides describe lengthening or shortening a vowel to connect two unconnected words, often with the effect, as the definition suggests, of juxtaposing two contrasting concepts in an amusing, thought-provoking, or ear-pleasing way. There may be more warrant in Mohrmann and den Boeft's reading of *adnominatio* in Quintilian. He explains that *adnominatio* "may be produced ... from some approximation to a preceding word with a change of case: for example, Domitius Afer, defending Cloatilla, says, '*mulier omnium rerum imperita, in omnibus rebus infelix*.'"[44] This example of *adnominatio* turns upon the shift from "*omnium rerum*" to "*omnibus rebus*." As I will discuss below, there is a place for such moves in technical etymology, but here there is no etymological force. The words are related, yes, but the purpose has nothing to do with highlighting or explaining any original meaning. Augustine's connection of Perpetua and Felicity to perpetual felicity is not *adnominatio* in the sense presented in the *Rhetoric to Herennius*. But is it

---

[42] Christine Mohrmann, *Études sur le Latin des Chrétiens* I, Storia e Letteratura: Raccolta di Studi e Testi 65 (Roma: Edizioni di Storia e Letteratura, 1958), 289. Quoted in den Boeft, "Some Etymologies," 245.
[43] *rhet. Her.* 4.21.29 (LCL 403:300–2).
[44] Quintilian, 9.3.66 (Latin original and English translation, LCL 127:138–39).

merely fulfilling the ornamental purpose that Quintilian has his inflected pair perform? If it is, then den Boeft would be justified in categorizing this passage as an example of *adnominatio*, at least according to Quintilian.

But something more is going on in Augustine's discussion of Perpetua and Felicity's names, and sussing it out is imperative for understanding Augustine's exemplary preaching on the martyrs because he makes similar moves with many other figures. Before turning to the discussion of etymology in the rhetorical handbooks, though, I want to turn to the philosophers and the grammarians to establish two key points: First, Augustine's nominal etymology bears resemblance to the linguistic theory presented in the *Cratylus* and to that which was systematized by the Stoics. Second, Augustine's method is evident in the grammatical work of Varro, who has much to say about techniques of etymology. Only after discussing these two points will I move to the rhetorical theory of etymology and Augustine's use of it to turn the names of the martyrs into exemplary resources.

The philosophical starting point for etymology is Plato's *Cratylus*.[45] The literary context is a debate about whether or not names (not necessarily proper ones, though these are the main examples given) are affiliated with their object by convention or by nature. Plato leads his interlocutor, Hermogenes, to conclude that names, if used properly and truthfully, must accord to the nature of the thing named. But this does not mean that there is only one possible name for a thing. For instance, both Hector and his son, Astyanax, share the same relative etymology: "For lord (ἄναξ) and holder (ἕκτωρ) mean almost the same thing, both being names of a king. For obviously a man is holder of that of which he is lord; for it is clear that he rules it and possesses it and has it."[46] This passage represents the key point I want to glean from the *Cratylus*: the etymology of names, for Plato, reveals something about the nature of the thing named. He may leave room for a plurality of possible names, but if any are true names, they must conform to something true about the thing named. A person's name, then, is not arbitrary; it is revelatory.

Augustine need not have read the *Cratylus* to get an appreciation for this feature of nominal etymology. The Stoics developed a notion of the materiality of the signifier that conformed to the materiality of the world. As Mark Amsler describes:

---

[45] For the philosophical background on etymology, see Dorothea Frede and Brad Inwood, *Language and Learning: Philosophy of Language in the Hellenistic Age* (Cambridge: Cambridge University Press, 2005), 14–35.

[46] Plato, *Cratylus*, 393a (LCL 167:38).

> The philosopher-grammarian uses etymological analysis to break through the surface of language and reveal the reasons why the original namers (identified with the philosopher-kings) established a set of primitive names keyed to the fundamental elements of the world. Working outward from this isomorphic cradle of words and elements, the philosopher-grammarian can then account for the general language system which stands for the order of things.... The Stoics distinguished derivation (*Romulus>Roma>Romanus*) from inflection (words marked for case, tense, and concord).[47]

We see here a similar emphasis on the naturalness of the correlation between names and the named, a relationship Amsler refers to as "isomorphic." In addition, we find a distinction between the relationship between the same word when it is declined or conjugated, on the one hand, and the relationship between distinct words with a common root. Both Augustine with Perpetua and Felicity and Plato with Hector and Astyanax are attending to derivation rather than mere inflection. This distinction further distinguishes *adnominatio* as described in Quintilian from the etymological work that Augustine is doing in his preaching on the martyrs. Augustine is not just offering various inflections of the same word; he is connecting the names to words with the same root to highlight their spiritual appropriateness.

Varro provides an example of this sort of derivative analysis in a passage defending the validity of even limited etymological discourse. "He who shows that *equitatus* is from *equites*, *equites* from *eques*, *eques* from *equus*, even though he does not give the source of the word *equus*, still gives several lessons and satisfies an appreciative person."[48] This movement from "cavalry" back to "horse" may be, to Varro's readers, an incomplete etymology because it limits itself to derivation, not providing an explanation for the base term. For Varro, however, even an incomplete etymology such as this is worthy of the grammarian's time and can reveal something about the significance of the derived words. This type of derivation is the exact kind of etymology that Augustine is performing when he elucidates the meaning of Perpetua and Felicity's names for his audience.

---

[47] Mark Amsler, *Etymology and Grammatical Discourse in Late Antiquity and the Early Middle Ages* (Amsterdam: John Benjamins Publishing Company, 1989), 22–23. See also A. C. Lloyd, "Grammar and Metaphysics in the Stoa," in *Hellenistic Philosophy*, ed. A. A. Long (New York: Charles Scribner's Sons, 1974), 58–74.

[48] Varro, *ling. Lat.* 7.4 (Latin original and English translation, LCL 333:270–71).

Having demonstrated that Augustine is not deploying *adnominatio* and that he does evince philosophical and grammatical understandings of etymology, it remains to examine the role of etymology within classical rhetoric.[49] Aristotle, though not using the word "etymology," describes a topic concerning "the meaning of a name." This topic, he says, "is also customarily spoken in praise of the gods. Conon called Thrasybulus 'the man of bold counsel (θρασύβουλον)' and Herodicus said of Thrasymachus, 'you are always bold in battle (θρασύμαχος);'" and so on.[50] Thus, for Aristotle, nominal etymology is associated with speeches of praise, much like the ones Augustine uses to honor the martyrs. Augustine, however, turns that praise into exhortation to imitate the qualities found in the martyrs' names.

Exempla and Ἐτυμολογία

"Martyr" is a loanword from Greek, where it refers to a witness. Augustine is aware of this linguistic debt and makes much of the term's original meaning.[51] At times the etymology leads to quite complex theological moves. For instance, in a sermon on St. Vincent, Augustine declares:

> The Lord bears great witness to his witnesses, when, after stiffening their hearts for the struggle, he does not abandon their bodies once they are dead, like the outstanding miracle he performed over the body of blessed Vincent. The enemy desired and took all necessary steps to ensure that it should completely disappear; but a divine sign gave its whereabouts away and revealed it for religious burial and veneration so promptly that it would continue as a lasting memorial to the victory of piety and impiety's defeat.... What, after all, is God doing when he performs miracles with the bodies of the departed saints but bearing witness to the truth that what dies does not perish as far as he himself is concerned.[52]

---

[49] Here I am indebted to den Boeft, "Some Etymologies," 244, and will echo his brief summary with my own emphases.

[50] Aristotle, *rhet.* 2.23.29 (1400b). See also Cicero, *inv.* 2.9.28, where the meanings associated with a cognomen can be used to draw suspicion upon the accused. Cicero, *top.* 8.35–37 describes the use of etymology in legal disputes but in a way not connected to proper names. Quintilian, *inst.* 1.6.29–38 provides a history of the various terms used to indicate etymology. He also laments that "some scholars have not hesitated to make every explanation of a name a matter of etymology."

[51] On Augustine's use of the etymology of "martyr," see den Boeft, "*Martyres sunt*," 122–24; Campenhausen, *Die Idee des Martyriums*, 162–75.

[52] *s.* 275.3 (PL 38:1255).

This passage is not, strictly speaking, exemplary. The details about Vincent's body can hardly be emulated. The heart of the excerpt lies in the double witness. God becomes Vincent's martyr, so to speak, so that he who witnessed to God is witnessed to by God after his death. In describing the preservation of Vincent's body, Augustine establishes the divine prerogative in establishing the cult of the martyrs around corporal relics. Yet, two exhortations are secreted within this play on human and divine "witnesses." First, the veneration of the martyr is to be done with piety if it is to commemorate its victory over impiety. Such is the point of God's witness to God's witnesses: to establish this implied cultic *exemplum*. Second, part of God's witness is testimony to the life that this world cannot destroy. If, then, we desire to emulate the martyrs, we ought to attend to what the witness of witnesses reveals about the virtues inherent in their martyrdoms.

Elsewhere, however, Augustine deploys the etymology of "martyr" in a more straightforward exemplary way. A common theme unites these instances: the difference between true and false martyrs. Augustine tells his audience that "'martyr,' a Greek word, is *testis* (witness) in Latin. If, therefore, they were true witnesses, they spoke the truth and speaking the truth they received their crowns. If, however, they were false witnesses—which of course they were not—they went to receive punishment, not crowns."[53] Though this passage has only the most minimal of exemplary power (one should be truthful), elsewhere Augustine opens up the potential of the distinction between true and false martyrs. In a sermon on the Scillitan martyrs, he again reminds his audience of the Greek meaning of "martyr." The heart of his description of true and false witnesses is a depiction of the martyrs' trial as they are demanded to deny Christ: "To deny Christ is false testimony. 'Say that Christ is not God and that those we worship are gods.' Both are false for on the one hand Christ is God and on the other they are not gods."[54] Here the veracity of a witness is tied to her maintenance of faith in Christ in the face of imminent death. No doubt, Augustine sees his own flock as in danger of such pagan influences. There is, then, a possible *exemplum* in such faithfulness. More compelling, however, is the explanation of truth and falsity that surrounds this narration of the martyrs' trial: "Therefore the holy martyrs, who are not false witnesses but true ones, testified by their blood that there is another life to be preferred to this life, because they so strongly disdained this

[53] *s.* 328.2: (RB 51:16). See also, *s.* 286.1, 315.2–3.
[54] *s.* 299F.2 (RB 50:21).

passing life. . . . True witnesses were holding onto this, seeing in their mind his future gifts."[55] In addition to the Scillitan martyrs' obvious faithfulness, then, Augustine depicts them as witnesses attesting to the truth of a better life beyond this terrestrial one. We have seen this theme, of course, repeatedly in Augustine's use of martyrial *exempla*. Here it is the etymology of the very term "martyr" that he deploys to establish members of that category as truthful witnesses.

More interesting is Augustine's use of isomorphic nominal etymology to illustrate the virtues of his *exempla*. The martyrs' names became signs of God's providential grace at work in them and indications of the values that ordinary Christians are to emulate if they want to honor the martyrs. For example, in a sermon on St. Agnes, Augustine declares that "The virgin was what she was called. Agnes signifies 'lamb' (*agnam*) in Latin and, in Greek, 'chaste.' She was what she was called."[56] As a lamb Agnes is innocently slaughtered; yet what stands out about this lamb is its chastity. Augustine's auditors might not be able to be sacrificed like lambs, but they can follow Agnes's chastity and, it is implied, earn a common heavenly reward. Similarly, in a sermon on St. Vincent, Augustine returns to a familiar theme: "The holy martyr Vincent was victorious (*vincentem*) everywhere. He was victorious (*vicit*) in words; he was victorious (*vicit*) in suffering; he was victorious (*vicit*) in confession; he was victorious (*vicit*) in tribulations; he was victorious (*vicit*) when burned by fire; he was victorious (*vicit*) when submerged by waves. . . . But all this ought to be referred not to the human but to the glory of God."[57] As we have seen, Augustine is eager to turn his audience's devotion from the martyrs to the God of the martyrs. In this passage, then, Augustine uses the etymology of "Vincent" first to praise his endurance, but then to point toward the God who makes such endurance possible, as if to say, "If you wish to conquer like Vincent, look not to his strength but to God's grace."

The most extended use of isomorphic nominal etymology comes in a sermon on St. Quadratus:

> The name of this martyr prompts us to say something about holy squaring (*quadratura*). Holy Noah was commanded to make the ark of squared beams. Why is squareness chosen; what is signified by it, if not that nobody is able to throw down a standing square [cube]? For however you move

---

[55] *s.* 299F.1, 3 (RB 50:21, 23).
[56] *s.* 273.6 (PL 38:1250).
[57] *s.* 274 (PL 38:1252–53). See also 275.3, 277A.1.

it, it will still stand. Exhaust yourself rolling it. Labor to turn it over. And when you turn it over, you will find that which you have turned over stands just as it did before it was turned over. Everywhere it stands. Financial loss was proposed, the things of those who confessed Christ were confiscated; Quadratus still stood. Exile was proposed, and the loss of his carnal homeland; cognizant of his spiritual homeland, Quadratus still stood. Savage torments and tortures were inflicted upon him; cognizant of the fearful pains of Gehenna, Quadratus still stood. Vast secular rewards were promised, so that Christ would be denied; cognizant of the celestial crown, Quadratus still stood. A Christian should be like that; but in order to be like that, Christ must be called upon. Let him square you.[58]

There is no better illustration of Augustine's use of isomorphic nominal etymology to deploy the martyrs as *exempla*. Augustine makes full use of the idea of squareness—or, in the illustration, something more like cubeness. A cube cannot be overturned without landing upright on another side. It will not topple over no matter the energy exerted against it. But this is not just a description of Quadratus; this should describe every Christian, and every Christian should call upon Christ for such stability in their faith. Augustine draws out the *exemplum* of Quadratus in an elegant rhetorical performance that in another age would be dismissed as an extended pun.

I want to conclude this look at Augustine's nominal etymology by highlighting his use of the tactic on four martyrs key to North African piety: Cyprian the martyr-bishop of Carthage in the mid-third century; Perpetua and Felicitas, martyrs in Carthage from the early second century; and the proto-martyr Stephen, himself not a North African, but whose relics arrived in the region in 415, soon to be enshrined. Taken together, the nominal etymology of these four martyrs encapsulates the journey of the one who desires to follow the *exempla* of the martyrs.

In one of his many sermons on Cyprian, Augustine compares him to some berries, *botrus cypri*, a reference to Song 1:13. This phrase "signifies through the most fragrant tree the most fragrant grace; surely, then, just as he [Cyprian] was made, through his right faith, a Christian in Christ, so in his sweet smell he was made a Cyprian by the *cyprus*." Here we see again the theme of Christ as the ultimate martyrial *exemplum exemplorum*. Cyprian himself becomes who he is by emulating Christ, by being drawn to imitation

[58] *s.* 306C.2–3 (MA 1:648).

of him by him. But the olfactory effect does not stop there. Cyprian himself emits the fragrance: "Thus, the sweet smell of Christ in our Cyprian goes out from this see, being enough not for this city alone, nor for Africa alone, of which this city is the capital, but spreading far and wide, from the rising of the sun to its setting, where the name of the Lord is praised. . . . [B]y suffering he preceded others who were going to imitate him."[59] Cyprian thus represents the appeal of the martyrs, the fragrant odor that draws others not only to honor him but also even to emulate him. Augustine suggests that the life and death of Cyprian are themselves effective rhetorical performances. Even though he does not make explicit the way his audience should imitate Cyprian, Augustine does illustrate the way in which Cyprian himself functioned as an *exemplum*.

For Stephen, Augustine plays on the name's Greek parallel, στέφανος, meaning a laurel crown. When speaking of a martyr, this word points immediately to the martyr's crown, her reward for endurance unto death. As we saw above, Augustine repeatedly highlights Stephen's emulation of Christ's *exemplum*. One aspect of this imitation is Stephen's prayer to forgive his murderers. Augustine thus urges his audience, "Quick, brothers, let us follow Stephen, that we might be crowned [playing on the Greek στέφανος]. Most of all he is to be followed and imitated in loving our enemies."[60] The στέφανος of Stephen is a steppingstone to the true lesson of the *exemplum*: if you want the crown, you have to love your enemies. Stephen, then, provides through his *exemplum* not only the goal of imitation but also, more importantly, the way to that goal.

Finally, we come to Perpetua and Felicitas. Referring to the larger group of Christians martyred with them, Augustine says:

> Perpetua, of course, and Felicity are the names of the two women, but that reward is for them all. I mean that all the martyrs labored bravely for a time in the contest of suffering and confessing only that they might rejoice in perpetual felicity. . . . For just as by the example of their glorious struggle they encourage us to imitate them, so also by their names they testify to the irremovable gift we are going to receive. Let them hold on to each other; let them bind themselves together. For we do not hope for one without

---

[59] s. 313C.2 (PLS 2:610).
[60] s. 314.2 (PL 38:1426).

the other. "Perpetual" profits not if there is no "felicity"; and "felicity" disappears if it is not "perpetual."[61]

Two aspects of this passage bear examination. First, Augustine makes the exemplary nature of the isomorphic nominal etymology explicit. As we have seen, this is not always the case and in other excerpts we have had to assume the presence of *exempla* to a certain degree. Here, however, he refers to their struggle as an example meant to be imitated. And that struggle is directly related to their promised reward of perpetual felicity. Second, the notion of perpetual felicity points toward a heavenly reward. This promised beatitude brings us back to the theme of distinguishing between the goods of this world and those of the next. Imitating the *exempla* of Perpetual and Felicitas, then, means not just struggling, but being willing to struggle precisely because of faith in the eternal goods of God.

From Cyprian to Stephen to Perpetua and Felicitas we see the progression of the martyrs' *exempla*. First, Cyprian's pleasant scent woos us toward the martyrial life. Stephen's Christomorphic behavior shows what the life and death of the martyr must look like. And, finally, the one who imitates the martyrs will share in their perpetual felicity.

The names of the martyrs are not incidental. They are not mere signs by which their parents chose to call them. They are divinely ordered, providential, and revelatory not only of the particular martyr's virtue but also of the common virtues and rewards of all martyrs. But these names do more than inform. They instruct the faithful, exhorting them to emulation so that they too might be worthy of the name "martyr." Moreover, Augustine's discussion of the martyrs' names is no mere ornamentation. Rather, it is central to his rhetorical purpose, an extension of his primary use of the martyrs as spiritual *exempla*.

Conclusion

Exempla represent Augustine's most common rhetorical use of martyrs and martyrdom. They allow him to promote spiritual virtues to his flock, work for reform in the cult, and connect the sacrifice of Christ to the lives of everyday Christians through mimetic heroic intermediaries. Indeed, Christ is

[61] *s*. 282.1 (PL 38:1285).

the ultimate *exemplum* whom the martyrs follow, but quotidian Christians may need something more proximate to follow. Throughout the rest of this study, the exemplary role of the martyrs will continue to shape the theological trajectory of Augustine's theology of martyrdom and my own analysis of that theology. At times, as in his contention of Donatist claims to martyrdom, Augustine will deploy *exempla* to prove his forensic point. For other topics, as in his discussion of martyrs and historiography, to which I turn next, the very idea of heroic *exempla* will be turned on its head.

3
The Time of the Martyrs

Introduction

For most Christians in the Roman Empire at the time of Augustine, martyrdom was the stuff of communal memory, not current experience. While the Donatists may have suffered persecution and thus laid claim to a continuation of martyrdom in their communion, the fact is that martyrdom had largely transitioned in Augustine's time from a threat to a cult, from something that people prepared to endure to something they ritually commemorated. But the time of the martyrs lay not only in the past. Through his theological rhetoric, Augustine works to make the past present, or rather, to establish a relationship between the time of the martyrs and that of his audience.

Yet Augustine is not satisfied to make mere connections between the past and present. Rather, he joins them together in a complete reimagining of history, divine providence, and timeless virtue. Here I use the term "history" in two senses: (1) the flow of time within the created world and (2) the way we narrate or make sense of that temporal flow. Augustine's rhetoric of martyrdom affects and is affected by both of these histories; just as the martyrs themselves are figures from the church's past, so the way martyrs and martyrdom are constructed shapes and is shaped by the way Christians rehearse that past. This universal feature of martyr discourse is what we encounter par excellence in Augustine's reconstitution of history, both temporal existence itself and our narration of the past.

To begin, I turn toward history as a literary discipline embodying the way a culture or community narrates its past. Again, I start not with Augustine's discussion of that history itself but with another way his audience connects to the martyrs of the past, in this case via the use of rhetorical *exempla*, with which we have already become acquainted in the previous chapter. I then connect Augustine's use of *exempla* to the paradigmatic use of them by Roman historians like Livy and Sallust. I argue that Augustine uses the martyrs as *exempla* in part to overturn the dominant Roman historical narrative of decline. It is not the case that the past alone is the domain of heroes, pagan or Christian. Any age can be the context for exercising virtue and for emulating the martyrs, whether or not there is imperial persecution.

Next, I take up the seemingly unrelated theme of the beauty of the martyrs. Through the use of antithesis, Augustine contrasts the ugliness of the martyrs' suffering with the beauty of the virtue they display through such suffering. This antithesis, I suggest, is not just a matter of style but also of accommodation and arrangement representing the ordering of divine providence, the guiding force in the sacred history in which martyrs are participants. This providential arrangement combines with the exemplary history of previous sections to establish a holistic picture of the martyrs' place and role within history.

Rhetoric, Historiography, and *Exempla* of Virtue

In the previous chapter, we saw how Augustine uses the martyrs as rhetorical *exempla* to promote the virtues of the Christian life, often as a way to rein in the alleged excesses of cultic venerations. If you want to honor the martyrs, Augustine says, emulate their sobriety, their integrity, and their love of God and of the church. But what of the other more obvious traits that made them martyrs, namely, suffering and dying? After all, if the martyrs are to serve as rhetorical *exempla*, surely they are to inspire the same mortal deeds. But how is Augustine's audience to respond to such *exempla* in a context without persecution?

The answer to this question lies at the heart of his treatment of the martyrs as *exempla*: "Do not think, beloved brothers, that you are not able to possess the merits of the martyrs because there are no persecutions like there were in those times when the martyrs were crowned. There are no longer persecutions, but temptations never cease."[1] At one level, this answer is simple and obvious: Augustine spiritualizes the virtues of martyrdom so that one need not actually suffer physically in order to imitate those who did. But there is a deeper significance in Augustine's use of the martyrs as spiritual *exempla*. His need to spiritualize them arises from the gap that exists between his own time, the age of Christian emperors, and the time of the martyrs, the age of persecution. The use of *exempla* requires some level of

---

[1] Augustine, *s.* 335D.3 (PLS 2:777).

continuity between the past of the source material and the present of the rhetorical audience. To understand Augustine's use of Christian martyrs as *exempla*, then, we must turn from rhetoric proper to a related classical discipline: historiography.

Augustine's use of the martyrs as *exempla* brings his rhetorical construction of martyrdom into conversation with history, both the past in which the martyrs lived and the narrative of that past as it is ideologically constructed.[2] In late antique education, the disciplines of rhetoric and history were intimately related.[3] Indeed, rhetoric depended upon history precisely for a knowledge of *exempla*. As Cicero proffers, "All of antiquity and a large body of *exempla* must be held [in the memory]."[4] Quintilian suggests that when a student has been passed from a *grammaticus* to a rhetor, the latter ought to guide the student in reading history, first Livy and then Sallust,[5] in order to cultivate, among other things, "a knowledge of events and *exempla*, which are among the foremost things with which the rhetor needs to be equipped."[6]

Whereas rhetoric needed to draw on history, Roman historiography was inherently rhetorical. While fictionalized speeches, conforming to the best rhetorical practice, make up much of classical histories,[7] the nature of good historiography itself was understood by some to be not only rhetorical but also exemplary in its narration of the past.[8] As Livy puts it, "That which is

---

[2] On Augustine's historiography, see Michael I. Allen, "Universal History 300–1000: Origins and Western Developments," in *Historiography in the Middle Ages*, ed. D. M. Deliyannis (Leiden: Brill, 2003), 17–42, esp. 26–32. Still authoritative is Robert A. Markus, *Saeculum: History and Society in the Theology of St. Augustine*, rev. ed. (Cambridge: Cambridge University Press, 1988), esp. 1–44. My reading of Augustine's historiographical arguments fits well with Markus's analysis. See esp. his observation of how, from the early 400s onward, Augustine comes to see the period of the Roman Empire as but one part of the larger historical period initiated by the incarnation and enduring until the parousia. This "sixth age" includes both the period of persecution and the period of privilege, so that, interpreted theologically, the meaning of both is subsumed under the larger, more significant period of salvation history. E.g., "Since the coming of Christ, until the end of the world, all history is homogenous" (20–21). And "contemporary history has been quietly removed from the perspective of sacred history. The scripture imposes no pattern upon it; or, if it does, the pattern is so open in its texture that anything—the 'established Church' of the Theodosian age no less than the age of the martyrs—will fit" (34). It is this "homogenous" view of history that I argue Augustine constructs with the help of his martyr *exempla* in contrast to traditional Roman narratives of decline.

[3] On the relationship between the two disciplines, see Peter Van Nuffelen, *Orosius and the Rhetoric of History* (Oxford: Oxford University Press, 2012), 76–82; Matthew Fox, *Cicero's Philosophy of History* (Oxford: Oxford University Press, 2007), 111–48.

[4] Cicero, *de orat.* 1.18 (LCL 348:14). See also 1.201. For a view dismissing the need to possess this knowledge of one's own, see 1.256.

[5] Quintilian, *inst.* 2.5.1, 2.5.19.

[6] Quintilian, *inst.* 10.1.34 (LCL 127:268, 270). See also 12.4.1.

[7] See John Marincola, "Speeches in Classical Hagiography," in *A Companion to Greek and Roman Historiography*, ed. John Marincola (Oxford: Wiley, 2009), 118–32.

[8] See esp. Jane D. Chaplin, *Livy's Exemplary History* (Oxford: Oxford University Press, 2000), 16–29.

especially wholesome and fruitful in the knowledge of history is that you may study the lessons of every type of *exemplum* set forth in a clear monument; from these you may seize upon what you and your republic will imitate."[9] Sallust offers a more suggestive depiction of history, memory, and *exempla*:

> I have often heard that Q. Maximus and P. Scipio, in addition to other illustrious men of our country, were in the habit of saying that, upon studying the images of their ancestors, their hearts would be set on fire most vehemently for the pursuit of virtue. Certainly neither the wax nor the figure had any power in itself, but the memory of past deeds stirred this flame in the breast of these excellent men and it would not settle until their own prowess equaled the fame and glory of their ancestors.[10]

Here the wax images confront the viewer with the power of memory—not personal memory but culturally constructed communal memory—inspiring admiration for past glory and a desire to emulate it in one's future actions. The wax figures represent the writing of history as well as one of its key purposes for Roman authors, namely, as rhetorical narration meant to stir the reader toward the proper virtues.

This exemplary use of history also supports the Roman historiographical tendency toward a narrative of decline.[11] Indeed, in the subsequent paragraph, Sallust laments that such *exempla* no longer inspire the way they once did:

> By contrast, who among all people in the current mores is there who does not contend with his ancestors in riches and luxury rather than in uprightness and diligence? Even new men, who previously would surpass the nobles through virtue, now pursue power and honors in stealth and through robbery rather than good character; just as if a praetorship, a consulship, and all other such things were noble and illustrious in and

---

[9] Livy, praef. 10 (LCL 114:6).
[10] Sallust, *Jug.* 4.5–6 (LCL 116:172).
[11] On Augustine's engagement with this theme, see Andrew R. Murphy, "Augustine and the Rhetoric of Roman Decline," in *Augustine and History*, ed. Christopher T. Daly, John Doody, and Kim Paffenroth (Lanham, MD: Lexington Books, 2008), 53–74. Murphy highlights the way Augustine "severs the longstanding and comforting assumption that our earthly prospects correlate, even in a rough way, with our spiritual health" (66), a view of history that lies at the heart of my own argument about his use of *exempla*.

of themselves and were not assessed according to the virtue of those who maintain them.[12]

This description fits with Sallust's general view of the arc of Roman history: a distant golden age gives way to decadence and decline. More significant is the way Sallust is using an *exemplum* to illustrate the failure of his contemporaries to emulate *exempla* properly. The story of Maximus and Scipio being inspired by the wax images of their ancestors is an historical *exemplum* about *exempla* and the proper role of memory. This meta-*exemplum* operates by contrariety to condemn the vicious corruption of contemporary Romans who misuse the memory of their ancestors, seeking not to imitate their virtue but to exceed their luxury. Thus, Sallust's *exemplum* of *exempla* both reaffirms the proper moral and civic role of *exempla* and situates the exemplary past in a ruptured relationship to the corrupt present within an overarching view of history.

Augustine knows well the historical perspective of Sallust, even quoting in *City of God* his opinion that "discord, greed, ambition, and the other evils that arise from wealth increased exceedingly after the destruction of Carthage" (a perspective I will discuss more in the next section).[13] The *City of God* itself, of course, comes in part as a response to the claims of "pagans" that Christianity is responsible for the recent decline of the empire as proximately demonstrated by the sack of Rome in 410. Augustine's response, in part, is to deny the legitimacy of the traditional Roman narrative of decline by undermining any era's claim to have been a golden age—thus his use of Sallust along with Livy and others to demonstrate the inaccuracy of such claims. For instance, how could the earliest Romans represent moral virtue in light of the rape of the Sabine women?

> Perhaps there were no laws established by the gods for the Roman people because, as Sallust says, "justice and goodness prevailed among them not as much by laws as by nature"? Out of this "justice and goodness," I suppose, the Sabine women were raped. For what is better and more just than to

---

[12] Sallust, *Jug.* 4.7–8 (LCL 116:172).
[13] Sallust, *hist.* 1.11, apud Augustine, *ciu.* 2.18 (CCSL 47:49). For Augustine's engagement with Sallust in *ciu.*, see Peter Busch, "On the Use and Disadvantage of History for the Afterlife," in *Augustine and History*, 21–24; and Paul C. Burns, "Augustine's Use of Sallust in the *City of God*: The Role of the Grammatical Tradition," *Augustinian Studies* 30 (1999): 105–14.

acquire foreign women not from their parents but by misleading them with the deceit of a show so that you would be able to carry them off by force?[14]

A historiographical narrative of decline cannot gloss over the moral failings that already existed within the supposedly pristine period.

More important for our purposes, Augustine also uses Christian martyrs as historical *exempla* to challenge the heroes of the traditional Roman narrative. After all, the Roman *exempla* function precisely because of their connection to an idealized and idolized past. The failure of present men to emulate their superior ancestors accounts for the supposed moral and political decline of Rome. But Augustine argues that the Christian martyrs represent a higher virtue, surpassing the culturally established standard *exempla*:

> And then there were the martyrs who outdid Scaevola and Curtius and the Decii not by urging punishment upon themselves but by bearing the punishments urged upon them and by their true virtue, which is true piety, and also by their innumerable multitudes. But since those Romans were of an earthly city, and since what was set before them as the end of all their duties on its behalf was its safety and sovereignty not in heaven but on earth, not in eternal life but the passing of the dying and a succession of those who are going to die, what else could they love but glory, by which they hope to live even after death on the mouths of those praising them?[15]

Augustine accomplishes much in this brief passage. First, he describes the martyrs as surpassing "Scaevola and Curtius and the Decii." In doing so, he directly challenges the canon of Roman *exempla* as well as the traditional narrative of decline. It is not the case that some idealized Republican past holds the key to the storehouse of *exempla*. Nor is it the case that Christianity represents the cause of decline. Rather, the relatively recent acts of Christian martyrs can serve as *exempla* superior to the most famous of antiquity.

Further, Augustine grounds the superiority of Christian martyrs as *exempla* in their virtue, itself defined as piety.[16] *Virtus* is a common theme

---

[14] Augustine, *ciu.* 2.17 (CCSL 47:47).
[15] Augustine, *ciu.* 5.14 (CCSL 47:148).
[16] *Virtus* as a theme for the martyrs goes back, in the West, at least to Cyprian (*laps.* 4, 31; *Fort.* 11). See also Ambrose, *virg.* 1.2.5, 1.2.8; and Paulinus, *ep.* 49.4, *carm.* 19.283, 21.129. For Augustine's contestation of the concept of virtue against traditional Roman culture, see (inter multa alia) Brian Harding, *Augustine and Roman Virtue* (London: Continuum, 2008); Robert Dodaro, *Christ and the Just Society in the Thought of Augustine* (Cambridge: Cambridge University Press, 2004); James Wetzel, *Augustine and the Limits of Virtue* (Cambridge: Cambridge University Press, 1992). Of

in Roman historiography, and one usually associated with narratives of decline.[17] The decline is a loss of *virtus* among leading Roman citizens, and many, like Sallust, explicitly trace its loss to the final defeat of Carthage at the end of the Punic wars. But Augustine's account of the martyrs as *exempla* superior to Scaevola and company subverts this narrative of decline by relativizing the virtue of these golden-age Romans. Augustine does not merely reject the exemplarity of such admirable self-sacrifice. Indeed, unlike some of his Christian contemporaries, Augustine permits the limited preservation of classical *exempla*.[18] But the noblest of Roman heroes could not hold a candle to the glory of the martyrs. As Augustine claims in the second half of the above passage, all that the most illustrious of Romans did they did for the sake of an earthly kingdom and ephemeral goods, rather than for the heavenly kingdom and its eternal life. Indeed, the greatest that any of the "pagan" heroes can hope for is future glory, defined here as a type of life after death "on the mouths of those praising them," that is, at least partly, to become *exempla*.

Yet because Augustine grounds the true virtue of the martyrs in Christian piety, which itself orients one's love toward the eternal kingdom rather than the temporal, his martyrs are superior to the Roman *exempla* not only in the virtues that they inspire but also in the goods that they themselves have received. Although, like Scaevola and the Decii, they live in this world well after their deaths through the culturally constructed communal memories of ritual and rhetoric, Augustine's martyrs also attain a true eternal life through their piety, that is, their faith.

Yet Augustine's depiction of Roman exemplary virtue should not be taken at face value. The idea that heroic deeds were only performed for the sake of earthly rewards and a place on the lips of future generations is a selective interpretation at best and a false caricature at worst. We have seen support for this depiction in Sallust, but the Roman hero was not a static cultural figure but a dynamic one prone to contestation. For example, the famous "Dream of

---

particular note is Jennifer Herdt, "The Theater of the Virtues: Augustine's Critique of Pagan Mimesis," in *Augustine's City of God: A Critical Guide*, ed. James Wetzel (Cambridge: Cambridge University Press), which engages the same phenomena that I do, but from the lens of philosophy and "spectacle," rather than rhetoric and historiography.

[17] On the significance of *virtus* in Roman and early Latin Christian historiography, see Jason M. Gehrke, "*Christus Exemplar*: The Politics of Virtue in Lactantius" (PhD diss., Marquette University, 2017), esp. 58–73.

[18] See Van Nuffelen, *Orosius and the Rhetoric of History*, 82–92.

Scipio" that ends Cicero's *Republic* is preceded by Scipio's claim that "though the consciousness of the worth of his deeds is the noblest reward of virtue for a wise man, yet that godlike virtue longs, not indeed for statues fixed in lead or triumphs with their fading laurels, but for rewards of a more stable and lasting nature"[19]—thus Scipio the Elder's promise that "all those who have preserved, aided, or enlarged their fatherland have a special place prepared for them in the heavens, where they may enjoy an eternal life of happiness."[20] This eternal heaven stands in contrast, Scipio continues, to the ephemeral nature of all human speech and institutions. This vision of virtue's reward seems consistent, *mutatis mutandis*, with Augustine's Christian version that he, nevertheless, depicts as a stark contrast to traditional Roman values.

Given Augustine's certain familiarity with Cicero's *Republic*, we may reach two conclusions about his one-dimensional depiction of Roman glory. First, he is not interested in giving a fair, comprehensive account of Roman virtue theory and heroic *exempla*. Rather, he is using one strand within Roman historiography as a foil for Christian martyrs. Complexifying that strand would problematize his argument. Second, and more important, in light of the "Dream of Scipio," we must see Augustine involved not only in a Christian versus "pagan" polemic but also in a preexisting internal Roman debate about the nature of virtue and its reward for the civic hero. It is a question that is still alive and well in the late fourth and early fifth centuries, as evident in Symmachus's third *relatio* and Macrobius's commentary on Scipio's dream. Within the Latin tradition, therefore, Augustine finds not only a foil for the virtue of the martyrs but also precedents for his Christian view of their eternal reward. Framing the matter as rejecting traditional Roman values allows him to claim the eternal reward as a uniquely Christian concept rather than as one shared with at least one strand of Roman virtue theory.

In *ciu*. 5.14, then, as throughout the work, Augustine appropriates classical cultural tools, in this case rhetorical *exempla*, and baptizes them for Christian use. He does not dismiss altogether the virtuous Roman heroes but instead depicts them as mere shadows of the Christian heroes, the former manifesting a virtue appropriate for earthly kingdoms, the latter a superior virtue befitting the heavenly one. Even this heavenly vision, though, has a precedent within Roman philosophy, as represented by Cicero's "Dream of Scipio." Thus, Augustine's use of the martyrs as *exempla* in his preaching is

---

[19] Cicero, *rep*. 6.8 (Latin original and English translation, LCL 213:260–61).
[20] Cicero, *rep*. 6.13 (Latin original and English translation, LCL 213:265).

more than a simple matter of instructing his congregation in the proper memorialization of the beloved dead. It is, rather, a matter of Christian culture-making through rhetorical means, establishing the new canon of *exempla*, not just the names and the deeds, but the moral lessons to be drawn from them as well, all in an attempt to subvert traditional Roman values while still drawing upon them.

A Trans-Historical Enemy

Yet, as we saw earlier, using the martyrs as *exempla* poses a particular problem: how can Augustine's contemporary Christians emulate the martyrs when they no longer suffer imperial persecution? While the superficial answer seemed obvious even in our initial reading of *s.* 335D—that is, emphasize the spiritual virtues over the physical suffering and death—this move can be better understood by placing it in the context of Augustine's reinterpretation of Roman historiography through the use of *exempla* that we have just explored. A full appreciation requires a further step in our analysis, however, because in *City of God* Augustine is not just challenging the way history is narrated but redefining what actually happens within history itself.

In particular, in this section I will show that, for Augustine, the martyrs are not merely *exempla* drawn from the past for the benefit of the present; rather, in their martyrdom itself, they accomplish within their proximate context the very rhetorical purpose for which Augustine deploys them in his preaching: moral exhortation that reorients one's desire from the material to the spiritual. Moreover, their ability to do this depends upon the same vision of history that allows Augustine's contemporaries to emulate the martyrs: every pre-eschatological age, regardless of imperial favor or persecution, faces the same enemy that the martyrs did.

We must bear in mind that Sallust, as representing traditional Roman historiography, and Augustine are both using historical *exempla* with an awareness of a rupture between the context of the source material and that of their own contemporary audiences. Whereas for Sallust the disconnect between an imagined glorious past and a decadent present requires a return of sorts to the old virtues, Augustine continues to deconstruct the traditional Roman historiography of decline by way of his martyr discourse in order to turn every historical period into a potential context for virtue. Like Sallust,

Augustine argues that a proper understanding of historical *exempla* provides the proper understanding of both history itself and true virtue.

My reading of Augustine's exemplary martyrs in this section again establishes a contrast with Sallust's narrative of decline, but now I focus particularly on Sallust's understanding of the historical significance of the defeat of Carthage. As mentioned earlier, Augustine quotes Sallust's assessment that the defeat of Carthage opened the door to moral decay and decline in the republic. Beneath this opinion lies a deeper analysis of what creates virtue: external conflict. Up until the annihilation of Carthage, Romans benefited from the presence of a true external threat, which resulted in a positive form of internal rivalry, each man striving for virtue in battle as well as in the forum. Without the Punic threat, Rome devolved into decadence, turning from external enemies to internal conflict and seeking wealth and status rather than virtue. This reading of Roman history might present a compelling precedent for lamenting the end of persecution—something not absent in modern assessments of the Constantinian turn—because without the empire as an enemy, Christians would no longer be able to cultivate their true virtue in conflict with such powers. But Augustine subverts this historiographical tendency by redefining what the martyrs were actually fighting, namely, a perennial threat that will never be removed from Christians until the end of history itself.

To illustrate this, I turn to *ciu.* 10.21 in order to demonstrate the various moves Augustine makes in relation to *exempla*, history, and true virtue. Augustine begins by explaining why God allowed the martyrs to suffer:

> For a moderate and predefined time, power was permitted to the demons so that, by stirring up those humans that they could, they might tyrannically exercise their enmity against the city of God. They were permitted not only to receive sacrifice from those offering and demand it from those willing but also indeed to extort it from the unwilling by persecuting them violently. This power was not simply not harmful to the church, but indeed it was found to be useful to the church so that the number of the martyrs might be fulfilled, those martyrs whom the city of God holds as the more glorious and honored among its citizens on account of how mightily they strove against the sin of impiety, even to the point of [shedding their] blood.[21]

---

[21] Augustine, *ciu.* 10.21 (CCSL 47:294–95). The idea that the martyrs were instruments of divine providence is not unique to Augustine. See, e.g., Paulinus, *carm.* 19.18–19 in which God spreads the tombs of the martyrs across the world like the stars in the sky to provide spiritual light in a dark world.

Not surprisingly, Augustine situates the period of persecution and martyrdom within the context of God's overarching providence. More significant is the ironic purpose at work in such suffering: in seeking to diminish the number of Christians, persecutions only increase the city of God's honor roll, building up the church triumphant and, by establishing such "glorious" and "honored" figures, providing a host of *exempla* for the church militant so that they too might strive against sin.

We find similar explanations for the period of persecutions and martyrdom throughout *City of God*. For instance, Augustine describes how God has overthrown superstition "through the highest humility of Christ, through the preaching of the apostles, and through the faith of the martyrs dying on behalf of the truth and [now living] with the truth," suggesting that the martyrs' deaths are part of the persuasive work of God's redemption, serving as *exempla* within history, not only as drawn from it.[22] Similarly, Augustine describes how Porphyry, seeing the persecution of Christians, supposed that Christianity could not represent the universal way of salvation. Porphyry, however, did not see how the martyrs' sufferings showed that "all bodily evils are to be tolerated for the sake of loyalty to the faith and commitment to the truth," and therefore, he was unable to "understand that that which disturbed him and which he feared to suffer in choosing [this path] actually resulted in a confirmation and more robust commendation of [that path]."[23] Again, the virtues demonstrated by the martyrs not only become fodder for later Christian emulation but also actually effect the transformation of their proximate context.

In the subsequent paragraphs of *ciu.* 10.21, Augustine offers an etymological argument that, I will show, connects the historical work of the martyrs to their later use as *exempla* via his overarching reinterpretation of Roman (indeed, of world) history. In lauding the martyrs, Augustine suggests that they would even be called "our heroes" if it were not for the fact that ecclesial usage does not permit it. In the brief phrase "our heroes" we see Augustine juxtaposing the Christian cultural tradition with that of the Romans, the same process of Christianization of classical culture that we have already seen and which lies at the heart of his discourse on martyrial *exempla*. But what stands out in this passage is the etymological interpretation of the word "hero":

---

[22] Augustine, *ciu.* 4.30 (CCSL 47:124).
[23] Augustine, *ciu.* 10.32 (CCSL 47:310–11).

> The name is said to derive from Juno, because Juno is named Hera in Greek, and for the reason that, according to the fables of the Greeks, one of her sons was named Heros. In a mystical way, this fable evidently signifies that the air is assigned to Juno and is where they think that heroes dwell along with the *daemones*. By the name "heroes" they mean the souls of dead people of some merit. By contrast, our martyrs would be called heroes ... not because they had communion with the *daemones* in the air but because they defeated those very same *daemones*, that is, those powers of the air, including among them Juno, whatever she is thought to signify.[24]

In Augustine's telling, Roman heroes are so called because, as a reward for their heroic earthly acts, they now live "in the air," in the realm of *daemones*. But Augustine refuses to accept a positive meaning for the term *daemon*, associating such beings of the air with the Christian understanding of demons or evil spirits. The martyrs do not associate with such demons as a reward for their labors; rather, fighting such demons is their labor.

Here then we see the heart of Augustine's connection between martyrial *exempla* and Roman historiography. For Sallust and others, the true heroes of Rome's golden age needed the military and political competition with Carthage to cultivate virtue. Without that external opponent, the classical *exempla* were no longer followed, and Romans strove against one another for wealth and decadence rather than for virtue. For Augustine, however, the real striving of the martyr is not against the human forces of competing cities and empires; it is against the spiritual forces of temptation, including those very same powers of the air that "pagans" falsely honor. The martyrs' physical endurance manifested the virtue cultivated in this spiritual struggle, and therefore it is the latter fight for which they serve as *exempla*.

Because Augustine has shifted the hero's adversary from a temporal, earthly enemy to spiritual forces of temptation, the narrative of decline no longer applies to the rhetorical use of historical *exempla* for Christians. The virtues that the martyrs model are not dependent upon earthly political, social, or historical circumstances, because spiritual temptation exists in many forms in every age and in every context. The martyrs are not heroes from some Christian golden age in which the external threat of persecution enabled feats of virtue. Their virtue is cultivated in response to an enemy,

---

[24] Augustine, *ciu.* 10.21 (CCSL 47:295). That the martyrs fight not against earthly enemies but demonic ones is a standard figure. See, e.g., Augustine's contemporary, Prudentius, *peri* 1.106–8, 2.505–8, 10.1088–90.

yes, but that enemy is spiritual, not mortal. Therefore, the agonistic pursuit of Christian virtue will never lack for adversaries, and the historical *exempla* of the martyrs can easily be promoted and emulated in a time of Christian empire because, in Augustine's vision of history, peace from adversity only comes with the eschaton.

Thus, when in *Sermon* 335D Augustine tells his congregation not to worry because, though persecutions have ceased, temptations never will, we ought to see this move as more than a spiritualization of the martyrs' struggle. It is a reinterpretation of the arc of history that highlights the common struggle of any Christian in any time and circumstance. Sallust was right: conflict cultivates virtue. But he was wrong, Augustine would say, to limit that conflict to earthly political and martial opponents. Such powers and principalities are wont to rise and fall, making one age more prone to virtue than another. It may be tempting to read the pre-Constantinian period and the often-mythic visions of ubiquitous persecutions within it as such a golden age, where Christians could manifest their true faith by enduring torture and sacrificing their lives. But this view would limit the exemplary role of the martyrs' memories, making them only heroes to honor and not models to emulate. As a Roman teacher of rhetoric, Augustine knows how to manipulate and represent heroic figures from history in order to inspire emulation. By developing the martyrs as *exempla*, though, he also constructs a Christian vision of history that stands in opposition to traditional Roman historiography. His spiritualization of the martyrs' struggle promotes an agonistic view of Christian life, always engaged in a battle against temptation and evil spirits, no matter the social status of the church in one age or another.

Antithetical Beauty

If any age of history can be the setting for imitating the martyrs' struggle, why would anyone want to do so? After all, the passions of the martyrs could be quite gruesome. Looking just at the account of the deaths of Perpetua and friends, we see Saturus emit such a bloody spurt from the bite of a leopard that the crowd mocked him as "washed and saved." And Perpetua, after being attacked by a wild cow, is stabbed between the ribs before guiding the gladiator's hand to her throat of her own accord.[25] And yet, such accounts

[25] *Perp.* 6.4.

elicited rapt attention when read on feast days, in worship, or at a shrine dedicated to a given martyr.

Why were such scenes so appealing? Indeed, one can imagine Augustine to be thinking of such stories when he writes the following in the *Confessions*: "Why is it that a person should wish to experience suffering by watching grievous and tragic events which he himself would not wish to endure? Nevertheless, he wants to suffer the pain given by being a spectator of these sufferings, and the pain itself is his pleasure. What is this but amazing folly?"[26] But, of course, in this quotation Augustine is speaking of the "pagan" spectacles, not the Christian ones.[27] When it comes to the gruesome spectacles of the martyrs' suffering, Augustine does not dismiss his audience's cathartic engagement with suffering and pain as folly; instead, he draws their attention and their hearts toward the beauty that is manifest in the midst of such ugliness.

In this section, I seek to demonstrate the rhetorical character of Augustine's preaching on the beauty[28] of the martyrs in light of the ugliness of their passions. I argue that Augustine is using antithesis, a rhetorical figure of juxtaposition, to highlight the beauty of virtue that shines brightest against the backdrop of suffering.[29] I will show that antithesis is operative at two levels for Augustine. First, he himself uses it in his preaching to draw his audience's desire toward the martyrs' virtues not in spite of but by way of the enticing spectacle of their suffering. In the next section, I will show how antithesis is a rhetorical figure not just for Augustine's preaching but also for his depiction of God's own rhetorical arrangement of history. Indeed, this providential arrangement of opposites allows for Augustine's own homiletical rhetoric. That is to say, the beauty of the martyrs is not just a rhetorical figure within Augustine's preaching but a rhetorical element within his larger theological worldview.

Augustine frequently contrasts the ugliness of the martyrs' suffering with the beauty of their virtue, but the best example of his use of antithesis

---

[26] Augustine, *conf.* 3.2.2 (O'Donnell, 23; English translation, Chadwick, 35–36).

[27] On the significance of such spectacles in Augustine, see Richard Lim, "Augustine and Roman Spectacles," in *A Companion to Augustine*, ed. Mark Vessey (Malden, MA: Wiley-Blackwell, 2012), 138–50.

[28] On Augustine's theology of beauty, see Sohn Hohyun, "The Beauty of Hell? Augustine's Aesthetic Theodicy and Its Critics," *Theology Today* 64 (2007): 47–57; Carol Harrison, *Beauty and Revelation in the Thought of Saint Augustine* (Oxford: Clarendon Press, 1992); Emmanuel Chapman, *Saint Augustine's Philosophy of Beauty* (London: Sheed & Ward, 1939).

[29] On the importance of antithesis in classical rhetoric, see Randy Allen Harris, "The Fourth Master Trope, Antithesis," *Advances in the History of Rhetoric* 22 (2019): 1–26.

to do so comes in his third tractate on the Gospel of John. In this sermon, Augustine reminds his audience of the Psalms—*enarrationes* on which were interspersed among his early tractates on the gospel—and of the lover who speaks in many of those songs, a lover with whose love the church is to unite. Upon the proclamation of Ps 26:4 that our joy will come from gazing upon the delight of the Lord, Augustine interrogates the nature of the longing desire that arises from gazing at the martyrs:

> I ask you, what do you desire? Can it be seen by the eyes? Can it be touched? Is it some beauty that delights the eyes? Do we not love the martyrs vehemently; and when we commemorate them, are we not enflamed with love? What do we love in them, brothers? Their limbs ripped apart by beasts? What could be uglier if you question the eyes of the flesh? What more beautiful if you question the eyes of the heart?[30]

These are rhetorical questions, of course; the congregation is expected to agree with Augustine's assessment that the beauty of the martyrs and of their suffering is seen not with the eyes of the flesh, which can only see carnage, but with the eyes of the heart, which perceive their faith.

It should be noted that this particular passage is not primarily about martyrs. Augustine is not trying here to contest who has the right to claim to be the church of the martyrs or who counts as a real martyr or even how the martyrs ought to be venerated and emulated. At least not explicitly. Rather, Augustine uses this flesh/heart distinction to exercise the spiritual senses of his congregation. Nevertheless, this passage represents the type of figure Augustine often uses when discussing the horrors of the martyrs' experience by pointing to the beauty of their virtue: that is, antithesis (*contrapositum* or ἀντίθετον).

Discussion of antithesis as a rhetorical figure goes back to Aristotle, who advised its use on the grounds that "it is a pleasing kind of style, because contraries are easily understood and even more so when placed side by side."[31] The anonymous *Rhetoric to Herennius* provides more material for understanding how antitheses are to be understood. While defining antithesis as "that through which contraries are proposed," the author delineates two types of antitheses: one according to words and one according to ideas

---

[30] Augustine, *Io. ev. tr.* 3.21 (CCSL 36:30).
[31] Aristotle, *rhet.* 3.9.8 (1410a) (Greek original and English translation, LCL 193:392–93),

(*sententiarum*). "The former is based upon a rapid juxtaposition of words; in the latter, contrary ideas (*sententiae*) ought to come together through comparison."[32] Ps.-Demetrius provides the same division of antitheses, illustrating the difference through a single sentence from Isocrates about Hercules and Helen: "for [Hercules] he made a laborious and perilous life; for [Helen] he established an admired and coveted beauty."[33] The parallel construction establishes the contrast of ideas through the contrast of words.

While Aristotle provides an appreciation for the effectiveness of antithesis and the *Rhetoric to Herennius* and Ps.-Demetrius describe the basic two-part division of word and thought, Quintilian offers the most helpful practical discussion for understanding Augustine's form of antithesis in our earlier sermon passage. Quintilian notes that antithesis can be further divided into subfigures, including "the figure in which words of similar terminations but different meanings come at the end" as in Cicero's *Pro Cluentio*: "So that what evil there was in the circumstances should do no harm (*nihil obstit*), and what good there was in the cause should do positive good (*prosit*)."[34] Similarly, Quintilian notes that "there is commonly an alternating pattern of repetition of first words" as in this passage from the *Pro Murena*: "You stay awake all night to find answers for your clients, he to get himself and his army to their destination in time; you are roused by cockcrow, he by the bugle; you are setting up proceedings, he is drawing up an army; you are taking care that your clients should not be caught out, he that cities and camps should not be captured."[35] The rhyme and rhythm of these two verbal constructions accentuate the contrast between the ideas or things to which they point.

Returning to Augustine's third tractate on the Gospel of John, then, we can see his use of antithesis clearly. While at one level his use of contrasts is obvious in his juxtaposition of flesh and spirit as well as the ugliness of the martyrs' suffering on the one hand and the beauty of their virtue on the other, Quintilian allows us to identify the rhetorical mechanics of this figure with more precision. When Augustine asks his audience, "What do we love in the martyrs, brothers? Their limbs pulled to pieces by beasts?" he answers with a pair of rhetorical questions: "What could be uglier if you question the eyes of the flesh? What more beautiful if you question the eyes of the heart?" Or, in Latin, "*quid foedius, si oculos carnis interroges? quid pulchrius, si oculos cordis*

---

[32] *rhet. Her.* 4.45.58 (LCL 403:376). See also Demetrius, *elocut.* 22–24.
[33] Demetrius, *elocut.* 23 (LCL 199:360).
[34] Quintilian, *inst.* 9.3.82 (Latin original and English translation, LCL 127:150–51).
[35] Quintilian, *inst.* 9.3.32 (Latin original and English translation, LCL 127:118).

interroges?" The questions exactly parallel each other in form, with only two words in each differing. The superlatives *foedius* and *pulchrius* are paired and contrasted with each other, as are the ocular genitives *carnis* and *cordis*. Clearly this is not just a generic contrast but a technical rhetorical antithesis befitting Cicero's advice on *suavitas*: "the choice of words should be from contraries, repetition to repetition and like to like."[36]

But what is the effect of this move and why is Augustine concerned to make it? The cult of the saints was strong in North Africa, and we know that some veneration practices observed there were viewed as aberrant and excessive in other parts of the Christian world, such as Augustine's own mother's practice of *refrigerium*. In considering this devotion to the martyrs and the liturgical role of *passiones* in feast day celebrations, we are drawn back to Augustine's concerns about the spectacles. Are these passion accounts not the same sort of gory indulgences that seduced his friend Alypius? Further, this talk of seduction reminds us that as a good Christian Platonist, Augustine knows that our love, our desire, draws us toward that which we perceive as beautiful. The games and spectacles of Rome are prime examples of the distorting effects of sin upon our hearts as we are drawn to a false beauty, indeed to the beauty of ugliness.

With this in mind, then, we can see Augustine's use of antithesis as a rhetorical salve, seeking to heal the eyes of both flesh and heart. We see this again in his exposition of Ps 64:

> Therefore, there is a certain beauty of justice, which we see with the eyes of the heart, and love, and kindle to, and which people have loved much in the martyrs themselves, when their limbs were torn apart by beasts. When they were all defiled with blood, when beastly bites were tearing out their guts, what would the eyes [of onlookers] behold but horror? What was there that they might love, except the untouched beauty of justice that was present in the foulness of shredded limbs?[37]

We see the antithesis artfully constructed in the closing contrast between *foeditate dilaniatorum membrorum* and *integra pulchritudo iustitiae*. And if we read *integra* not just as "untouched" but as "intact," we see a stronger dimension to the contrast as the beauty of righteousness refuses to be torn

---

[36] Cicero, *part. or.* 6.21 (LCL 349:326).
[37] Augustine, *en. Ps.* 64.8 (CCSL 39:831).

apart like the martyrs' bodies. More important, though, with this use of antithesis, Augustine acknowledges that people are in fact attracted to the gruesome accounts of limbs being torn apart even as he invites his audience to find a different sort of beauty, a truer beauty, in those stories.

But we should be careful not to see Augustine's use of contrasts here as a stark dualism between the eyes of the flesh and the eyes of the heart, or between the ugliness of the passions and the beauty of righteousness. In a dynamic that echoes his Christology, Augustine suggests that, when we see aright, we do not see the beauty instead of the horror; rather, we see the beauty through the horror. The antithesis works because the righteousness of the martyrs shines brightest against the grim backdrop of the violence they endure. This is important because Augustine does not want to tell his flock not to find pleasure in hearing these stories. He cannot tell them to, as Alypius famously tried to do, close their eyes to the ugly brutality of these stories and think only of the martyrs' virtue. Rather, he directs how they should consume the tantalizing details of the passions. We should allow ourselves to be drawn in by their beauty, but we must recognize that that beauty is on display not in the acts of violence or suffering themselves but in how and why they are endured.

The Martyrs within Antithetical History

But there is still more going on in Augustine's use of antithesis to depict the martyrs' beauty. While we have looked so far at how Augustine deploys the figure to guide his congregation through passion into virtue, I now want to explore the larger role this juxtaposition plays in his theology. In short, I argue that, for Augustine, God uses the rhetorical figure of antithesis and the beauty of the martyrs within the providential arrangement of history to woo and heal those who will be saved.

The idea that God providentially arranges the economy of creation and history according to rhetorical standards of aptness and decorum—and here I am deeply indebted to recent work by Brian Gronewoller[38]—is a theme that runs throughout Augustine's corpus. To appreciate its basic contours, we need only turn to one example from *On the Nature of the Good*:

---

[38] Brian Gronewoller, *Rhetorical Economy in Augustine's Theology* (New York: Oxford University Press, 2021).

[Created things] were so ordered, so that more unstable things yield to more stable ones, weaker things to stronger ones, and more impotent things to more powerful ones; and thus, earthly things harmonize with celestial ones, as subordinate things to surpassing ones. Moreover, with things passing away and succeeding, a certain temporal beauty, in its kind, comes about, so that those very things, which die or cease to be what they were, do not defile or confuse the measure, form, and order of the entire universe. In the same way, a well-composed speech is undoubtedly beautiful, even though, in it, the syllables and all the sounds pass by, as if being born and dying.[39]

In this early text, Augustine explicitly compares the divine ordering of creation to the well-ordered oration. But we also note Augustine's repeated use of antithesis throughout the passage—weaker and stronger, unstable and stable, earthly and celestial—contraries creating balance and harmony in the cosmos. This is God's own rhetoric.

Moreover, within the economy of salvation, particularly in the incarnation, Augustine again depicts God's use of contraries. In the first book of *On Christian Teaching*, he describes the medical nature of God's salvific work:

The medicine of Wisdom was accommodated to our wounds through the assumption of a human, curing some of our wounds by their contraries . . . just as the one who heals a wound of the body sometimes applies contraries, like cold to heat, or moist to dry, or other things of that kind. . . . Therefore, because humanity fell through pride, [Wisdom] applied humility in order to heal. We were deceived by the wisdom of the serpent; we are freed by the foolishness of God. . . . We used immortality wickedly, so that we died; Christ used our mortality well, so that we might live. . . . The disease entered through the corrupted mind of a woman; health ushered forth from the intact body of a woman. To these same contraries belong the fact that our vices are cured by the example of his virtues.[40]

While this is a medical analogy and owes much to the theory of opposites in that discipline, it fits well with the more explicitly rhetorical imagery of our previous passage. And so we see that, for Augustine, God's rhetorical

---

[39] Augustine, *nat. b.* 8. (CSEL 25.2:858; English translation from Gronewoller, *Rhetorical Economy*, 57).
[40] Augustine, *doct. christ.* 1.14.13 (CCSL 32:13–14).

arrangement of creation includes not only the general order of the cosmos but also the particular elements of sacred and salvation history, even the incarnation itself. Moreover, although antithesis is not the only means of divine arrangement in salvation history, the juxtaposition of contraries represented by antithesis plays a large role in the work of providence within history.

Returning to the beauty of the martyrs, let us see them now within this vision of a rhetorically ordered creation. Allow the violence and death that they are said to have suffered be juxtaposed with the righteousness and faith that they are believed to have manifest. And hear Augustine's words from *City of God* 4: "For [God], through the most high humility of Christ, through the preaching of the apostles, through the faith of the martyrs who died for the truth and now live with the Truth, has cast down superstition."[41] Along with the paradoxically most high lowliness of Christ and the proclamation of the apostles, the faith of the martyrs is part of God's persuasive work in the world. And their role lies in a rhetorical antithesis: dying they live, and as witnesses to the truth they destroy superstition.

To conclude this discussion of antithesis, both the antithetical beauty of the martyr and the martyrs' place in God's antithetical arrangement of history, I offer this extended quotation from one of Augustine's sermons on the martyrdom of St. Vincent:

> We have seen in the mind and inspected in thought how much he endured, what he heard, what he answered, and in what way a wondrous spectacle was staged before our eyes: the wicked judge, the cruel torturer, the unconquered martyr, a contest between cruelty and piety; here insanity, there victory. With the reading sounding in our ears, charity flared up in our hearts; we wish, if it had been possible, to embrace and to kiss those shredded limbs, which amazed us by being able to take such punishment, and with inexpressible affection we wished them not to be tormented. For who would wish to see an executioner doing his savage deed, and a human, having lost his humanity, attacking the body of another human? Who would be pleased observing limbs stretched apart on the torture machine? Who would not be against the natural figure ruined by human technique, bones separated by stretching, stripped bare by the flesh being clawed off them? Who would not be horrified? Nevertheless, the justice of the martyr

---

[41] *ciu.* 4.30 (CCSL 47:124).

was making all this horror beautiful; and that marvelous fortitude which he showed for the faith, for piety, for the hope of the future age, for the love of Christ, was pouring forth the appearance of glory over his hideous torments and deadly wounds.[42]

Antitheses are spread throughout this passage. The entire scene is one of contrast. At its center lies the suffering of the martyr, through which ugliness he manifests a virtuous beauty. But we must note that, for Augustine, who himself is so adept at the rhetorical figure of antithesis, this powerful juxtaposition is the work of God, for it is God who, for a time, disposes the ordering of history such that the wicked are able to torture and kill the righteous. Such events may seem to some to threaten the survival of Christianity and to promise the victory of ugly brutality within the order of the world. But those who look with faith, who trust in God's providential ordering of history, know how to view this scene: as a divinely crafted antithesis in which the gruesome horror of persecution only serves to heighten the beauty of the martyrs and the faith for which they suffer.

Conclusion

Historiography on early Christian martyrdom has shifted much in the last few decades. The rhetorical turn has meant scholars no longer focus so much on questions of historicity as on the constructive purposes of martyr discourse. Attending to Augustine's use of classical rhetoric allows us to see another type of historiography at work, a theological account of the providential ordering of the ages. With exemplarity, Augustine challenges the traditional Roman narrative of decline. Whereas for an historian like Sallust the loss of Carthaginian challenges led to decadence, for Augustine every age, regardless of external peace or conflict, is ripe for combat against a host of spiritual enemies. With antithesis, he situates the martyrs within a history of contrasts where God orders the created world according to contrasts, creating an ordered whole. The suffering of the martyrs, then, has its place within God's overarching economy.

---

[42] Augustine, *s.* 277A.1 (PLS 2:417–18).

Augustine's conflicts were not just with spiritual enemies, however, and the martyrs themselves were the subject of polemical antitheses, nowhere more so than in his fight with the Donatists. These last three chapters have demonstrated the rhetorical and theological power of the martyrs. I turn now to the Donatist controversy to examine how Augustine not only constructs but also contests the martyrs against a communion that deemed themselves "the church of the martyrs."

4
The Court of the Martyrs

Introduction

In previous chapters, I have examined Augustine's deployment of the martyrs as rhetorical tools to help craft a certain type of Catholic faith in his congregation, a faith built on the martyrs' virtues—as defined by Augustine—and promoting fidelity not only to God but also to the church. But martyrdom is not simply about piety. At its heart is the reality (or communal memory) of state-sanctioned violence perpetrated upon a particular group. Martyrdom thus entails practical issues of law, power, and coercion. Much the same could be said about classical rhetoric as well. Rhetoric is the way by which various legal officials are persuaded to inscribe and enforce both official laws and unofficial policies. Therefore, in this chapter I turn to forensic rhetoric, the branch associated with contestations around civil and criminal claims. And I likewise turn to Augustine's writings against the Donatists, with whom he competed not just for theological supremacy but also for imperial legitimacy and its accompanying privileges.

This chapter takes up Augustine's slogan *non poena sed causa*, that it is not the penalty but the cause that makes a martyr. In denying that Donatists can truly be called martyrs, Augustine seeks to undercut their claim to be the true "church of the martyrs" that ought to be recognized as the legitimate Christian communion in North Africa. Augustine's argument draws upon forensic rhetoric, especially classical issue theory and the issue of definition. This rhetorical approach has implications for the interpretation of scripture as illustrated by Augustine's use of Matt 5:10. The second half of the chapter takes up a related Donatist claim, namely, that the Catholics are persecutors. Augustine again has recourse to forensic issue theory, this time an issue of quality that brings us back to the perennial theme of *exempla*, now used not for mimetic exhortation but as argumentative evidence.

By examining Augustine's use of forensic issue theory in his rhetorical theology of martyrdom, we move beyond the spiritual formation of his flock, local conflicts over ritual practice and power, and even competing Christian communions and authors. We move into the realm of political theology and Augustine's part in shaping Western Christendom and its understandings of faith, coercion, and the proper role of civil power in a Christian society. With that in mind, I begin with an exchange between a bishop and a tribune around these very issues.

Non poena sed causa

Augustine sounds a bit exasperated when he writes to Dulcitius in 418. The tribune had asked the bishop to refute the teachings of Gaudentius, the Donatist bishop of Thamugadi. But, seven years after the definitive Conference of Carthage, Augustine has reached his limit:

> I am busy, and I have refuted this type of empty speech in my many other little works. For I do not know how often I have shown in disputing and in writing that they are unable to have the death of martyrs because they do not have the life of Christians, since not the punishment but the cause makes a martyr.[1]

Indeed, Augustine had by this point repeated his dictum, *non poena sed causa*—not the punishment but the cause—ad nauseam in numerous letters, sermons, and treatises,[2] to the point that in this late exchange with Dulcitius, he rattles off the slogan in passing with no further elucidation.[3] The problem was that the Donatists styled themselves the "Church of the Martyrs," and, as imperial coercion intensified following the Edict of Unity in 405 and the Conference of 411, they re-entrenched under this banner to declare themselves "the true church that suffers persecution rather than inflicts it."[4] It

---

[1] *ep.* 204.4 (CSEL 57:319).

[2] This list of genres suggests the wide range of audiences for Augustine's *non poena sed causa* argument. He is addressing not only Donatists directly but also members of his own church as well as imperial officials adjudicating between the two communions and enforcing anti-Donatist legislation. No matter the particular audience, the rhetorical structure of the argument that I describe in this article remains consistent.

[3] Inter multa alia, see *ep.* 89.2, 108.5, 185.2; *en. Ps.* 34.2.1, 34.2.13, 68.1.9; *s.* 53A.13, 94A.1, 277A, 285.6-7, 306A, 327, 328.4, 331.2, 335C.5, 335G.2; *Cresc.* 3.47.51. The most substantial treatment of Augustine's *non poena sed causa* is Wojciech Lazewski, "La Sentenza Agostiniana *Martyrem Facit Non Poena Sed Causa*" (PhD diss., Pontificia Universitas Lateranensis, 1987). Lazewski explores many of the theological implications of Augustine's phrase, but he does not identify or examine the rhetorical arguments that give it shape and meaning.

[4] This is Petilian's declaration at the Conference of Carthage, 411 (*conl. Carth.* 3.22 [CCSL 149A:184]): "*apud nos est enim uera catholica, quae persecutionem patitur, non quae facit.*" This slogan

was, undoubtedly, a smart and powerful strategy in the context of North Africa where the blood of the martyrs had long been the seed of church pride and conflict. Augustine's slogan, *non poena sed causa*, sought to deny the Donatists the title of martyr and the rhetorical power that went with it. Perhaps more consequentially, *non poena sed causa* also helped to justify his embrace of imperial coercion in religious matters.

To understand the full scope and significance of the *non poena sed causa* argument, however, I believe we need to place it within the context of late antique theories of issue and argumentation that guided invention in forensic speeches. In this section I will show how two types of forensic arguments— one on the issue of definition and the other on the contested interpretation of a legal text—shape Augustine's response to the Donatists' claim to martyrdom. Further, through this lens we will see the competing Christian communities act as rival claimants to the martyrs' reward and as would-be heirs to the kingdom haggling over the Lord's own will and testament.

The Rhetoric of Definition

In classical rhetorical theory, "definition" (ὅρος, *finitio*, *nomen*) is one of the three primary forensic "issues" (στάσις in Greek and *status* in most Latin texts).[5] An "issue" is the point upon which a given dispute turns. Originating with Hermagoras of Temnos in the first century BCE, by the time of Augustine "issue theory" had become a standard aspect of rhetorical handbooks as

---

is repeated throughout the proceedings of the conference by various Donatist representatives. See *conl. Carth.* 3.251, 3.258. On this conference, see Burns and Jensen, *Christianity in Roman Africa*, 54–57; Serge Lancel, *Saint Augustine*, trans. Antonia Nevill (London: SCM Press, 2002), 287–305; Erika T. Hermanowicz, *Possidius of Calama: A Study in the North African Episcopate at the Time of Augustine* (Oxford: Oxford University Press, 2008), 188–220; For the significance of martyr imagery in Donatism, see Bernard Kriegbaum, *Kirche der Traditoren oder Kirche der Märtyrer? Die Vorgeschichte des Donatismus* (Vienna: Tyrolia, 1986); and Maureen Tilley, "Introduction" and "Legal and Literary Notes," in *Donatist Martyr Stories: The Church in Conflict in Roman North Africa* (Liverpool: Liverpool University Press, 1996), xi–xxxvi.

[5] The most significant scholarship on issue theory has come from Malcolm Heath, who is to be credited for resurrecting attention to this feature of classical rhetoric. See especially the Prolegomena and commentary for his translation of Hermogenes, *On Issues: Strategies of Argument in Later Greek Rhetoric* (Oxford: Clarendon Press, 1995); Heath, "The Substructure of *stasis*-Theory from Hermagoras to Hermogenes," *Classical Quarterly* 44 (1994): 114–29; Heath, "Zeno the Rhetor and the Thirteen *staseis*," *Eranos* 92 (1994): 17–22; Heath, "στάσις-Theory in Homeric Commentary," *Mnemosyne* 46 (1993): 356–63. Prior to Heath, the most important treatment is Ray Nadeau, "Classical Systems of Stases in Greek: Hermagoras to Hermogenes," *Greek, Roman, and Byzantine Studies* 2 (1959): 53–71.

exemplified by Cicero and Quintilian in the West and Hermogenes in the East.[6] The three most common forensic issues are conjecture, definition, and quality. These conform to three disputed questions: "Did it happen? How is what happened to be categorized? How is what happened to be evaluated?"[7] Unfortunately the initial issue of conjecture is unavailable to Augustine. Because such categorical denial is difficult to support given the reality of imperial prosecution of the Donatists at various times and ways, Augustine typically moves to the other judicial issues, namely, definition and quality. Although the condemnation of the Donatist *causae*, their distorted motives, has implications for the quality question, I believe that Augustine's *non poena sed causa* slogan fits most appropriately under the issue of definition.

Before showing why this is the case, I want to take a closer look at what an issue of definition entails. In his *On Invention*, Cicero says an issue of definition occurs "when there is agreement concerning the fact but a name by which to call that which has been done is sought."[8] Similarly, Quintilian explains that in an issue of definition "someone who is not able to say he did nothing will next say that he did not do that with which he is charged."[9] In brief, the issue of definition concerns the apt correspondence between a *lex* and a *factum*, between a law and the deed committed.[10] The dispute is not around what actually happened, but rather whether what happened is properly labeled in the legal charge.

One standard example, found in Quintilian, Cicero, and Hermogenes, will clarify what such an issue looks like: "Someone has taken private money from a temple and is charged with sacrilege."[11] The perpetrator's guilt is not in question. He admits to taking the money from the temple. The question is whether "sacrilege" is the correct legal category for what has happened. The defendant will argue that he only committed "theft," a less serious crime,

---

[6] Issue theory also composes the bulk of the *de rhetorica* attributed to Augustine. Although most scholars still treat this as an erroneous attribution, the judgment is not as universal as it once was. For a recent affirmation of Augustinian authorship, see Jeffery Aubin, "Le *De rhetorica* du Pseudo-Augustin: réexamen des objections contre l'authenticité augustinienne," *Revue d'études augustiniennes et patristiques* 59 (2013), 117–34. For a summary of the earlier debates on the *de rhetorica*'s authenticity as well as an English translation, see Otto Alvin Loeb Dieter and William Charles Kurth, "The *De Rhetorica* of Aurelius Augustine," *Speech Monographs* 35 (1968): 90–108. If the *de rhetorica* is authentic, it further supports my argument about Augustine's use of rhetorical issue theory. However, I am not confident enough in its legitimacy to use it for more than further evidence of the prevalence of issue theory in late antique rhetorical handbooks.

[7] Heath, Prolegomena to *Hermogenes, On Issues*, 21 n.27.
[8] Cicero, *inv.* 1.11 (LCL 386:22).
[9] Quintilian, *inst.* 7.3.1 (LCL 126:216).
[10] Lausberg, *Handbook of Literary Rhetoric*, §105, §167.
[11] Quintilian, *inst.* 7.3.21 (LCL 126:228). See also Cicero, *inv.* 1.11; Hermogenes, *stas.*, 37.8–14.

because the money itself was not sacred. The prosecution would argue that sacrilege includes stealing anything from a temple, not just items that are themselves sacred.

As we see in this stock example, the arguments in an issue of definition deny the validity of an opponent's definition while defending one's own. A definition can be attacked in two ways. It can simply be false: for example, if one defined a horse as a rational animal.[12] More often, however, a definition is *parum plena*, not complete enough. A *parum plena* definition, in turn, can either be too broad or too narrow in its scope.[13] For instance, in the temple theft example, the prosecution could say, as Quintilian suggests, that sacrilege is stealing from a sacred place (*ex sacro*). Quintilian suggests that the defense will say such a definition is false, claiming that, as in the rational animal definition of horse, this definition does not accurately represent the true nature of sacrilege; instead, they will say that sacrilege is stealing something that itself is sacred (*aliquid sacrum*). The prosecution will condemn this definition as *parum plena* for being too narrow and not including the full range of sacrilegious acts. Thus, the key question in an issue of definition is the *proprium*, the one qualification that properly separates the particular term from other members of the larger genus while not excluding anything that should fall under the specific term.[14] This type of conflict over the semantic range of a term and its defining *proprium* represents the rhetorical

---

[12] Quintilian, *inst.* 7.3.24 (LCL 126:228): "*Falsa est si dicas 'equus est animal rationale': nam est equus animal, sed inrationale.*"

[13] Quintilian's distinction between a *falsa* and a *parum plena* definition is difficult to parse, partly because the text of 7.3.23–24 is contested. Lausberg, *Handbook of Literary Rhetoric* §113, n.32, interprets it in this way: "The incorrect definition can ... be too narrow or too broad. The definition which is too narrow is called *parum plena* (Quint. *Inst.* 7.3.23): it covers too few (possible) offenses. The definition which is too broad is called *falsa* (Quint. *Inst.* 7.3.23): it covers too many (possible) offenses." But Quintilian gives the example of a horse defined as a rational animal and calls this a false definition. Clearly that is not a situation where the definition covers "too many" referents. Rather, it simply has an incorrect property included in the definition. Similarly, in his example of a *parum plena* definition, Quintilian points to the defendant in the temple theft case who would define sacrilege as "to steal something sacred (*surripere aliquid sacri*)." The prosecutor would say this is *parum plena* and insist on adding "or from something sacred (*aut ex sacro*)" (7.3.24). The key here is that something more needs to be added to the definition in order for it to be *plena*. Yes, in this case the definition is too narrow without the addition. But presumably a definition could be too broad and need something added to it to narrow it down, as if I said a horse is an "irrational animal." This would not be false, but it would be *parum plena*, incomplete. (In fact, George Ludwig Spalding suggests exactly this example for explaining *parum plena* when working to establish the text of *inst.* 7.3.24 in his edition of the work [Leipzig, 1808].) For the sake of my argument, therefore, I will take *falsa* to refer to a definition that (the opposition claims) has an erroneous property included (such as "rational" in the horse example), and *parum plena* to refer to definitions that lack some necessary property that would either narrow or expand its referent range, as appropriate.

[14] Quintilian, *inst.* 7.3.27.

frame for Augustine's contestation of the meaning of martyrdom against the Donatists.

Claiming Rewards for Tyrannicide and Martyrdom

The temple theft example represents the basics of an issue of definition. To show why this type of forensic rhetorical approach fits with Augustine's denial of Donatist claims to martyrdom, I turn now to another stock example, one that parallels the *non poena sed causa* argument quite closely. The case entails the reward for killing a tyrant, a common topic for declamations and rhetorical handbooks that assumes something like the following law: "Whoever kills a tyrant shall receive the rewards of the Olympic games and shall request whatever thing he wishes for himself from the magistrate and the magistrate shall give it to him."[15] This then provides the basis for a whole host of judicial and legal questions: Is a man who kills two tyrants owed two rewards? What if another law precludes someone from claiming the reward he wants? What if someone deposes the despot through rational appeal instead of killing?

The version of this forensic theme that I want to highlight appears in Seneca the Elder[16] but receives more significant theoretical engagement in Quintilian, who presents the following hypothetical dispute: A man is committing adultery with a tyrant's wife. He is caught in the act by the tyrant. He slays the tyrant. Is this man rightly to be considered a tyrannicide and therefore eligible for the appropriate reward?[17] Quintilian shows how definition is the primary issue here. What makes someone a tyrannicide? "If on account of etymology it is said, 'the *proprium* of tyrannicide is to kill a tyrant,' we should deny [by saying]: 'An executioner is not called a tyrannicide if [a tyrant] is handed over to him; nor would someone [who kills a tyrant] unintentionally or unwillingly [be called a tyrannicide]."[18] A definition whose

---

[15] Cicero, *inv.* 2.49.144 (LCL 386:312). It should be noted that the context for Cicero's citation of this law is not a discussion of the issue of definition but rather an issue of conflicting laws in the context of the larger forensic issue of document interpretation. I cite this line here only to suggest what the relevant law about tyrannicide might be for the more resonant example I discuss below from Quintilian's explanation of definitional disputes. That Cicero mentions this law in relation to the interpretation of documents is not unimportant, however. As I will show later, an issue of definition often arises in connection to an interpretive dispute. Indeed, such complex intertwining of issues is one reason that few classical handbooks agree on how to categorize them.
[16] Seneca, *contr.* 4.7.
[17] Quintilian, *inst.* 5.10.36 (LCL 125:384).
[18] Quintilian, *inst.* 5.10.59 (LCL 125:394).

proprium is only the killing of a tyrant is *parum plena*, incomplete, because it is too broad.

So what would be an appropriate *proprium*? Quintilian says it is the *causa*, the motive, that distinguishes a true tyrannicide from others who happen to kill a tyrant.[19] *Causa* is a standard rhetorical locus, that is, one of the traditional argumentative topoi taught in rhetorical handbooks for guiding the process of invention and crafting an argument.[20] Quintilian divides the different psychological *causae* into those that seek to acquire, increase, conserve, or use something good and those that seek to avoid, get rid of, decrease, or endure bad things.[21] Errors in motive arise from mistaken beliefs about what is good or bad, and thus the *locus a causa* can be used to either convict or defend someone of a given charge.[22] In the case of the adulterous tyrannicide, one could argue that the claimant is ineligible for the reward because his *causa* was dishonorable: he merely wanted to defend himself against retribution for his adultery.

This example of the *locus a causa* providing the *proprium* for an issue of definition should be read as the rhetorical archetype for Augustine's *non poena sed causa* argument against Donatist claims to martyrdom. Augustine's emphasis on *causa* as the delineating factor for true martyrdom is an explicit application of the *locus a causa* to a definitional issue. Moreover, Augustine repeatedly mocks the Donatists' claim to martyrdom by showing that their definition is *parum plena*, incomplete, because it includes too wide a range of deaths within its scope. For instance, he deploys the example of the two criminals crucified next to Christ:

> For the Lord himself was crucified along with thieves; but those whom *passio* joined, *causa* separated. Therefore, in the psalm we ought to understand the voice of the true martyrs wishing to distinguish themselves from false martyrs: "Judge me, God, and distinguish my *causam* from an unholy people" (Ps 43:1). He did not say, "distinguish my *poenam*" but "distinguish my *causam*."[23]

---

[19] Quintilian, *inst.* 5.10.36. The role of *causae* in issues of definition is the context for Quintilian's use of the adulterous tyrannicide example.

[20] For a brief summary of the role of *loci* in invention and argumentation, see Lausberg, *Handbook of Literary Rhetoric*, §260, §373.

[21] Quintilian, *inst.* 5.10.33 (LCL 125:382).

[22] Quintilian, *inst.* 5.10.34–35 (LCL 125:382).

[23] *ep.* 185.2.9 (CSEL 57:8). For similar discussions of the thieves crucified with Christ, see *s.* 285.2, 335.2, 335C.12; *ep.* 93.2.

If the *poena*, the punishment, is the *proprium* that makes a martyr, then the thieves are equally to be honored in their death as Christ is in his.[24] Only the *proprium* of motive can provide a proper definition for martyrdom and establish the legitimacy of a claimant's pursuit of the reward.

Further, Augustine's denial of Donatist martyrdom is not a dispute over a charge of wrongdoing (though such a charge is connected to this issue); rather, it is, as in the tyrannicide case, a dispute over a claim to a reward. Like the tyrannicide desiring his prize for ridding the city of a tyrant, the martyrs want to claim the reward they are due, namely, recognition as the one true church. But upon what basis do they make this claim? Not surprisingly, the answer is scripture. Although several texts appear repeatedly in the conflict over Donatist martyrdom, the most significant for the *non poena sed causa* argument is Matt 5:10: "Blessed are those who suffer persecution for the sake of righteousness, for theirs is the kingdom of God."[25]

The Donatists use Matt 5:10 as a law similar to that promising a reward to tyrannicides. For example, in the letters of Petilian preserved by Augustine, the Donatist bishop runs through each of the beatitudes in turn, showing how Augustine and the Catholics lack the respective virtue. Finally, he comes to the key text: "'Blessed are those who suffer persecution on account of righteousness, for theirs is the kingdom of heaven.' But you are not blessed, but you make martyrs who are blessed, whose souls fill the heavens and whose memories flourish on the earth."[26] Similarly, in *Letter* 44 Augustine describes a debate he had with the Donatist bishop Fortunius, who also references Matt 5:10 to support his claim that the Donatists are the true church:

> [Fortunius] turned from there [a previous argument] to exaggerating the persecution that his party often said they suffered, wishing to show from this that they are Christians, because they suffer persecution. Therefore, he first cited the passage where the Lord says, "Blessed are those who suffer persecution on account of righteousness, for theirs is the kingdom of heaven."[27]

---

[24] Elsewhere Augustine suggests that even the devil would be saved according to Donatist logic on account of how much Christians cause him pain. See *s.* 328.4.

[25] For the role of Matt 5:10 and other "persecution" texts in Donatist self-understanding, see Maureen A. Tilley, *The Bible in Christian North Africa: The Donatist World* (Minneapolis: Fortress Press, 1997), 153–54.

[26] Quoted in Augustine, *c. litt. Pet.* 2.71.159 (CSEL 52:101–2).

[27] *ep.* 44.2.4 (CSEL 34.2:112).

When we read these Donatist uses of Matt 5:10 in the context of North African martyrdom tradition, which since Tertullian has been steeped in the imagery of the martyr's crown and other *praemia* given to those who remain faithful in persecution,[28] we see the weight of Petilian's and Fortunius's claims. The true church is the church of the martyrs.[29] Only they can lay claim to Christ's promised reward of the kingdom. To support their claim to be the true church, the Donatists appeal to Matt 5:10 as the *lex* that entitles them to the *praemium* of the kingdom.

We have seen how Augustine uses the *locus a causa* to undermine the Donatists' claim to this reward. Now we can see how Matt 5:10, the very text the Donatists use to stake their claim, provides Augustine with the necessary *proprium* for the definitional issue. For instance, in his debate with Fortunius, Augustine reports that he was grateful to have Matt 5:10 brought forth and "immediately proposed that it should be inquired whether they [the Donatists] suffered persecution on account of righteousness" or on account of something else.[30] The text that the Donatists used to claim the reward of martyrdom and the right to be recognized as the true church now becomes the main piece of evidence in what Augustine has made an issue of definition. The *lex* assigning the reward contains within itself the *proprium* for defining true martyrdom.

From Definition to *Interpretatio Scripti*

So far, I have focused on the rhetorical issue of definition to show how Augustine uses the rhetorical arguments associated with this forensic theme to deny the Donatists their claim to martyrdom. But the issue of definition

---

[28] See *inter multa alia*, Tertullian, *mart.* 2; Cyprian, *unit. eccl.* 19; Cyprian, *Fort.* 11–13 (Cyprian even uses Matt 5:10 at *Fort.* 12); Cyprian, *ep.* 76.1.2, 76.7.1, 77.2.2.

[29] There may seem to be a logical fallacy here: one need not necessarily continue to produce martyrs in order to qualify as the true church. Indeed, to be the "church of the martyrs" one could simply maintain the martyrs' fidelity to Christ. For the Donatists, the claim to be the true church that *still* suffers martyrdom works most effectively when contrasted with the *traditores* who betray the memory of the martyrs through complicity with persecutors, apostates, and collaborators. In short, a communion need not necessarily produce martyrs in order to be the true church that maintains fidelity to Christ; but if a communion can claim to be experiencing persecution and martyrdom, then in the context of Christian North Africa they may have a better claim to be the true church than those who, they allege, commit or collaborate in the persecutions. Thus, although Augustine could hypothetically problematize martyrdom as an ecclesiological criterion, the identification of the church with martyrs is so ingrained in his cultural context that he must redefine martyrdom itself.

[30] *ep.* 44.2.4 (CSEL 34.2:112). Augustine makes the same *proprium* argument from Matt 5:10 in *ep.* 87.7, 93.2.8, 108.5.14, 185.2.9; *Io. ev. tr.* 88.2–3; *en. Ps.* 34.2.13, 43.1, 118.1.3; *c. Gaud.* 1.20.23, 1.30.35.

is not the only argumentative approach that Augustine uses in this dispute. In his polemical interpretation of Matt 5:10, Augustine pushes the argument beyond the issue of definition and to the more basic question of scriptural interpretation. While the Donatists use the verse to legitimate their claim to the *praemium* of martyrdom, Augustine will use the arguments of legal literary analysis to accuse the Donatists of being sloppy readers of scripture, inappropriately appealing to a divine law they do not even understand. In doing so, he will connect his primary issue of definition to the more hermeneutical concerns of the *genus legale* and *interpretatio scripti*.[31] This phrase keeps us within the realm of forensic rhetoric but redirects our attention to disputes over how a text is to be interpreted within a particular case. This includes conflicts between the letter of the law and the intent of the lawgiver, ambiguity created by confusing syntax, conflict between various laws, and the applicability of a specific law to an analogous case. Although this branch of rhetorical argumentation exerts a ubiquitous influence in early Christian exegesis, from Paul to Augustine and beyond, I want to highlight two themes from Cicero and Quintilian that will illuminate what Augustine is doing with Matt 5:10.

First, many of the examples for these issues in rhetorical handbooks describe disputes between competing heirs regarding the meaning of a dead man's will and testament. Cicero provides this hypothetical case:

> A father, when he was making his son his heir, bequeathed to his wife one hundred pounds of silver dishes in the following way: "Let my heir give to my wife one hundred pounds of silver dishes, the ones that ___ shall want (*quae uolet*)." After his death, the mother requests splendid and preciously embossed dishes from the son. He says that he is required to give to her what *he* wants.[32]

This dispute arises over the ambiguous subject of the verb *uolet*. Who gets to choose the dishes: the son or the mother? One argument that Cicero suggests the mother could make would be to say that, had her dead husband intended his heir to choose the dishes, then he would not have added *quae uolet*.[33]

---

[31] On these themes, see Lausberg, *Handbook of Literary Rhetoric*, §§198–223 (n.32). In addition to Lausberg, I am indebted to Kathy Eden, *Hermeneutics and the Rhetorical Tradition: Chapters in the Ancient Legacy and Its Humanist Reception* (New Haven, CT: Yale University Press, 1997) for my understanding of this topic in classical rhetoric. For a brief but rich summary of the role of *interpretatio scripti* in Augustine's biblical exegesis, see Cameron, *Christ Meets Me Everywhere*, 29–30.

[32] Cicero, *inv.* 2.40.116 (LCL 386:284).

[33] Cicero, *inv.* 2.41.120 (LCL 386:288).

Without these extra words, Cicero suggests, it would be clear that the dishes were to be chosen by the son. The only reason for the additional phrase would be to specify the widow as the one who is to choose. In fact, Cicero clarifies, this type of argument is useful in many disputes over a law or a testament. Whoever wants to stick to a strict reading of a text in opposition to a proposed appeal to the author's unspecified *uoluntas* will say things like, "He wrote it in this way" or "He would not have used this word" or "He would not have placed this word in this place."[34] In short, the disputant will argue that there is neither ambiguity nor confusion as to the text and the author's intent so long as one attends to and respects the perspicacity of the language used by the testator or lawgiver, whose honor and expediency are to be lauded for so carefully constructing his text.

A second pertinent textual argument involves extending a particular judgment to cover an analogous case. Cicero calls this *ratiocinatio*, while Quintilian names it syllogism.[35] In such a dispute, one litigant will appeal to the similarity between the present case and the situation imagined in the specific law. The opponent, however, will "diminish the similarity, which he will do if he demonstrates that the cases being compared are different according to kind, nature, meaning, magnitude, time, place, person, or reputation."[36] Moreover, this type of textual legal dispute can pair well with the dispute described above about the intent of the dead man who wants his heir to give his wife some dishes. There, the wife emphasizes the way in which a close reading of the text reveals her late husband's intent. Here, in a dispute where one party wants to show that a law can be argued to extend beyond its written specificity to cover an analogous case, the opponent to this extension will argue in favor of a strict reading of the *scriptum* to prevent "anything other than what is written" from being done.[37] Again, this type of argument, rejecting the extension of a law by analogy, will emphasize the wisdom and diligence of the law-giver or testator to write with such clarity and precision.

Augustine responds to the Donatists' claim to be the true church of the martyrs—a claim bolstered by their appeal to Matt 5:10 as a testament granting their ecclesial inheritance—by arguing that the Donatists are bad readers of scripture. To do so he uses the above rhetorical arguments for interpreting disputed legal documents. For instance, in a letter to the

---

[34] Cicero, *inv.* 2.41.121 (LCL 386:288).
[35] Cicero, *inv.* 2.40.116. Quintilian, *inst.* 7.8.1. See Lausberg, *Handbook of Literary Rhetoric*, §221.
[36] Cicero, *inv.* 2.50.151 (LCL 386:318–20).
[37] Quintilian, *inv.* 7.8.1 (LCL 126:277).

Donatist bishop Emeritus, Augustine draws his opponent's attention to the limits set by Matt 5:10 itself: "Therefore with the greatest providence the Lord did not say simply, 'Blessed are those who suffer persecution,' but he added 'on account of righteousness.' Therefore I wish to know from you if it is righteousness that you work in that dissension in which you still remain."[38] We see here the same type of textual argument that Cicero suggests in the dispute over silver dishes. Augustine, like the widow, emphasizes the author's careful limiting of the scope of the reward offered for suffering persecution. Christ, had he intended to bless all who suffer punishment or even death, would have left out the qualifier *propter iustitiam*. This legalistic parsing of the sentence allows Augustine to deny the Donatists' claim to martyrdom by showing that their definition is too broad according to the terms of the divine testament they themselves bring forth.

Similarly, in his response to Fortunius, Augustine emphasizes the difference between the Donatists' actions and those of a true martyr in order to prevent the extension of the beatific law and its consequent reward to a disparate situation:

> Those who wish to see whether they had suffered persecution on account of righteousness should attend more to this: whether they rightly cut themselves off from the unity of the whole world. Because if they were found to have done so unjustly, it would be manifest that they suffered persecution on account of unrighteousness rather than on account of righteousness and therefore are not able to be added to the number of the blessed, of whom it was said, "Blessed are those who suffer persecution on account of righteousness."[39]

Elsewhere Augustine uses the examples of Hagar and Sarah or of David and Saul to illustrate further the difference between suffering on account of righteousness and suffering on account of unrighteousness.[40] Again we see Augustine using the approaches suggested by Cicero and Quintilian to limit the scope of a legal text in his dispute with the Donatists over who can lay claim to be the church of the martyrs. In this way the *causa* distinction not only arises from a strict adherence to the letter of Matt 5:10 but also gives

---

[38] *ep.* 87.7 (CSEL 34.2:403). Augustine makes this same argument in *ep.* 93.2.8, 108.5.14; *s. Dom. mon.* 1.13; *en. Ps.* 34.2.13, 43.1; *s. Caes.* 7; *c. Gaud.* 1.36.46.
[39] *ep.* 44.2.4 (CSEL 34.2, 112).
[40] See esp. *ep.* 185.2.9–11.

Augustine the key dissimilarity needed to separate the Donatists' experience from that of those whom Matt 5:10 intends to bless.

Therefore, Matt 5:10 does more than provide Augustine with his definitional *proprium* for true martyrdom. In addition, because the Donatists have used the text as the basis for their claim to the reward of martyrdom, the kingdom of God, and ecclesial legitimacy, Augustine can treat the verse like a legal document and bring his forensic rhetorical training to bear upon the disputed text. The Donatists thus become pretenders to the legacy of the martyrs, usurpers of the rightful heirs, and, as Augustine would have it, willful misreaders of the Lord's own testament.

But Augustine had to not only confront the Donatist claims to be the church of the martyrs but also fend off accusations that his communion were persecutors and therefore guilty of betraying the martyrs, thus forfeiting their own claim to ecclesial legitimacy. It is to this related accusation and Augustine's similarly forensic response that I now turn.

For Their Own Good

In the second half of this chapter, I examine Augustine's response to the Donatist charge that he and the Catholic Church are persecutors and thus have no rightful claim to ecclesial legitimacy. Because this argument is so closely entwined with the previous one, it is no surprise that Augustine again turns to forensic rhetoric, this time deploying techniques associated with an issue of quality. Augustine also returns to scripture, but here he does so to call upon *exempla* much like we saw in chapter 2, now with a forensic frame.

"With us is found the true Catholic Church, that which suffers persecution, not that which inflicts it."[41] What could the self-styled "church of the martyrs" offer that would more viscerally evince their claim to be the rightful heirs to the tradition of Perpetua, Tertullian, and Cyprian? In fact, this was, arguably, the strongest plank in the Donatists' anti-Catholic platform.[42] Communal memory of persecutions and martyrdoms—regardless of their objective reality—so defined North African Christianity that even after

---

[41] *conl. Carth.* 3.22. See note 4 above.
[42] Lenski, "Imperial Legislation," 187: "To be a Donatist was to endure persecution, so that the continuation of persecution even after the establishment of Christian state religion was in many ways optimal for the ongoing identity construction of the dissident church."

"winning" the debate in 411, Augustine and his fellow Catholics still risked losing the larger battle for the hearts and minds of the Donatists.

Following their initial failed attempts to win imperial support[43]—attempts of which Augustine often reminds them[44]—Donatists quickly adopted the polemical posture of the persecuted, condemning the imperially sanctioned Catholics for colluding with the powers of this world and betraying the memory of the martyrs. Sporadic efforts by Constantine and his successors throughout the fourth century to force the Donatists back into unity with the Catholics only perpetuated the Donatists' view of themselves as the true church that suffers persecution.[45] Finally, in response to the Edict of Unity in 405[46] and at the Conference of Carthage in 411,[47] Donatists like Petilian sought to condemn the Catholics for embracing imperial power. Continuing to inhabit an apocalyptic worldview similar to earlier Christian martyrs, the Donatists maintained (at least rhetorically) a strict delineation between their holy community and the evil powers of the world that are most manifest in persecution. How could a church claim to be legitimate if it supported such persecution against other Christians? Or, as Donatus himself said, "What has the emperor to do with the church?"[48]

The Quality of Forensic Rhetoric

Augustine's justification of persecution ought to be understood in terms of forensic rhetoric, especially as an issue of *qualitas* in which the justice of a seemingly wrongful act is defended. In a dispute over quality, the defendant attempts to justify an act that might usually be seen as dishonorable or criminal. Cicero offers several suggestions for how one might make such

---

[43] See the letters relating to the Council of Arles (314) and Constantine preserved by Optatus as appendices to *Parm.*, esp. appendices 4–7. Lenski, "Constantine and the Donatists," provides the most thorough analysis of Constantine's efforts to restrain the Donatists while still maintaining his commitment to some form of religious toleration.

[44] E.g., *c. litt. Pet.* 2.93.205. More damning than their appeal to Constantine, however, was the Donatists' use of civil authorities to enforce unity upon their own schismatics, the so-called Maximianists. On how the Catholics subsequently adopted the Donatists' own legal playbook, see Hermanowicz, *Possidius of Calama*, 126–36; and Lenski, "Imperial Legislation," 178–81.

[45] See the discussion of these events, which include beatings, imprisonment, and killings of both laity and clergy, in Burns and Jensen, *Christianity in Roman Africa*, 48–50; Shaw, *Sacred Violence*, 146–94, 822–24; Gaddis, *There Is No Crime*, 103–11.

[46] Honorius's edict only survives in fragments. See *Codex Theodosianus* 16.5.38, 16.6.3–5.

[47] Technically this was not a "council" or *concilium* but a "conference" or *conlatio*. On the intentional legal ambiguities of this gathering, see Hermanowicz, *Possidius of Calama*, 200–203.

[48] Reported in Optatus, *Parm.* 3.3.

an argument. First, one might use *relatio criminis*, whereby "the defendant, having confessed to that with which he is charged, shows that he acted justly because he was led into it by an offense of his opponent."[49] In describing this approach, though he uses the Greek term instead of the Latin, Quintilian offers more detail:

> The strongest approach of this type (assumptive quality) is to defend the crime by the motive of the deed, and of this type are the defenses of Orestes, Horatius, and Milo. This is called ᾿Αντέκλημα, because our entire defense depends upon our accusation against the victim which claims: "He was killed, but he was a thief" or "He was blinded but he was a robber."[50]

The examples of Orestes and Horatius appear in both Cicero and Quintilian and provide vivid illustrations of an issue of quality in which a crime is justified on account of the wicked deeds of the victim. Orestes kills Clytemnestra because she first killed his father, Agamemnon. Horatius kills his sister because she shamefully wept for the death of his enemies rather than the death of her own brothers. The key here is that the blame for the act is shifted onto the victim, whose own baseness or crime becomes the supposed justification for the defendant's action.

To enhance the *relatio criminis* argument, Cicero recommends using *ekphrasis*,[51] vivid verbal description:

> He will confirm this *relationem* first by augmenting the guilt and audacity of the one onto whom he is transferring the crime, and then by placing [the scene] before the eyes [of the jury] with the greatest indignation; and second by demonstrating that he punished [the victim] more lightly than he deserved, and by comparing the defendant's act of punishment to the crime of the supposed victim.[52]

The key here is to describe the victim's own crime with the utmost disdain while contrasting the tempered response of the defendant with the severity of the victim's precipitating wickedness. In the case of Horatius, he would

---

[49] Cicero, *inv.* 2.78 (LCL 386:242).
[50] Quintilian, *inst.* 7.4.8 (LCL 126:240).
[51] For an analysis of the role of ἔκφρασις in Augustine's depiction of martyrdom, see Diane Fruchtman, "Living in a Martyrial World: Living Martyrs and the Creation of Martyrial Consciousness in the Late Antique West" (PhD diss., Indiana University, 2014), 215–53.
[52] Cicero, *inv.* 2.83 (LCL 386:248).

elaborate the brave honor of his dead brothers in order to accentuate the shameful tears of his sister who disgraces her family in such misplaced grief. Surely, he might suggest, such shameful actions deserve worse punishment than death, but he, in order to maintain honor against one so devoid of it, provided mercy in death.

In addition to *relatio criminis*, where the defendant blames the victim, Cicero recommends the use of *comparatio*, "when some deed which is not able to be approved in itself is defended by the reason on account of which it was done."[53] At first glance this seems similar to the *relatio criminis*, but the reason here is not the preceding crime of the victim but the intended goal of the defendant. In particular, a *comparatio* points to the consequences of not having done the act in order to show that by doing what in itself seems wrong the defendant avoided a greater negative outcome. Cicero's example here is Gaius Popilius:

> A certain general, when he was surrounded by the enemy and was unable to escape, came to terms with them that he would leave the weapons and baggage behind and lead his soldiers away. Thus he did. And though the weapons and baggage were lost, he saved his soldiers when there seemed to be no hope. He is accused of treason.[54]

In this situation, Cicero suggests, the defendant would again defend himself through *ekphrasis*, vividly describing the events so that the audience "will judge that they would have done the same thing" had they been in the general's shoes.[55] In addition, Cicero recommends bringing two common topics into play for *comparatio*. The first says that no act should be judged good or bad unless the intent (*animo*) and the reason (*causa*) are known. For instance, one cannot condemn Popilius without knowing that he sacrificed his weapons in order to save the lives of his men. The second common topic emphasizes the magnitude of the benefit (*utilitas*) accrued by the act; for example, Popilius will show how much service and honor the living soldiers will bring to the republic.[56]

When Cicero discusses this last point—the benefit, advantage, or *utilitas* that the otherwise wrongful act sought—the beneficiary of the *utilitas*

---

[53] Cicero, *inv.* 2.72 (LCL 386:236).
[54] Cicero, *inv.* 2.72 (LCL 386:236).
[55] Cicero, *inv.* 2.78 (LCL 386:242).
[56] Cicero, *inv.* 2.77.

is normally a third party, often the state itself or the general good of the people. But Quintilian offers a more intriguing option. In discussing this approach to an issue of quality, he says that the act may be justified "by some *utilitas* . . . even to our opponent himself."[57] That is to say, the defendant can argue that he did it for the victim's own good.

To illustrate this type of quality issue in which the victim's own benefit justifies the crime, we must turn from the Latin sources to the Greek. Hermogenes provides the following example in his treatise on rhetorical issue theory from the late second century CE:

> A hero killed his son for prostituting himself, and is charged with homicide. . . . The defendant will use intent (*dianoia*), asserting that the argument should be based not just on what was done, but also on the intention with which it was done: first, that he was not hostile to or scheming against his son; secondly, that he acted reluctantly, but out of necessity. . . . [I]n this case a counteraccusation is relevant—he deserved it; and he [the defendant] will develop the common topic against a male prostitute. . . . He will also say something by the way of counterstatement, that he did this on behalf of the victim himself.[58]

Here we see an otherwise wrongful action—killing one's son—justified by the crimes of the victim and the defendant's desire to benefit the victim. Presumably the common topic would emphasize the baseness and shame of the son's prostitution, stirring up indignation in the audience, so that they would side with the father in believing that death was preferable to dishonor for the son.[59] This lurid example from Hermogenes prepares us well for what we will now see in Augustine.

Letter 185 and the Issue of Quality

Although Augustine's justification of persecution against the Donatists appears in a wide range of texts, the most significant and sustained argument

---

[57] Quintilian, *inst.* 7.4.9 (LCL 126:240).
[58] Translation from Malcolm Heath, *Hermogenes: On Issues*, 50. Greek text from H. Rabe, *Hermogenis opera* (Leipzig: Teubner, 1913), 72.
[59] See Heath's commentary on 73.2–9 in *On Issues*, 126.

appears in *Letter* 185,[60] written to Boniface, the African tribune responsible for enforcing the anti-Donatist policies. Here we see all the approaches discussed above: blaming the victim, comparing the consequences of persecution to the perils of inaction, and ultimately claiming that everything is done for the Donatists' own good.

Before unpacking Augustine's use of those arguments, however, it is worth noting that he sometimes attempts to treat the persecution allegation as an issue of definition. What the Donatists suffer, he proffers, is not "persecution" but "correction." For instance, in his response to Petilian's appeal to Matt 5:10—"Blessed are those who suffer persecution on account of righteousness"—Augustine challenges the Donatist bishop to examine why his communion suffers what it does: "If it is on account of righteousness, then they [the imperial officials] are truly your persecutors ... but if it is on account of the iniquity of your schism, what are they but your correctors?"[61] Similarly, when reviewing his writings late in life, Augustine treats *Letter* 185 as a book in itself, giving it the title *The Correction of the Donatists*.[62] Augustine knows how damning the label "persecutor" is and therefore tries to rebrand the anti-Donatist actions as loving correction instead.

Unfortunately for Augustine, *persecutio* is a more generic word in Latin than the English cognate suggests, and as such it refers generally to prosecution or any effort to hold someone accountable by legal means.[63] Given the imperial actions levied against the Donatist church following the Edict of Unity in 405 and the Conference of Carthage in 411,[64] Augustine must accept that the empire and the Catholic Church are in fact engaged in persecution. While the broad meaning of *persecutio* obstructs his use of the definitional stasis, it allows him to shift to the next option: the issue of quality. The real question, Augustine now suggests, is not whether his church is committing

---

[60] On this epistle, see Robert Dodaro, *Christ and the Just Society in the Thought of Augustine* (Cambridge: Cambridge University Press, 2004), 200–214.

[61] Augustine, *c. litt. Pet.* 2.84.186 (CSEL 52:116).

[62] Augustine, *retr.* 2.48.

[63] See "persecution," in *Thesaurus linguae Latinae (TLL) Online* (Berlin, Boston: De Gruyter, n.d.). Accessed July 21, 2016, at http://www.degruyter.com/view/TLL/10-1-11/10_1_11_persecutio_v2 007.xml. Compare this to the distinction made between "persecution" and "prosecution" in Moss, *The Myth of Persecution*.

[64] Although these actions were primarily concerned with seizing Donatist churches and related property, violence could result when such actions were resisted. See, e.g., the events in Thamugadi reported in Augustine, *ep.* 204. In addition, laity could be fined and clergy exiled. See *Codex Theodosianus* 16.5.52–55. These details are helpfully summarized in Burns and Jensen, *Christianity in Roman Africa*, 54–57. Lenski, "Imperial Legislation," 180–86 offers more detailed analysis of the legal particulars involved.

persecution by means of coercive imperial power but whether they are doing so justly.

And so in *Letter* 185—a long, dense epistle from which I will only highlight a few examples—we find Augustine resorting to the issue of quality by using the arguments suggested by Cicero, Quintilian, and Hermogenes. His most sensational points come as a *relatio criminis* in which he condemns the actions of his opponents. He describes as "criminal impudence" the Donatists' condemnation of the universal church's communion because of the alleged crimes of Caecilian or one of his consecrators.[65] But for greater effect, he lingers on his opponents' vile madness with vivid description:

> They love murder so much that they commit it upon themselves when they are unable to perpetrate it upon others. . . . Certain [Donatists], in order that they might be butchered, even thrust themselves upon armed travelers, threatening fearfully to beat [the travelers] unless [the Donatists] were killed by [the travelers]. Sometimes they would violently extort transient judges in order to be killed by the executioners or an official. . . . Truly it was a daily game for them to kill themselves by steep heights or by water and flames.[66]

This description is part of Augustine's most notorious depiction of the Donatists.[67] These supposed victims of persecution, Augustine suggests, must be seen as the vile death seekers that they are. What great mercy the Catholic Church shows to gather them back, even by force, setting them free from these evils, like the demoniacs healed by Christ.

Augustine's most explicit use of *relatio criminis* against the Donatists comes when he describes the brutality allegedly suffered by Catholics at the hands of the Donatists or the Circumcellions.[68] He laments that "many Catholics, and especially bishops and clerics, have endured horrid and cruel things, which it would take a long time to put on record, when the eyes of some were destroyed and the hand and tongue of a certain bishop were cut off, and several were even slaughtered."[69] Augustine keeps going, employing ἀπόφασις or παράλειψις to say that he will not speak of a host of

---

[65] Augustine, *ep*. 185.1.4 (CSEL 57:4).
[66] Augustine, *ep*. 185.2.11–3.12 (CSEL 57:9–10).
[67] On the theme of Donatist suicides, see Shaw, *Sacred Violence*, 721–70.
[68] On the difficulty of identifying and defining the Circumcellions, as well as significant historiographical analysis, see Shaw, *Sacred Violence*, 828–39.
[69] Augustine, *ep*. 185.7.30 (CSEL 57:28).

other atrocities. Of course, in saying that he will not speak of such things, he succeeds in listing all the horrible deeds of which he will not speak. Acting as the defendant in a case alleging persecution, Augustine effectively paints his accusers, the victims of persecution, as wicked criminals deserving no sympathy. Augustine here is Orestes to the Donatists' Clytemnestra. Whatever the Donatists suffer by way of Catholic persecution is nothing compared to the horrors they have inflicted.

In addition to *relatio criminis*, Augustine also deploys *comparatio* to show how irresponsible it would be of him, of the Catholic Church in general, and indeed of Boniface the tribune and the Roman government to fail to persecute the Donatists. Per Cicero's suggestion, he paints the dilemma in which the Catholic bishops found themselves in order to convince his audience that there was no other good option and any virtuous person in that position would have done the same thing:

> For either the truth ought to be kept silent or they had to bear [the Donatists'] brutality. But if the truth were to be silent, not only would no one be set free by this silence, but many people would also be lost by the Donatists' seduction. If, however, [the Donatists'] furor would be provoked to the point of rage by the preaching of the truth, some people would be set free and our own people strengthened, but again fear would prevent the weaker ones from following the truth. Since, therefore, the church was afflicted by these difficulties, whoever thinks it better for the church to have endured all these things rather than seeking the help of God to be brought by the Christian emperors—whoever thinks this attends too little to the fact that no good reason can be given for this negligence.[70]

Like Gaius Popilius defending the surrender of his arms in order to save his men, Augustine shows that there was no good option left besides calling upon the service of Christian emperors. Even persuasive preaching presented too many perils without the backing of imperial coercion. The consequences of not acting, he suggests, would be much worse than any negative result of persecution.

And, of course, implicit in all of these *comparationes* is the claim that the persecution of the Donatists is for their own good. Augustine depicts the imperial church as "a doctor to a raging madman or a father to an undisciplined

---

[70] Augustine, *ep.* 185.4.18 (CSEL 57:16–17).

son."⁷¹ Both act out of the best interests of their charge, even when the patient or child finds the actions painful or burdensome. In such cases, failing to act would be a "false gentleness" that is more like cruelty. Similarly, as a revived patient will thank the doctor for the previously unwanted pain, so, Augustine claims, a host of former Donatists now thank the ones they previously cursed:

> It was a great mercy to them when, by these laws of the emperors, they were rescued against their wills from that sect where they learned those evil things from the teachings of lying demons, so that in the Catholic church afterwards they might be healed, having become familiar with her good precepts and ways.⁷²

Augustine here plays the role of the father in Hermogenes's example where the justifying utility of the act benefits the presumed victim himself.

Yet whereas the father's disgraced son can only benefit from a death that puts an end to his dishonor, Augustine's opponents, whom by *relatio criminis* he has painted as the most disturbed madmen one could contrive, are able to enjoy the benefit of sound faith and sound morals, if only they will suffer the harsh medicine of imperial coercion. By this combination of *comparatio* and *relatio criminis*, Augustine treats the Donatists' accusation of persecution as an issue of quality, not by denying the charge, but by showing that the Catholics and the empire perform such persecution justly, indeed for the Donatists' own good.

The Role of Scriptural *Exempla*

Yet something is still missing. All of these arguments raise the indignation of Augustine's readers against the shameful crimes of the Donatists, convince them that it would have been worse not to persecute them, and even show how such actions might be seen to be in the Donatists' own interests. But a more basic question remains: Given the deeply rooted and viscerally felt

---

[71] Augustine, *ep.* 185.2.7 (CSEL 57:6). For further analysis of medical imagery used to describe punitive measures, see Eric Fournier, "Amputation Metaphors and the Rhetoric of Exile: Purity and Pollution in Late Antique Christianity," in *Clerical Exile in Late Antiquity*, ed. Julia Hillner, Jacob Enberg, and Jörg Ulrich (Frankfurt am Main: Peter Lang, 2016), 231–49.

[72] Augustine, *ep.* 185.3.13 (CSEL 57:12).

abhorrence for persecution among Christians who still see themselves as the church of the martyrs, can persecution for whatever reason ever be justified? In the example from Hermogenes, the son-killing father could appeal to the principle that death is preferable to dishonor, especially given the shame associated with male prostitution. Similar principles would undergird the defense of Orestes or Horatius. In fact, someone finding themself on trial for murder might point to the story of Orestes or Horatius as an authoritative example for the general principle that murder could be justified based on the crimes or baseness of the victim.

Within a forensic dispute, the rhetorical *exemplum*—more famously, as we have seen, used for exhortation or moral inspiration—helps to establish a general principle as the basis for judgment in the specific case at hand. *Exempla* are normally drawn from history, including mythological history, and are therefore assumed to represent shared cultural norms that can be applied to the present case through similarity or dissimilarity. For instance, to illustrate how an *exemplum* can be used as a proof from similarity, Quintilian offers the following: "Saturninus was killed justly, just as the Gracchi were."[73] The orator seeks to draw a parallel between the demagoguery of the Gracchi and that of Saturninus in order to show that the killing of the latter should be judged like that of the former. For an *exemplum* of dissimilarity, Quintilian offers the following: "Brutus killed his sons for planning treason; Manlius punished his son's virtue with death."[74] Here the deeds are the same, but the orator highlights the dissimilarity in motives and circumstances, accentuating Manlius's wickedness by contrasting the place of honor in the two sets of fathers and sons. In both these examples, the orators bring culturally ubiquitous historical figures—the Gracchi and Lucius Junius Brutus—to bear upon their present cases, appealing to popular sentiment about the former as the basis for judgment in the latter.

If Augustine is to defend the justice of persecution, he needs some sort of normative precedent, an *exemplum* that can establish the principle that persecution can in fact be performed justly, just as the *exemplum* of Horatius might establish such a principle for sororicide. Augustine draws his definitive *exempla* not from the *Aeneid* or Homer or the annals of Roman history, but from scripture. Several Old Testament figures serve as *exempla* for just persecution. Nebuchadnezzar once unjustly persecuted by means of a

---

[73] Quintilian, *inst.* 5.11.7 (LCL 125:432).
[74] Quintilian, *inst.* 5.11.7 (LCL 125:432).

"sacrilegious law" those who would not worship an image, but after being corrected, he "established a laudable law so that whosoever spoke blasphemy against the God of Shadrach, Meschach, and Abednego should die with their whole household."[75] The contrast between the sacrilegious and laudable laws of a single ruler suggests, Augustine proposes, that laws regarding religious coercion are not in themselves wrong; rather, their justice turns upon the truth of the religion being promoted. For Augustine, of course, only the Catholic Church meets the standard of truth for legitimate coercive promotion. Moreover, in the transformation of Nebuchadnezzar, Augustine may also intend his audience to see the transformation of the Roman imperial authority, once punishing Christians for refusing to worship false gods but now using the same authority for its proper end, that is, to promote true religion. In any case, Augustine does not leave the significance of the *exemplum* to his readers' imagination: anyone who condemned Nebuchadnezzar's second law and suffered the consequences "ought to say what [the Donatists] say, that they are just because they suffer persecution from a king's law."[76] If such a claim would appear nonsensical in the case of Nebuchadnezzar's second law, then so may the Donatists' condemnation of imperial persecution. The justice of persecution, this *exemplum* proves, depends upon the justice of the law and its purpose, not upon the act of persecution itself.

But Augustine's most significant repeated *exemplum* is that of Sarah and her maidservant, Hagar. In Gal 4, Paul had already established these women as contrasting figures: Hagar representing the present Jerusalem and slavery to the law, Sarah representing the heavenly Jerusalem and freedom. The church, Paul suggests, has Sarah as its mother and therefore ought to live free from the law. In addition to this ecclesiological connection, Paul also uses the word "persecute" (ἐδίωκεν, *persequebatur*) to describe how Hagar's offspring treats Sarah's (Gal 4:29). He concludes, however, by reminding the Galatians that Sarah commanded Abraham to cast out Hagar and Ishmael so that Sarah's child would not have to share his inheritance (Gal 4:30). Thus, Paul has already used Sarah and Hagar as an *exemplum* to exhort the Galatians to live in freedom from the law.

Augustine expands upon Paul's use of Sarah and Hagar, accentuating the contrast between the two figures and the role of persecution between them: "For Hagar also suffered persecution by Sarah, and she who did the

---

[75] Augustine, *ep.* 185.2.8 (CSEL 57:7–8).
[76] Augustine, *ep.* 185.2.8 (CSEL 57:8). On God's use of Nebuchadnezzar, see *s.* 296.

persecution was holy while she who suffered it was unjust."[77] Whereas the Nebuchadnezzar *exemplum* proved that kings might persecute both justly and unjustly, Paul's depiction of Sarah and Hagar allows Augustine to draw a more direct parallel to the Catholic and Donatist churches:

> If the true church is that which suffers persecution not that which commits it, let [the Donatists] seek from the Apostle which church Sarah signified when she persecuted her servant. Of course [Paul] says that our free mother, the heavenly Jerusalem, i.e., the true church of God, was figured in this woman who afflicted her servant. Yet if we examine more, [Hagar] persecuted Sarah more by being prideful than Sarah did by punishing her. For [Hagar] committed an injury against her mistress, but [Sarah] imposed discipline upon pride.[78]

Augustine's analysis of the Sarah and Hagar *exemplum* accomplishes three things: First, it reaffirms the principle that persecution in and of itself is not necessarily wrong but can in fact be pursued justly. This is the most basic move necessary for Augustine to treat the Donatist accusation as an issue of quality. All of his other moves depend upon this premise of just persecution. Second, Augustine uses the argument of *relatio criminis* within the *exemplum* to show that Hagar herself is guilty of a more serious persecution than that which she receives from Sarah. Similarly, he suggests a *comparatio* by showing that Sarah's intent was to curb the dangerous pride of her servant. Third, by highlighting the vice of pride in Hagar and reminding his audience that Paul sees the church as Sarah, Augustine associates the Donatists with the former, who suffers a just persecution. By implication, Augustine suggests that the Donatists are committing the truly unjust persecution, a point he makes more explicitly in an earlier sermon where he describes how they persecute by leading away from the true church, offering rebaptism, and generally persecuting not the body but the soul.[79]

Augustine summarizes the significance of both the Nebuchadnezzar and the Hagar and Sarah *exempla* by highlighting the contrast between Catholic and Donatist persecutions:

---

[77] Augustine, *ep.* 185.2.9 (CSEL 57:8).
[78] Augustine, *ep.* 185.2.11 (CSEL 57:9–10).
[79] See Augustine, *Io. ev. tr.* 11.13.

If, therefore, we wish to speak or acknowledge the truth, it is unjust persecution that the wicked commit against the church of Christ, and it is just persecution that the church of Christ commits against the wicked. . . . We persecute by loving; they by hating. We persecute in order to correct; they in order to ruin.[80]

Augustine has brought us back to the matter of intent and to the *utilitas* sought from the act, again contrasting his own communion's actions with the shameful behavior of his opponents. This is a textbook defense in an issue of quality enhanced by the deployment of scriptural *exempla*.

Conclusion

Having analyzed Augustine's deployment of forensic rhetorical arguments—especially the issues of definition and quality—to deny the Donatists' claim to be the true church of the martyrs who suffer persecution at the hands of the Catholics, I return to where I began: with Augustine's letter to the tribune Dulcitius. We do well to remember that the rhetorical performances Augustine is conducting with his *non poena sed causa* slogan and his argument for beneficial persecutions are not just for the benefit of his Donatist opponents or his own faithful flock. It is a public dispute often explicitly directed to imperial authorities such as Dulcitius, Boniface (*ep.* 185 especially), or Marcellinus (at the Conference of Carthage in 411). Whether they are rival claimants to a reward or squabbling siblings trying to cut each other out of dad's will, Augustine and the Donatists are arguing not just about ecclesiology but about who should receive the benefit of imperial legitimation.[81] *Non poena sed causa*, then, as well as the justification of persecution,

---

[80] Augustine, *ep.* 185.2.11 (CSEL 57:10).

[81] The most thorough recent summary of Donatist and Catholic appeals to imperial support—from Constantine to Honorius—is Lenski, "Imperial Legislation and the Donatist Controversy," esp. 197–219. Lenski lists over one hundred pieces of legislation, including rescripts, edicts, petitions, etc. It is important to note that the Donatists, despite their anti-imperial rhetoric, continued to petition for legal support for their cause into the fifth century. Further, in his analysis of how Catholics and Donatists competed in the legal realm, Lenski notes, "The law was not a monolithic artifact but an intersubjective dialogue that came into being and was invigorated by ever-unfolding interplay between (on the one hand) petitioners, plaintiffs and appellants and (on the other) the emperor or his officials. Those groups or individuals most skilled at manipulating this dialogue were themselves most likely to benefit from it" ("Imperial Legislation," 169). Lenski's study offers a good example of the more general use of "rhetoric" as he discusses the different "rhetorical strategies" used by Augustine, the Donatists, and others. He does not connect these strategies to actual practices or techniques taught in classical rhetorical handbooks. This is not a criticism of Lenski's excellent analysis but an example

represents not only classical rhetorical theory but also, to borrow a phrase from Averil Cameron, "the rhetoric of empire."[82] Throughout his career, the bishop of Hippo sought to bring the "pagan" liberal arts into the service of Christian faith while also negotiating the uneasy relationship between the church and imperial power. In his use of forensic rhetoric to reject the Donatists' claim to martyrdom and refute their accusations of persecution, we catch a glimpse of the cultural tools and practice methods needed for both efforts.

---

of where more precise work is still needed. As Lenski states, Catholic success in the Donatist controversy came "by the Catholics out-competing their Donatist opponents in the discursive realm" (189). For the legal disputes at the time of Augustine, see Hermanowicz, *Possidius of Calama*.

[82] Averil Cameron, *Christianity and the Rhetoric of Empire: The Development of Christian Discourse* (Berkeley: University of California Press, 1994).

5
The Rhetoric of the Martyrs

Introduction

This study set out to examine what it means to call Augustine's martyr discourse "rhetorical." So far, we have seen two options. First, in a more generic sense of the term, the contexts in which Augustine deploys notions of martyrdom are rhetorical in that they represent spaces in which the significance of martyrs and martyrdom bears persuasive force, both culturally and theologically. Second, the previous three chapters have examined the ways Augustine uses classical rhetorical techniques to construct and contest the meaning of martyrdom in ways that promote his pastoral and political aims.

We come now to the third way in which we can understand Augustine's martyrs to be rhetorical: they themselves should be understood as ideal Christian rhetors. This is not to say that historically the martyrs themselves played this part. Nor is it merely to repeat the claim that Augustine uses them for the purpose of persuasion. Rather, I mean that, within Augustine's constructed world of martyrdom, the characters of the martyrs function as and embody the ideals of Augustine's Christian rhetor. More than this, though, they also fulfill the role of the rhetor-statesman as described in Cicero and as Christianized by Augustine. The statesman role is further redefined within the martyrial context by the fact that the martyrs are statesmen serving the heavenly kingdom while on sojourn in the world under a hostile regime. In crafting his martyrs as rhetor-statesmen, Augustine furthers the agendas we have already observed, namely, promoting a Christian transvaluation of earthly goods in favor of eternal ones and confirming the role of God's providence within history even in the midst of pagan rule.

This chapter proceeds in three parts. First, I trace the classical ideals associated with the figure of the rhetor and the rhetor-statesman. Here I draw primarily on Quintilian and on Cicero's *On Invention* and *On the Republic*. Second, I discuss Augustine's transformation of both the rhetor and the statesman, emphasizing his *On Christian Teaching*, the *City of God*, and *Letter 155* to Macedonius. Finally, I turn to Augustine's martyr texts to demonstrate

Augustine, Martyrdom, and Classical Rhetoric. Adam Ployd, Oxford University Press. © Oxford University Press 2023.
DOI: 10.1093/oso/9780190914141.003.0006

how his martyrs fit a combination of the classical and Christian ideals of the rhetor and the statesman, looking at a combination of sermons and passages from *City of God*.

Classical Ideals

Vir bonus dicendi peritus

Cicero has much to say on what makes a good orator. In the *Brutus*, the *Orator*, *On the Orator*, and *On the Best Kind of Orator*, he takes up the question again and again. Consistently, he describes the superior orator, whether historical or ideal, as one who can deploy various styles appropriately to fit diverse audiences and purposes. Although moral concerns are not wholly absent, they are, nevertheless, not central to his consideration.[1] Yet Cicero's approach lies a bit outside the norm, or, at least, it represents but one trend in classical rhetorical theory. In this section I trace a countertrend that extends from Plato to Quintilian, one that intertwines the questions of just what rhetoric is and how it relates to the moral character of the orator. It is to this latter rhetorical tradition that, I will argue, Augustine's martyr-rhetors belong.

Plato's *Gorgias* and *Phaedrus* represent the appropriate starting point for considering Greco-Roman understandings of rhetoric and the virtues of the ideal rhetor. In the *Gorgias*, Plato's Socrates appears rather negative toward rhetoric precisely because it does not seem to be a true ἐπιστήμη or τέχνη but merely a knack of some sort. In fact, Socrates gets Gorgias to admit, an orator would be better served by ignorance than wisdom in his efforts to convince.[2] Socrates is most concerned, however, that the rhetor would need to be one who possesses knowledge of what is just and unjust, shameful and admirable, good and bad, and thus that the orator must actually be a just, admirable, and good person (459c–60b).[3] This is the point at which Gorgias bows out of the

---

[1] As we will see below, Cicero is indeed concerned with the virtues possessed by the rhetor in his role as statesman. These simply do not appear to the same degree in his discussions of the ideal orator qua orator, at least not to the extent as they do in Quintilian.

[2] For the difference between Plato's character of Gorgias and the actual rhetoric of the historical figure, see Bruce McComiskey, *Gorgias and the New Sophistic Rhetoric* (Carbondale: Southern Illinois University Press, 2002), 17–54.

[3] For an analysis of this section of the *Gorgias*, see Seth Benardete, *The Rhetoric of Morality and Philosophy: Plato's* Gorgias *and* Phaedrus (Chicago: University of Chicago Press, 1991), 5–30; Marina McCoy, *Plato on the Rhetoric of Philosophers and Sophists* (Cambridge: Cambridge University Press, 2008), 87–92.

argument, unable to confront the moral challenge posed by Socrates about the necessarily just character of a true orator.

In the *Phaedrus*, Socrates is a bit more sanguine on the subject of rhetoric. Unlike in the *Gorgias*, he is here willing to treat rhetoric as a τέχνη for "directing the soul by means of speech" (261a).[4] To do so effectively, the orator must know the nature of the soul and indeed of the truth itself. Therefore, as in the *Gorgias*, Plato prioritizes philosophy over rhetoric, making the true orator first and foremost a philosopher. From the beginning, therefore, questions about the nature of rhetoric turn to questions about the moral character and philosophical preparation of the orator.

Within the Latin tradition, this approach to rhetoric can be summed up in the phrase *vir bonus dicendi peritus*.[5] Originally a maxim of Cato the Elder, the saying is preserved in a number of authors. Seneca the Elder quotes it in the first book of his *Controversies*.[6] Apuleius quotes it in his *Apology*.[7] Ambrose of Milan and Jerome both quote the maxim, the former in his *On Abraham*,[8] the latter in a letter to Oceanus in 397.[9] These uses all suggest that *vir bonus dicendi peritus* had become an agreed-upon shorthand definition for what makes an orator. The adjective *bonus* may admit some ambiguity, but it is unambiguously attached to *vir*, identifying goodness, however we are to define it, as a necessary quality not just of an orator's speech but of the orator themself.

The most significant use of this formula comes in Quintilian's *On the Orator's Education*.[10] Turning to that text, then, will allow us to unpack at least one possible way in which an orator can be considered *bonus*. The phrase arises in Quintilian's final book where he considers the necessary character of the ideal orator. Lamenting that Cicero is concerned with style but not moral character,[11] Quintilian declares for himself, "Let the orator

---

[4] See Benardete, *The Rhetoric of Morality and Philosophy*, 169–74; and David A. White, *Rhetoric and Reality in Plato's* Phaedrus (Albany: State University of New York Press, 1993), 175–202.

[5] On the history of this phrase, see William M. Calder III, "Vir bonus, discendi peritus," *American Journal of Philology* 108 (1987): 168–71.

[6] Seneca, *contr.* 1.praef.9.

[7] Apuleius, *apol.* 94.

[8] Ambrose, *Abr.* 2.10.76.

[9] Jerome, *ep.* 69.8.

[10] For a more nuanced treatment of Quintilian's ideal, see George Kennedy, *Quintilian* (New York: Twayne, 1969), 123–35. On the *vir bonus* in Quintilian, see Arthur E. Walzer, "Quintilian's 'Vir Bonus' and the Stoic Wise Man," *Rhetoric Society Quarterly* 33 (2003): 25–41; Alan Brinton, "Quintilian, Plato, and the 'Vir Bonus,'" *Philosophy & Rhetoric* 16 (1983): 167–84; Prentice A. Meador Jr., "Quintilian's 'Vir Bonus,'" *Western Speech* 34 (1970): 162–69; Michael Winterbottom, "Quintilian and the *Vir Bonus*," *Journal of Roman Studies* 54 (1964): 90–97.

[11] Consider Quintilian's regret that even Cicero does not go far enough in describing the perfect orator, emphasizing style but ignoring morality: "*Unum modo in illa inmensa vastitate cernere videmur*

whom we are establishing be, as Cato defines him, 'a good man skilled in speaking'; indeed, as Cato put first, and what is by nature more important and greater, by all means let him be 'a good man.'"[12] Quintilian is precise about the implications of this claim: "I am not only saying that he who would be an orator ought to be a good man, but that only a good man will be an orator."[13] He offers a series of proofs for his claim but holds to this strong assertion against every opposition he brings before himself. Ultimately, even if a wicked man might be considered eloquent, he is no orator.[14] A good moral character, then, is the *sine qua non* of a true orator for Quintilian. But this relationship goes even deeper.

As in Plato, Quintilian's discussion of an orator's morality is connected to the question of how rhetoric itself is to be classified. In seeking to answer what rhetoric is, Quintilian opines that "the first and most significant difference of opinion is that some think that bad men also are able to be called orators, while others, with whose opinion I agree, wish this name and the art of which we are speaking to be assigned only to the good."[15] Those who disagree with Quintilian suggest that rhetoric may be labeled a power (*uim*), a science (*scientiam*), an art (*artem*), or even an evil art (κακοτεχνίαν), but they all agree that rhetoric is primarily about persuasion, "for this can be done also by one who is not a good man."[16] Under this heading of theorists describing rhetoric as merely the power (here he uses the term δύναμιν) of persuasion (some specifying "by speaking," some not) without clear regard for the moral character of the orator, he includes Isocrates, Gorgias as represented by Plato, and Cicero.

But for Quintilian himself, "the first [requirement of the perfect orator] is that he should be a good man."[17] This qualification guides his embrace of possible definitions for rhetoric. Ultimately, though, he puts forward a definition originally attributed to Xenocrates: "rhetoric is the science of speaking well." Such a definition, he tells us, "covers all the virtues of speech at once as

---

M. Tullium, qui tamen ipse, quamvis tanta atque ita instructa nave hoc mare ingressus, contrahit vela inhibetque remos et de ipso demum genere dicendi quo sit usurus perfectus orator satis habet dicere. At nostra temeritas etiam mores ei conabitur dare et adsignabit officia" (Quintilian, inst. 12.proem.4 [LCL 494:196]).

[12] Quintilian, *inst.* 12.1.1 (LCL 494:196).
[13] Quintilian, *inst.* 12.1.3 (LCL 494:198).
[14] Quintilian, *inst.* 12.1.23 (LCL 494:208).
[15] Quintilian, *inst.* 2.15.1 (LCL 124:350).
[16] Quintilian, *inst.* 2.15.3 (LCL 124:350).
[17] Quintilian, *inst.* 2.15.33 (LCL 124:366).

well as the character of the orator, because only a good man is able to speak well."[18] Under this definition, therefore, he includes those of Chrysippus and Cleanthes, that rhetoric is "the science of speaking rightly" (*recte*), and that of Areus's "to speak according to the virtue of oration." Quintilian approves of calling rhetoric a *scientia* so long as *scientia* is associated with *uirtus*, and *ars* and τέχνη also suffice as ways to distinguish rhetoric from a mere knack or talent. All of these classifications, however, must be connected to the moral quality of the orator. Without the latter, the former can be neither complete nor effective.

While not unanimous, the Latin rhetorical tradition, as attested to and represented by Quintilian, contains a strong thread emphasizing the necessary moral character of the ideal orator. Moreover, this concern is connected to debates over the nature and classification of rhetoric such that Quintilian can define rhetoric as the *scientia* of speaking well, where *bene* is understood to include questions of virtue in both the speech and the speaker.

The Rhetor as Statesman

While Cicero may not have quite the moral bent in his description of the ideal rhetor as Quintilian does, he nonetheless affirms the necessary utility of the rhetor for society in a way that requires consideration of the virtues, as we will see in the next section. For now, however, I turn to Cicero to advance our understanding of the ideal rhetor from the purely oratorical to the political. For Cicero, the ideal rhetor is necessarily a statesman, necessarily active in the governance and direction of the state. No appreciation of the rhetorical ideal, therefore, is complete without considering its public function.

In the introductory chapters of *On Invention*, Cicero offers an historical description of the significance of an orator for the very concept of society:

> For there was a time when men wandered at large in the fields like animals and lived on wild fare; they did nothing by the guidance of reason, but relied chiefly on physical strength; there was as yet no ordered system of religious worship nor of social duties; no one had seen legitimate marriage nor had anyone looked upon children whom he knew to be his own; nor had they learned the advantages of an equitable code of law. And so

---

[18] Quintilian, *inst.* 2.15.34 (LCL 124:366).

through their ignorance and error blind and unreasoning passion satisfied itself by misuse of bodily strength, which is a very dangerous servant.[19]

Cicero depicts a chaotic human wilderness without custom, law, or reason. The very building blocks of society, as he sees them, are nowhere to be seen. Religion either does not exist or is disordered. The lack of legal marriage leads to a sexual free-for-all that leaves no man with certainty as to which child is his. This feral condition allows passion and bodily strength to rule in place of reason. But into this horrid condition steps the rhetor:

> At this juncture a man—great and wise (*sapiens*) I am sure—became aware of the power latent in man and the wide field offered by his mind for great achievements if one could develop this power and improve it by instruction. Men were scattered in the fields and hidden in sylvan retreats when he assembled and gathered them in accordance with a plan; he introduced them to every useful and honorable occupation, though they cried out against it at first because of its novelty, and then when through reason and eloquence they had listened with greater attention, he transformed them from wild savages into a kind and gentle folk. To me, at least, it does not seem possible that a mute and voiceless wisdom could have turned men suddenly from their habits and introduced them to different patterns of life.[20]

It is the rhetor who brings order out of chaos, who uses their eloquence and their wisdom to woo humanity to a better way of living. If this person possessed only wisdom regarding human society, they would be unable to achieve anything without the power of persuasion according to which the resistant are subdued and convinced of their own good. The state, with its legal foundations for social life, depends upon the rhetor for its very existence and, this account suggests, for its continued survival. The rhetor stands between civilization and barbarism, pointing toward and guarding the former through reason and eloquence. The rhetor, it seems, is the necessary and ultimate statesman.

The necessity and ability of the rhetor to function as a statesman is a constant theme throughout Cicero's work. Indeed, many of the historical figures

---

[19] Cicero, *inv.* 1.2.2 (Latin original and English translation, LCL 386:4–5).
[20] Cicero, *inv.* 1.2.2–3 (Latin original and English translation, LCL 386:4–7).

he praises as exemplars of oratory are themselves statesmen, whether Roman or Greek. For example, in *On the Orator*, he allows Crassus to articulate the importance of the rhetor-statesman:

> Moreover, there is to my mind no more excellent thing than the power by means of oration, to get a hold on assemblies of men, win their good will, direct their inclinations wherever the speaker wishes, or divert them from whatever he wishes. In every free nation, and most of all in communities which have attained the enjoyment of peace and tranquility, this one art has always flourished above the rest and ever reigned supreme.[21]

For Crassus—or, we may say, for Cicero—the art of rhetoric is inherently connected to the government of the state. At least in the best of societies, in which freedom and peace reign, the art of rhetoric will naturally emerge. This raises the question, however, as to what will happen to the rhetor-statesman in an unjust society? What will it mean for them to use the powers of oratory in the assemblies, to direct and divert from potential actions? We will return to these questions when we discuss Augustine's martyrs below.

The Ideal Statesman

If the ideal orator should, at least to Cicero, be understood as a statesman, then it follows that the qualities of a good orator will also be connected to those of a good statesman. To appreciate Cicero's understanding of the ideal statesman, I turn to his fragmentary *On the Republic*. Here we find, among other characteristics, the role of the virtues in shaping both the statesman and the state he himself helps to shape.

Cicero begins with a discussion of the opposite of a good statesman, the tyrant. He represents the latter as a devolved version of the former: "For when this king [Tarquin] turned himself toward a less just form of rule, he immediately became a tyrant, than which no creature more vile or wretched to gods and men can be thought; for, although he has the form of a human, he nevertheless surpasses the most monstrous beasts in his savage behavior."[22] The tyrant is reminiscent of the pre-rhetorical state of humanity described

---

[21] Cicero, *de or.* 1.8.30 (Latin original and English translation, LCL 348:22).
[22] Cicero, *rep.* 2.48 (LCL 213:156).

by Cicero in *inv.* 1.2. His is the basest condition imaginable, his humanity replaced by wild ferocity. Passion has replaced reason, and he is no longer able to lead the people, neither with wisdom nor with persuasion. That is to say, he is neither a rhetor nor a statesman.

Cicero's purpose in describing the inhuman devolution of the tyrant is to use it as a foil to his main interest, the ideal statesman:

> To him we may oppose an alternative, one who is a *bonus*, *sapiens*, and *peritus* guardian and protector of the necessities and dignity of the citizens of the republic; for so is named one who is the [proper] leader and pilot of the city. Make sure you can recognize such a man; for he it is who is able to uphold the city by counsel and by deeds.[23]

"Good, wise, and skillful" are the main attributes of this ruler. We notice, again, the pairing of *bonus* and *peritus*, suggesting that Cicero has not completely ignored the formula for the ideal rhetor found in the Latin tradition but merely transposed it to the ideal statesman, adding the necessary virtue of wisdom. But Cicero has much more to say about how, by both counsel and action, the statesman is able to be the opposite of the inhuman tyrant.

Cicero most frequently associates two virtues with the statesman: prudence/wisdom and justice. Scipio and Laelius agree that the ideal statesman should be "a prudent person." They describe such a prudent person as like one who rides and guides an elephant. While such a feat is impressive, the prudent man is even more so: "that which is hidden in human minds and forms a part of the human, and which is called reason (*mens*), controls and subdues not only one animal nor only that which is easily subdued . . . ."[24] Unfortunately the text cuts off before we can presumably read Cicero clarify that reason can guide and control many animals, that is, humans, who may not be as easily controlled as an elephant. Prudence here refers, then, to the practical application of reason to a particular end. And what is that end in the case of the statesman? Justice, the other virtue necessary for the rhetor-statesman. Like one who governs the working of the fields should know the soil, plants, and rainfall, so the statesman "should certainly have studied in order to understand justice and laws and should have examined their origin."[25] Once again it is a practical application of one's cultivated reason that

---

[23] Cicero, *rep.* 2.51 (LCL 213:160).
[24] Cicero, *rep.* 2.67 (LCL 213:180).
[25] Cicero, *rep.* 5.5 (LCL 213:248).

is necessary to be a successful stateman. One should not be surprised, then, that this discussion of intellectual gifts of the statesman parallels the debate over the role of philosophy in Cicero's dialogues on the orator. It is Cicero's mediated position that philosophical training is absolutely necessary if the orator is going to discern the true from the false, the just from the unjust.

But justice is not the only goal of the statesman for their people. They are also responsible for guaranteeing the flourishing of the state and its citizens:

> For just as the aim of the pilot is a successful voyage, of the physician, health, and of the general, victory, so this director of the republic has as his aim for his fellow-citizens a happy life, fortified by wealth, rich in material resources, great in glory, and honored for virtue. I want him to bring to perfection this achievement, which is the greatest and best possible among men.[26]

The people's welfare must be as much the goal of the statesman as is justice itself. What is justice worth if people are not allowed to enjoy its benefits? Justice serves the preservation of these goods—financial and material goods as well as civic virtues. As we have seen in previous chapters, the martyrs, if they are to be understood as rhetor-statesmen, will have different aims for their *ciuitas*.

The role of the ideal statesman, however, lies not simply in the execution of their duties but in the conduct of their life as well. "Of course, he should be given almost no other duties than this one ... of improving and examining himself continually, urging others to imitate him, and furnishing in himself, as it were, a mirror to his fellow-citizens by reason of the supreme excellence of his life and character."[27] We have seen the significance of *exempla* before, and here Cicero makes explicit the rhetorical power of one's behavior. The ideal put forth itself suggests, though, that many statesmen fail to live up to this exemplary goal.

From this survey of the ideal rhetor, the rhetor as statesman, and the ideal statesman, we can make the following summary. First, there is a strand of Latin rhetorical thought that promotes an oratorical ideal that goes beyond issues of style or even effective persuasion. While these qualities are necessary, they do not in and of themselves constitute a true rhetor. As Quintilian

---

[26] Cicero, *rep.* 5.8 (Latin original and English translation, LCL 213:250–51).
[27] Cicero, *rep.* 2.69 (Latin original and English translation, LCL 213:180–81).

claims, if the orator is not also *bonus* in a moral sense, they do not deserve the title of orator. Second, the rhetor bears responsibility for establishing and maintaining society. After all, it is through persuasion and eloquence that wise people were able to draw feral humanity into a type of civilization. Within a state, therefore, it falls on the rhetors to lead through persuasion and instruction, to convince the citizens of what is good and just. Third, then, the rhetor-statesman must themself possess the virtues of justice and wisdom (as well as courage and moderation) in order to govern with equity and promote the welfare of the state, both through just laws and by moral example.[28]

Augustinian Transformations

The Christian Rhetor

Augustine's struggle with classical rhetoric is well known. It represents a key plot point in the autobiographical portions of his *Confessions* as he wrestles with his rhetorical profession and its moral implications. Consider how he describes an early exercise in his own rhetorical training:

> Permit me, my God, to say something also about my intelligence, your gift, and in what follies it was wasted by me. A task was given to me, which quite disturbed my soul with the reward of praise and fear of shame and blows, that I should recite the speech of Juno, angry and grieving that she "could not divert the Trojan king from Italy," which I heard that Juno never said. But we were compelled to follow the wandering footsteps of the poetic fictions and to speak in prose what the poet said in verse. And that speech was said to be most laudable in which, for the sake of the dignity of made-up characters, feelings most resembling anger and grief stood out, with the ideas appropriately dressed in words.[29]

According to Augustine, rhetoric as he was taught it was inherently concerned with fictions and follies. It took human skill in speaking, a true gift from God, and applied it to the raising of mythic passions rather than the promotion of true wisdom. And such activities were motivated, at their best,

---

[28] See J. G. F. Powell, "Cicero's *De Re Publica* and the Virtues of the Statesman," in *Cicero's Practical Philosophy*, ed. Walter Nicgorski (Notre Dame, IN: University of Notre Dame Press, 2012), 14–42.
[29] Augustine, *conf.* 1.17.27 (O'Donnell, 13).

by a proud desire for praise and, at worst, by fear of shame and corporal punishment. Rhetoric was, in his experience, concerned neither with cultivating the moral character of the orator nor with the good of the auditor.

The more his rhetorical education advanced, the more problematic it became: "My studies, which were called honorable, had the purpose of leading one to ligation in the courts, in which I might excel, the one being more laudable who is more fraudulent. The blindness of humanity is so great that they glory in their blindness."[30] And as a teacher himself, he attempts to find a happy balance in the morality of his instruction. Preferring to have "virtuous" students, he "taught them the tricks [of rhetoric], not that they should bring them to bear against the life of an innocent, but that sometimes they might use them on behalf of the life of a guilty person."[31] As he grows in his longing for God, Augustine comes to see that "something ought not be seen as true because it is eloquently spoken, nor false because the signs that the lips make sound uncomposed. Again, something is not true because it is enunciated incorrectly, nor false because the speech is splendid."[32]

And yet, Augustine, the celebrated preacher, does not reject rhetoric as irreparably profane. The error lies not in the art but in its application, not in the speech but in the speaker. As early as *On Order* he proposes a crucial role for rhetoric in leading souls toward the good, the just, and the true.[33] But it is his *On Christian Teaching*, and especially book 4, that offers a full-throated presentation of a Christian rhetoric.[34] Turning to that work, I want to highlight two related themes in Augustine's discussion of Christian rhetoric: the relationship between wisdom and eloquence, and the character of the preacher.

Augustine argues that the role of the preacher or of the Christian rhetor is to "teach what is good and unteach what is bad."[35] There is thus an inherent moral component to his understanding of Christian rhetoric as the preacher is supposed to move the soul of the hearer toward what is good and true as defined by the Catholic faith. But doing so requires not just eloquence but eloquence joined with wisdom. In fact, eloquence on its own can be dangerous because an audience is wont to "believe that somebody they hear speaking

---

[30] Augustine, *conf.* 3.3.6 (O'Donnell, 25).
[31] Augustine, *conf.* 4.2.2 (O'Donnell, 33).
[32] Augustine, *conf.* 5.6.10 (O'Donnell, 50).
[33] Augustine, *ord.* 2.13.38.
[34] On the idea of a Christian rhetoric, see James J. Murphy, "Saint Augustine and the Debate about a Christian Rhetoric," in *The Rhetoric of St. Augustine*, ed. Enos et al., 187–204; and Ernest J. Fortin, "Augustine and the Problem of Christian Rhetoric," in *The Rhetoric of St. Augustine*, ed. Enos et al., 219–34.
[35] Augustine, *doct. christ.* 4.4.6 (CCSL 32:119).

eloquently is also speaking the truth."[36] Thus, for Augustine, eloquence properly deployed must be joined to wisdom, a knowledge of what is true and good.[37] We see here echoes of Plato's concerns that the rhetor responsible for promoting justice must possess knowledge of what is just.

Plato's correlative also holds for Augustine. Just as in the *Gorgias* Plato held that the one who would promote justice must know justice and therefore also be just, so Augustine holds that one who would promote wisdom through Christian rhetoric must live according to that wisdom in their own moral character. At the beginning of *On Christian Teaching* 4, Augustine suggests that the basic prerequisite for someone wanting to study the rules of rhetoric is that they first be "a good man (*bono viro*)."[38] After winding his way through the rhetorical skill of the biblical authors and the proper use of the low, middle, and high styles to teach, delight, and move, he returns to this moral theme at the end of the work: "Of more weight than any amount of grandeur of style to those of us who want to be listened to obediently is the life of the speaker."[39] For Augustine, the moral speaker will be a better testament to the truth of which they speak, making their eloquence truly fruitful. In good Augustinian fashion, the ideal speaker has a properly directed love that will in turn properly direct the hearts of their audience, "since not even the love which is the end of the commandment and the fulfillment of the law can be ordered rightly if the things which are loved are not true but false."[40] Even the ineloquent, those incapable of speaking well even in the simplest of styles, can still be rhetors inasmuch as they "are able to live in such a way that they not only gain a reward for themselves but also provide an example to others, and their form of life becomes like an abundance of eloquence."[41] Already we see that an *exemplum* is not only a tool for rhetors but indeed what a rhetor themself should be. We also glimpse a bit of the Ciceronian statesman here, serving as an example for those they govern, an appropriate corollary for the priest or bishop within a Christian community.

Thus, we can derive a picture of Augustine's ideal orator. They are wise through familiarity with scripture and can therefore promote what is good

---

[36] Augustine, *doct. christ.* 4.5.7 (CCSL 32:120).
[37] On the joining of Christian wisdom and classical eloquence, see Amy K. Hermanson, "Religion's Rhetoric: Saint Augustine's Union of Christian Wisdom and Sophistic Eloquence," in *The Rhetoric of St. Augustine*, ed. Enos et al., 311–14.
[38] Augustine, *doct. christ.* 4.1.2 (CCSL 32:117).
[39] Augustine, *doct. christ.* 4.27.59 (CCSL 32:163).
[40] Augustine, *doct. christ.* 4.28.61 (CCSL 32:165).
[41] Augustine, *doct. christ.* 4.29.61 (CCSL 32:165).

and true, and they will promote it not only through their eloquence, though that helps, but also through the conformity of their life to that truth. In short, Augustine's ideal Christian rhetor is a *vir bonus dicendi peritus*, where the term *bonus* has been given a clear Christian moral gloss and *dicendi* is extended to include the way one's life speaks. In this way Augustine baptizes the Latin rhetorical tradition we observed above and saw especially embodied by Quintilian. To be clear, I am not making an argument for Augustine's necessary debt to Quintilian here. Rather, I am arguing that Augustine's approach to the ideal rhetor fits within the tradition that Quintilian epitomizes, but within a particular Christian idiom.

The Christian Statesman

In addition to the rhetorical ideal, Augustine also provides a Christian gloss for the political ideal of the statesman. In what follows, I adhere closely to Robert Dodaro, whose work on Augustine's political theology I have found the most fruitful for understanding Augustine's transformation of the classical tradition. I begin at the obvious location, the *City of God*, before turning to Dodaro's other favorite text, *Letter* 155 to Macedonius. What we will find is a concern for the virtue of the statesman akin to Cicero but filtered through the lens of the theological virtues of faith, hope, and love.

First, we must establish the context for the Christian statesman within Augustine's complex political theology. Above I drew upon Cicero's *On the Republic* precisely because of Augustine's use of it in *City of God* and his argument that, on Cicero's own terms, Rome never was a true republic or commonwealth. Augustine quotes Cicero's Scipio's definition of a republic as "the common good of a people," an ideal that requires the highest degree of justice in order to produce true concord among the different levels of society. Likewise, in every constitution—monarchy, aristocracy, or democracy—a republic requires justice in its rulers in order to promote justice among the citizenry as a whole. This concern for justice is the lynchpin for Augustine's critique. While Cicero explicitly says that the republic has ceased to exist in his time, Augustine claims

> according to Cicero's own definitions of what a republic is and of what a people is ... that republic never actually was one, because there was no true justice in it. Yet, according to more plausible definitions, it was a republic

in its own way, and it was better administered by the more ancient Romans than by their descendants. There is no true justice, however, except in the republic whose founder and ruler is Christ, if indeed it pleases us to call this, too, a republic, since we cannot deny that it is the common good of the people (*rem populi*).[42]

If the common good of the people requires the presence of justice but justice is absent, then there is no common good and, therefore, by Cicero's definition, no republic. Under no merely human government can justice arise because only Christ, as both founder and ruler—noticeably playing the roles ascribed to the rhetor-statesman in Cicero's *On Invention*—can provide such a good.

Why this is the case requires us to turn to *City of God* 19, where Augustine takes up this question again. Here, he famously defines a people as "a multitude of rational beings joined together by common agreement on the objects of their love."[43] This definition allows him on the one hand to establish the Romans as a people, and even as a sort of imperfect earthly republic guided by its love to its own desired goods. But "the city of the impious, is neither ruled by God nor obedient to him and therefore does not offer sacrifices to God alone, on account of which in that city the soul does not rightly and faithfully rule the body, nor reason the vices. And, thus, it lacks true justice."[44] Here Augustine has taken the traditional Roman virtue of piety, connected it to worship of the Christian God, and made it not the result of justice but the prerequisite for it. Rome was never a republic in the true sense because its love was pointed in the wrong direction, toward the things of this world and not those of the heavenly. The only true republic, as Augustine said, is the one founded and ruled by Christ because only the members of that republic have their loves properly directed and can therefore receive their true common goods.

In this context, therefore, we can begin to explore the meaning of statesmanship for citizens of the heavenly city who find themselves on sojourn within this foreign country. We have numerous examples of Augustine offering advice or admonition to imperial rulers, but the best example for our purposes is his letter to Macedonius. The first characteristic of the Christian statesman can be summarized as a piety that cultivates virtue oriented toward heavenly beatitude. Key to this summary is the way in which piety is foundational; it is not one virtue among others or a good that derives from other more primary

---

[42] *ciu.* 2.21 (CCSL 47:55).
[43] *ciu.* 19.24 (CCSL 48:695).
[44] *ciu.* 19.24 (CCSL 48:696).

goods. It is the *sine qua non* of civic virtue. "In the present age, this wisdom consists in the true worship of the true God in order that in the age to come its enjoyment may be certain and complete. Here there is a most solid piety, there everlasting happiness."[45] Here we see how true piety, proper worship of the true God, reorients the heart toward true happiness, only achievable beyond this life, in heaven. Finally, Augustine ties Macedonius's personal piety to that of Rome. "Because we know that you love the republic, see how it is clear in those sacred books that a human being is happy from the same source as the city.... You see that a people is not called happy because of the accumulation of earthly happiness except by strangers, that is, by those who have no share in the rebirth by which we become children of God."[46] Thus, the role of the Christian statesman is to promote within the state that which she herself has cultivated within herself by the grace of God: piety oriented toward heavenly goods. Earthly, material goods, which are typically seen to characterize a successful state, are relativized as insignificant in relationship to eternal goods.

We also see in Augustine's prioritizing of piety the beginning of a redefinition of the traditional civic virtues. Augustine defines the civic virtue of wisdom as piety. Thus, wisdom is baptized and transformed into a distinctly Christian type of prudence that properly values the things of this world and the next and knows to prioritize worship of the one true God, both in the individual statesman and subsequently within the republic that he governs. But this identification of wisdom with piety raises a question: can the Christian statesman govern in a way that is in conformity with that piety? Augustine, in Dodaro's reading, with which I agree, believes that he can to some degree, in particular by transforming the other civic virtues by the influence of the theological virtues of faith, hope, and love—much in the same way wisdom is transformed through piety.

First, Augustine redefines all the civic virtues as expressions of holy love: "And yet even in this life there is no virtue but to love what one should love. To choose it is prudence; to be turned away from it by no difficulties is courage; to be turned away from it by no enticement is temperance; to be turned away from it by no pride is justice."[47] This description depicts what the theological virtues look like on sojourn as they transform the civic virtues. Love of God—and, Augustine emphasizes, the necessary correlative of love of neighbor—grounds the virtues in the wisdom that is piety. Faith and hope allow the soul to maintain this adherence to God despite temptations or

---

[45] *ep.* 155.2.5 (CSEL 44:435–36).
[46] *ep.* 155.2.7–8 (CSEL 44:437–38).
[47] *ep.* 155.4.13 (CSEL 44:443). See also *ep.* 155.4.16.

hardships. The point of the statesman governing with these virtues is to promote them within his people, via love both of God and of neighbor. Only in this way can a republic of justice truly exist, but of course such a republic only exists fully in heaven. The goal of the Christian statesman, then, is to rule in this world in a way that conforms as closely as possible to the virtues that govern the heavenly city.

The Martyrs as Ideal Christian Rhetor-Statesmen

So far we have not discussed Augustine's understanding of martyrs or martyrdom within this chapter. We have instead surveyed classical and Augustinian understandings of the ideal rhetor and the ideal statesman. Only with this background in mind can I begin to demonstrate my argument, namely that Augustine's martyrs can be understood as ideal Christian rhetors as well as ideal Christian statesmen. As we have seen, these ideals are intimately connected in the classical imagination, and therefore moving from one to the other seems natural, even though it will require several caveats that I will offer in due course. For now, allow me to clarify that I am not arguing that we should understand historical martyrs to have functioned in this way. Rather, I mean that Augustine's depiction of the martyrs constructs them in such a way that within his version of their history they serve as and represent Christian rhetors and rhetor-statesmen.

The Martyrs as Christian Rhetors

I begin by showing how Augustine's martyrs function as rhetors within their literary context. The best depiction of a martyr as a rhetor in Augustine comes in *Sermon* 300 on the topic of the Maccabean martyrs. After spending most of the sermon explaining that dying prior to Christ's birth does not prohibit one's identification as a Christian martyr, Augustine turns to the story of the mother and her seven sons from 2 Mac 7. The mother becomes a model of martyrial endurance. "Being made the mother of seven martyrs, she was a martyr seven-fold; watching, she was not separated from her sons, and dying she added to her sons."[48] But her words are what distinguish her:

---

[48] *s*. 300.6 (PL 38:1379).

Antiochus, the persecutor, considered this woman a mother like other mothers. "Persuade," he said, "your son, lest he perish." And she said, "Surely I will persuade my son to live, by exhorting him to die; you want to persuade him to die by sparing himself." But what an address! How pious! How maternal! How evenly balanced between spiritual and carnal things! "Son, take pity on me. Son," she said, "take pity on me, who bore you for nine months in my womb; I gave you milk for three years and led you to this age; take pity on me" (2 Mac 7:27).[49]

Here Augustine combines his own version of the mother's speech with text from 2 Mac itself to present her as an effective rhetor persuading her sons to save their lives by losing them in martyrdom. He even pauses to praise the quality of her well-balanced and appropriately intimate address.

But Augustine is not content just to show how well-spoken a martyr can be. He also wants to make a larger point about the difference between the rhetorical performance of the martyrs and the uncultured speech of their persecutors. For example, in a sermon on the Scillitan martyrs, Augustine paints the scene in ekphrastic detail, focusing on the changing psychological states of the imperial official: "Now set before your eyes the contest of the martyrs. The opponent comes, and he tries to compel them to deny Christ. But let us lead him in flattering, not yet raging. He promises riches and honors."[50] At first the official himself wants to be an orator, a persuader who can woo the Christians away from Christ. But again deploying prosopopoeia, Augustine provides a powerful rhetorical response for the faithful man:

Shall I deny Christ for the sake of riches? Shall I deny riches for the sake of riches? Shall I deny the treasure trove for the sake of gold? Truly, he it is "who became poor for our sakes, though he was rich, so that we might be enriched by his poverty" (2 Cor 8:9). Truly, he's the one about whom the apostle says, "in whom are all the treasure troves of wisdom and knowledge hidden" (Col 2:30).[51]

In light of this rhetorical performance, the imperial official is reduced to savagery. The condition of his mind has now changed, as if an entirely new

---

[49] *s.* 300.7 (PL 38:1380).
[50] *s.* 299D.4 (*MA* 1:77).
[51] *s.* 299D.4 (*MA* 1:77).

character has entered the contest: "The promiser has been derided; another approaches, that is, the persecutor. Flattering, he was derided; he begins raging. The snake that was derided has turned into a lion."[52] The persecutor is exposed as animalistic in his rage. Unable to compete in the realm of argument or persuasion against such an opponent, the persecutor manifests his own defeat, his own inhumanity, in succumbing to his passions and losing the ability for rational, persuasive speech. In fact, to drive the point home, the martyr responds to the savage threats of the persecutor with another well-balanced speech on the true good.

It should be noted, of course, that these rhetorical performances of the martyrs do not only come by way of speeches. Perhaps the best example of a martyr retaining his ability to speak effectively in contrast to a raving persecutor comes in the story Augustine repeats from the martyrdom of St. Lawrence. Lawrence, having been roasted on a gridiron by a persecutor "burning with rage," was himself "even more so [burning] with love in his soul." This condition, presumably, is what allowed Lawrence to exclaim, "It's done cooking. The only thing left is to turn me over and eat!"[53]

Further, one celebrated North African martyr receives special treatment as a rhetor: Cyprian of Carthage. As a bishop trained in the art of rhetoric, Cyprian, like Augustine, would have deployed his training in the service of his preaching. Augustine, in discussing Cyprian's own martyrdom, highlights his rhetorical role in inspiring other martyrs before joining them: "Many martyrs proceeded from Cyprian, having been inflamed by his exhortations to conquer the devil."[54] By connecting Cyprian's own martyrdom to the rhetorical inspiration of his predecessors, Augustine brings the rhetoric of martyrdom full circle: the martyr serves as a rhetor in order to inspire other martyrs. I now turn to this theme of rhetorical audience and goals.

So far we have seen the martyrs operate as rhetors within their own stories. But these accounts are written and presented for the audience external to the story, that is, in these cases, Augustine's contemporary congregations. This is even more the case when we are considering the prosopopoetic speeches Augustine places in their mouths. Or, to put it another way, these instances represent the constructed nature of the whole enterprise. Augustine is presenting the martyrs as rhetors partly because it allows him to contrast

---

[52] *s.* 299D.4 (*MA* 1:78).
[53] *s.* 303.1 (PL 38:1394).
[54] *s.* 309.6 (PL 38:1412).

their virtue with that of their persecutors. But he is also depicting them as rhetors because he wants them to function as such for his present audience.

Consider again the mother and her seven sons. "Let a desire to imitate them burn in our hearts," Augustine tells his audience. "Let men learn to die for the truth. Let women learn from the great patience, the ineffable virtue of that mother."[55] Similarly, in the sermon on the Scillitan martyrs, where the faithful martyr chastised the persecutor for supposing that worldly things could appeal to one who has Christ, Augustine urges his hearers to "let Christ . . . not be denied for the sake of necessities," before chastising those in attendance who would deny Christ for their own well-being even without the context of persecution.[56] Even Lawrence's *bon mot* elicits an invitation of imitation: "Let us follow his footsteps in faith, and let us follow in contempt of the world."[57] And Augustine encourages his audience to share in the very speech of Cyprian: "What should erupt from our hearts and our mouths, but the final words of that venerable martyr? . . . 'Thanks be to God!' "[58] The martyrs, therefore, function as rhetors not only within their own stories but also, and more importantly, external to their stories as they are deployed to persuade those who venerate their memory.

These martyr-rhetors are not simply oratorical in a generic way; they also embody the Augustinian vision of a Christian rhetor and his transformation of the ideal of *vir bonus peritus dicendi*. I return, therefore, to the Maccabean mother, the Scillitan martyrs, Lawrence, and Cyprian to examine the content of their martyrial performance, which fits within Augustine's understanding of divine wisdom and Christian morality.

Beginning this time with Cyprian, we note that the martyrs all embody a certain congruity between their speech and their actions. Augustine claims that the martyr-bishop

> taught faithfully what he was going to do and did bravely what he had taught. Living justly he came to a precious death, and dying unjustly he came to a glorious life; and he gained the triumphant name of martyr, because he fought for truth to the point of blood.[59]

---

[55] *s.* 300.6 (PL 38:1380).
[56] *s.* 299D.6 (MA 1).
[57] *s.* 303.2 (PL 38:1394)
[58] *s.* 309.6 (PL 38:1412).
[59] *s.* 310.3 (PL 38:1413).

The quality of Cyprian's living and dying provides the legitimacy for his Christian rhetoric. Had he not been willing to suffer the fate of those he urged to martyrdom, or had he not died for the sake of truth and justice, Cyprian's rhetoric would have been empty.

Returning to Augustine's prosopopoeia as the Maccabean mother, we see her support her plea to her sons with the following vision of the true good: "Consent to God, do not desert your brothers. If it seems like you desert me, then you do not desert me. I would have you there, where I will not fear losing you anymore. There Christ will preserve you for me, there whence Antiochus will not take you."[60] The mother's vision of a heavenly reunion with her son has a distinctly Augustinian flair: to be truly blessed, one must possess the good eternally without fear of losing it. This includes the good of the love by which we love one another. An earthly love leaves us susceptible to the loss of our beloved, and such misdirected fear can be manipulated to inspire apostasy. But a heavenly love, a love of the other within God, assures us that we will never lose them as we are both held in God's eternality.

Similarly, returning to the sermon on the Scillitan martyrs, we see the faithful man continue his speech on true riches and those things that are truly to be desired. We have already seen him quote Col 2:3, praising the "hoard of wisdom and knowledge" hidden in Christ. But his speech continues, ostensibly addressing his persecutor, but really teaching Augustine's audience:

> You attend to what you promise because you are unable to see what you are trying to take [from me]. I, by faith, see what you wish to take from me; you, with the eyes of the flesh, see what you wish to give. There are better things, which the eye of the heart sees, than that which the eye of the flesh sees. [He quotes 2 Cor 4:18] . . . Therefore, I despise your gifts . . . because they are temporal, they are superfluous, they rot, they fly away, they're full of dangers, full of temptations.[61]

This is his speech when offered riches and honors. He promotes the pursuit of eternal, spiritual goods and the disregard of earthly, material goods, using a host of Pauline texts to support this transvaluation (including, in addition to those already cited, 2 Cor 8:9 and 1 Tim 6:7–8, 17–19). Thus, we find continuity between this martyr speech and that of the Maccabean mother. Both promote an awareness of the distinction between the earthly and the

---

[60] *s.* 300.7 (PL 38:1380).
[61] Augustine, *s.* 299D.4 (*MA* 1:77–78).

heavenly, the material and the spiritual, encouraging their hearers to pursue the higher things of God while forsaking the lower things as "superfluities." This distinction lies at the heart of Augustine's understanding of Christian wisdom, so it should come as no surprise that it is a repeated theme within the speeches he puts into the mouths of his martyrs.

Finally, we see a similar rhetorical performance of Christian wisdom in the account of St. Lawrence. First, in his agreement to deliver carts filled with all the treasures of the church, only to bring the poor and declare them to be the riches of the church, Lawrence brings wisdom to bear against greed: "Avarice," Augustine says, "opened its jaws, but wisdom knew what it was doing."[62] This account of Lawrence's pious cleverness extends the realm of rhetorical performance beyond the work of words and into that of the rhetor's behavior. This approach to persuasion is further manifest in Lawrence's playful words on the gridiron as he proclaims himself done on one side and ready to be flipped. It is a good line, indeed, but its power lies in its manifestation of equanimity in the face of bodily pain. As Augustine describes it, "He is said to have borne with such tranquility those torments, that in him it was fulfilled what we heard just now in the gospel: 'In patience you will possess your souls' (Luke 21:19)."[63] It is not just in his words but, primarily, in his actions that Augustine wants Lawrence to be seen as persuasive. This fits well with Augustine's claim in *On Christian Teaching* that what is most important, even more important than eloquence or wisdom, is the teacher's behavior by which they might have the greatest effect as an example.

Indeed, it is as moral exemplars that Augustine's martyrs have the most persuasive effect. But we should not limit their exemplarity to being mere *exempla* that the real rhetor can draw upon and use. The martyrs are not simply rhetorical tools. Rather, as we have seen Augustine construct them as rhetors themselves, specifically as Christian rhetors promoting divine wisdom through their virtuous speech, we should bear in mind the concern expressed by Augustine and others in the Latin rhetorical tradition that the character of the rhetor be considered essential to his work. And so, the martyrs are constructed as rhetors not only in their oral promotion of virtue and wisdom but also, ideally, in their living out of those virtues and wisdom. That is to say, in their speaking and also in their dying, Augustine's martyrs fulfill his own ideal of the Christian rhetor.

---

[62] Augustine, *s.* 303.1 (PL 38:1394).
[63] Augustine, *s.* 303.1 (PL 38:1394).

The Martyrs as Christian Statesmen

If, as I have argued, we can understand Augustine's martyrs as themselves rhetors in their performances (as Augustine depicts them, of course), then, knowing what we know about the political significance of rhetoric in the Roman tradition, we may investigate whether and how the martyrs might be understood to operate politically, that is, I suggest, as rhetor-statesmen. In this section I describe how we may view them as such, performing the function of an Augustinian statesman for the city of God but under the earthly rule of a hostile regime.

In *City of God* 20, Augustine takes up the question of eschatology, especially the millennial binding of Satan and reign of Christ described in Revelation. For our purposes, the most significant verse is Rev 20:4, "the souls of those who were slain for their testimony to Jesus and for the word of God reigned with Jesus for a thousand years." Augustine makes clear that this verse is speaking about "the souls of the martyrs whose bodies have not yet been given back to them. For the souls of the pious dead are not separated from the church, which even now is the kingdom of Christ."[64] In a very literal sense, then, the martyrs may be understood as statesmen within the city of God, serving in the administration of the king. But Augustine is concerned here about the dead, about the saints who have already tasted their martyrdom. I believe we can push this a bit further and see these statesmen at work even prior to their deaths, while still on sojourn. To serve as a statesman in a pre-Christian and persecuting empire will obviously look different than Macedonius' imperial service under a Christian emperor. Yet, even under a hostile regime, the same Christianized version of the Ciceronian rhetor-statesman ideal can be found in Augustine's depiction of martyrdom.

First, as in our discussion of Augustine's statesman, we must set the political scene for our martyrs. I do not mean rehearsing the state of the empire or its governance at the various times of persecution. I mean the moral state of the persecutors as consistently depicted by Augustine. Running throughout Augustine's preaching on the martyrs is a theme expressed in a single word (well, single root): *saevus/saevio*. In a sermon on St. Vincent, Augustine describes how the martyr stood "against the fiercest conflict, against the insidiousness of the ancient enemy, against the savagery of the impious judge, against the pains of mortal flesh, surviving it all with the help of the Lord."[65]

---

[64] *ciu.* 20.9 (CCSL 48:718).
[65] *s.* 275.1 (PL 38:1254).

And in a sermon on the Maccabees, Augustine turns his audience to the three youths in the fire of Daniel: "While a human burned with rage, the flames spared them."[66] Or on the death of John the Baptist: "When the holy gospel was read, a crude spectacle was presented before our eyes—the head of Saint John on a platter—along with a mission of savage cruelty, due to hatred of the truth. A girl dances, and the mother rages. And among the lascivious luxuries of the partygoers an oath is sworn rashly, and what is sworn is impiously implemented."[67] In all these examples, we see the ruling powers lacking the virtues of good statesmen. Whether it is the Roman imperial judge, the king of Babylon, or Herod, all these rulers are associated with savagery, an intemperate lack of wisdom or prudence. They are the opposite of Augustine's Christian statesman and evince it through their savagery. In them there is no piety, no wisdom, and no justice.

If this is the context in which the martyrs perform their rhetoric—an unjust city of savage statesmen lacking piety, wisdom, justice, or any true virtue—how does that rhetoric function under such a hostile regime? Clearly, they are not performing a statesman role as agents of that earthly city that rages so savagely against them. But we may understand them to be performing such a role within the earthly city as agents of the city of God. We should recall that in Cicero civilization itself arises from a state of savagery, of feral chaos. It is the rhetor who brings order through persuasion. We see the martyrs play similar roles in Augustine's sermons. For example, Augustine repeatedly contrasts the savagery of the original martyr context with the piety of his contemporary celebration. In a sermon on Perpetua and Felicitas he declares, "Now, however, the successors of those whose voices raged impiously against the flesh of the martyrs praise the merits of the martyrs with pious voices."[68] Similarly, in a sermon on Cyprian, he describes how "in the very place where he laid aside the goods of the flesh, a savage crowd gathered then, which on account of [their] hatred of Christ would shed the blood of Cyprian; there today a reverent multitude gathers, which on account of the birthday of Cyprian drinks the blood of Christ."[69] Augustine depicts a shift from savagery to piety, a shift in which the martyrs and their festivals play a key role. Elsewhere, Augustine makes the nature of this role more explicit.

---

[66] *s*. 301.2 (PL 38:1380).
[67] *s*. 307.1 (PL 38:1406).
[68] *s*. 280.2 (PL 38:1281).
[69] *s*. 310.2 (PL 38:1413).

Echoing Tertullian's famous dictum, Augustine claims that the resurrection and immortality of the flesh

> were sown with the blood of the martyrs to sprout up even more fecundly throughout the world. For the preceding proclamations of the prophets were read, manifest works of power confirmed them, and the truth, new to custom but not contrary to reason, worked to persuade until the whole world, which was persecuting the truth in fury, followed it in faith.[70]

Key here is that the force that spread the gospel was, to Augustine, not military might or some other form of coercion, but persuasion. Moreover, the martyrs, as witnesses to the truth, play a central role in this effort.

Taking this sense of the martyrs' role in persuading the world of the truth of Christ along with Augustine's contrast between the savagery of the past persecutors and the piety of present believers, we can see the martyrs as performing the duty of Cicero's primal statesman. The martyrs are the ones who lead people out of savagery and into piety by their testimony to the truth. Ultimately, of course, it is Christ who accomplishes this through divine persuasion and the gift of grace, but the martyrs are the instruments of this work, statesmen working on behalf of the king with whom they reign to bring sinful humanity into the city, not of Rome, but of God.

Moreover, these martyr-rhetor-statesmen also embody the ideal that Augustine describes to Macedonius in *ep.* 155. They manifest the virtues of the traditional statesmen as transformed by Augustine's emphasis on piety and love. In a sermon on Cyprian, Augustine describes how

> there [at Cyprian's church in Carthage] he served as a bishop, and there he accomplished his martyrdom. In the very place where he laid aside the goods of the flesh, a savage crowd gathered then, which on account of [their] hatred of Christ would shed the blood of Cyprian; there today a reverent multitude gathers, which on account of the birthday of Cyprian drinks the blood of Christ. And just as the blood of Christ is drunk more sweetly in that place on account of the birthday of Cyprian, so the blood of Cyprian was shed there more faithfully on account of the name of Christ.[71]

---

[70] *ciu.* 22.7 (CCSL 48:815).
[71] *s.* 310.2 (PL 38:1413).

We see again the contrast between the savagery of the persecutors and the piety of Augustine's fellow feasters. But this passage provides more details about the relationship between the martyrdom and the celebration. Cyprian's martyrdom is characterized not only by his dying but also by the piety that leads to that death. By becoming a bishop, he had "laid aside the trappings of the flesh," committing himself to that life of devotion to Christ and his eternal goods. His reverence is reflected in that of the crowd that now expresses their piety by not only celebrating his but also imitating it through partaking in the blood of Christ. Cyprian's blood was shed for his faith in the blood of Christ. His martyrdom itself, then, is a demonstration of proper piety whose persuasive force Augustine sees manifest in proper observance of his festival. In fact, Augustine makes explicit the rhetorical importance of Cyprian's role as a martyr-bishop: "His sound has gone forth to all the earth, and his words to the ends of the whole wide world. He faithfully preached what he was going to practice; he bravely practiced what he had preached."[72] In the first sentence, Augustine blends the work of Christ with the work of the bishop by the ambiguous referent for "his." But the second sentence is clearly about Cyprian, who, as a preacher, exhorted many to martyrdom, the very sacrifice of piety for which he himself would provide an example, manifesting the ideal of the statesman who both promotes piety and serves as an example of that which he promotes.

In addition to piety, Augustine's martyrs also manifest the transformation of the traditional civic virtues through the theological virtues of faith, hope, and love. As Dodaro summarizes, "The soul in heaven acts prudently when it clings to God as the good which it can never lose; it acts with fortitude because it clings tenaciously to this good and will not be torn from it; it acts temperately in that it clings to this good in a pure manner, because it can no longer be corrupted; and it acts justly because it is right for it to cling to this good, to which it is deservedly subordinate."[73] The job of the Christian statesman is to live as closely to these ideals as possible within the fallen world. As we have seen repeatedly, the martyrs serve as examples of these virtues, both living them themselves and exhorting their audience to imitate them by both word and deed. They cling to God as the good beyond all earthly goods, even earthly life. Despite temptations and threat, they cling tenaciously to that one good. Even those martyrs who have previously fallen

---

[72] *s.* 310.3 (PL 38:1413).
[73] Dodaro, "Political and Theological Virtues in Augustine," 441. See *ep.* 155.12.

through corruption of fear and improper desire regain the purity of their adherence and attain the crown of martyrdom. And ultimately the justice of the martyrs stands in contrast to the justice that is meted out against them, a justice that is blatantly impious and oriented toward material, earthly goods.

The martyrs, then, are statesmen of the heavenly city who reign with Christ. But, I have argued, this is not limited to the period after their death. The martyrs fulfill the role of the martyr-statesman in their lives and deaths. They do so not within a Christian empire, as with Macedonius, but under a hostile, pagan regime. As rhetor-statesmen, they participate in God's providential work of leading the world out of savagery and into piety, from the wilderness of the world into the civilization of heaven. But they are not only instrumental in the founding of the city, which, anyway, exists from Abel; they also promote the well-being of the city. Rather than material and financial goods, they promote piety, love of God and neighbor, and the eternal goods of heaven that can never be lost. They relativize the goods of this world, seeing even their earthly lives as worthy to be sacrificed in pursuit of eternal life in God. These martyr-statesmen may not do this by laws, but they do accomplish it by the original tool of the statesman: rhetoric, persuasion through word and deed.

Conclusion

Throughout this study, we have seen Augustine appropriate the tools of classical rhetoric to construct and deploy a vision of martyrdom that promotes his understanding of true Christian values while articulating a vision of God's providential work within the history of salvation and denying his opponents access to that powerful symbolic legacy. In this chapter, Augustine redefines the nature of the ideal rhetor to lift the martyrs up as ideal Christian expressions of the profession. But he also recognizes that the rhetorical world is at home in the political arena. Therefore, in reconceiving the rhetor in Christian dress, he also reimagines the classical ideal of the stateman, a role traditionally associated with rhetorical prowess. The martyrs, then, become more than victims of imperial persecution. They are, instead, agents of the divine city operating in the midst of the earthly city. They are covert rhetor-statesmen who perform the work of bringing pious order out of pagan chaos while modeling the civic virtues of the city of God. For Augustine, to be a martyr is to be an instrument and emissary of Christ, speaking for him, pointing toward him, in speech as well as in death.

Conclusion

This is a short book. It might seem odd to name that fact as I come to the conclusion. But I believe this work's brevity speaks to its purpose. It has never been my goal to say all that could or should be said about Augustine and martyrdom, nor even about Augustine, martyrdom, and rhetoric. I have left many passages unquoted and many rhetorical techniques unexamined. Yet I am convinced that chasing every rabbit would result in a list rather than an argument. Moreover, I have attempted to be suggestive rather than comprehensive, to offer an argument rather than an overview. In brief, I have sought to answer one question: if martyr discourse is rhetorical, what does that mean for its construction by someone like Augustine who is an expert in the techniques of classical rhetoric?

The answer to this question comes in three parts. First, in a more general sense, Augustine's construction of martyrdom must be understood within particular rhetorical contexts, contexts in which martyrs and martyrdom carried cultural weight and could be rhetorically constructed and contested for various purposes. Chapter 1 highlighted the historical emergence of martyr theology in North Africa, from the Scillitan martyrs to the Donatists, including contexts of persecution and imperial favor. Of particular note was the cult of the martyrs as experienced by Augustine both in Milan and in North Africa, as evidenced by his earliest writings on the subject in letters and the *Confessions*. The second half of the chapter continued this look at rhetorical contexts for martyr discourse by discussing Augustine's polemical engagements with the Manichaeans and the Pelagians. Through a close reading of texts from each of these disputes, we came to see the true ubiquity of martyr discourse due to its appearance and power within otherwise unrelated disputes.

The second way in which martyrs are rhetorical for Augustine is that he deploys rhetorical techniques and argumentative forms to construct them. Chapter 2 brought us into the meat of the argument as I turned to the rhetorical use of *exempla*. Taking first a broad look at the concept, we saw the way in which martyrs served as *exempla* within Augustine's sermons.

In particular, I highlighted their role as moral models seeking to shift Christians' love from the things of this world to the true goods of heaven. At the same time, Augustine used the supposed values of the martyrs to tame their cults, attempting to rid them of excessive drinking and dancing. A final discussion of nominal etymology reinforced the argument of this chapter by demonstrating how Augustine used even the martyrs' names to promote his favorite Christian values.

Chapter 3 used *exempla* to connect the disciplines of rhetoric and historiography. Here I argued that Augustine replaced traditional Roman *exempla* with the Christian martyrs. But doing so had larger theological ramifications. With his new martyrial *exempla*, Augustine rejected the traditional narrative of decline associated with historians like Sallust and replaced it with a view of history as defined by God's saving work in Christ. In doing so, he undercuts those who might lament the end of state persecution by establishing every era as ripe for spiritual battle and heroic endurance. The second half of this chapter added to this theological approach to history by examining the ironic beauty of the martyrs' deaths. This technique of antithesis echoes God's providential arrangement of history, ordering the good and bad, the ugly and beautiful, within sacred history.

Chapter 4 took on the more specific field of forensic rhetoric as well as the polemical context of the Donatist schism. Any account of Augustine's treatment of martyrdom must tackle his conflict with the Donatists as they styled themselves the "church of the martyrs" who still suffer persecution at the hands of the state. The Catholics, in the Donatists' eyes, only testify to their own villainy by aligning themselves with the persecuting empire. To this challenge, Augustine brings a double-pronged attack. First, using a *status* of definition, he argues that the Donatists are in fact not martyrs because, no matter what they suffer, they do not do so for the values of the martyrs. Not the penalty, his slogan says, but the cause makes a martyr. Second, using a *status* of quality, Augustine denies their claims that the persecution his Catholic Church commits is unjust. While in earlier texts he denies that it is persecution altogether, his mature writings adopt the forensic rhetorical approach to show that any persecution that is for the persecuted's own good is itself good.

Finally, Chapter 5 represents the third way Augustine's martyrs may be considered rhetorical: they themselves, as he depicts them, represent ideal rhetors. This brings us back to the quotation from Tertullian with which I began this book. Tertullian depicted the martyrs as rhetorical in their performance of death, agents Christ used to woo onlookers to consider the faith for which these men and women were willing to die. But Augustine goes further than Tertullian, in part, I believe, because he elsewhere delves deeper into what it means to be a Christian rhetor in general. The martyrs, then, become the embodiment of Augustine's rhetorical ideal. But Augustine is also part of a Ciceronian political tradition that emphasizes the social significance of the rhetor for the city. The rhetor is by nature a statesman, bringing order out of social chaos and modeling the civic virtues by his own example. Thus, we should understand Augustine's martyrs to be not just rhetors but rhetor-statesmen serving as Christ's agents in forming the city of God.

Augustine's martyrs, then, are *exempla* pointing to the true virtues of heaven, in their deeds and in their very names. But their exemplarity is connected to the history of salvation and God's providential ordering of the world. Augustine's martyrs are used to deny other communions the claim to martyrdom as well as to justify imperial coercion and persecution. Yet these same martyrs are ultimately agents not of an earthly empire but of a heavenly city. It is through them, through their *exempla*, that Christ builds his kingdom.

I began this study with a passage from Tertullian's *Apology*, written approximately two hundred years before Augustine's episcopacy. There Tertullian describes the rhetorical effect that martyrdom had on inspiring new adherents to the Christian faith, using his own rhetorical prowess to describe God's rhetorical use of the martyrs. His approach sounds markedly like what I have described Augustine to be doing. This is indeed the case. What I have analyzed in Augustine represents, *mutatis mutandis*, a standard approach to martyrdom within early Christian discourse. To conclude my analysis, therefore, I want to look at a series of martyrial homilies from Greek sources to highlight how an appreciation for the rhetorical and theological insights gleaned from reading Augustine help us see marks of continuity beyond his own context.

I turn first to a brief homily from Asterius of Amasea on the martyr Phocas to highlight the most widely shared theme from Augustine's martyr discourse: exemplarity. This theme emerges from the first lines of the sermon. "The commemoration of the saints is good and useful," Asterius proclaims, "especially for those who strive for what is noble. Those who long for virtue and true religion are not only taught by words but also have in front of them, as visible lessons, the deeds of people who lived in a just way."[1] The point

---

[1] Asterius, *hom. Phoc.* 1.1 All primary texts in this chapter are from Pauline Allen et al., eds. and trans., *Let Us Die That We May Live: Greek Homilies on Christian Martyrs from Asia Minor, Palestine and Syria c.350–c.450 AD* (London: Routledge, 2003). Here, Allen et al., 168.

of martyrs, Asterius suggests, at least as they relate to future generations, is as *exempla*, models for imitation. For all the miracles and intercessions they might provide, martyrs ought to be looked to first as models of virtue and piety.

Asterius further places this observation within the context of a larger theory of education:

> Theoretical education is a lesser and weaker teacher than real actions. . . . The doctor, even labouring on Hippocrates and the other authorities, remains inexperienced until he has visited many sick and has learned from those who are ill how to heal them. So we also as disciples of the martyrs take the deeds of these valiant people as teaching our confession and learn to preserve the true religion even in extreme danger; and therefore we keep our eyes on their holy shrines as inscribed monuments showing us precisely their struggle of martyrdom.[2]

Here we find an understanding of the pedagogical role of *exempla* that would be at home in Quintilian's description of the rhetor's education. Though Asterius would not have had recourse to Quintilian, other models of rhetorical pedagogy would have been available to him in the Greek tradition, such as the practice of προγυμνάσματα in which students move from the grammarian's study of language and literature to the rhetor's practice of crafting and delivering elements of oration.

Asterius's pedagogical theory, however, is also connected to historiography. Much like Augustine's Christian reconfiguration of Roman exemplary historiography, Asterius redefines what the canon of historical *exempla* includes:

> People who approach the oak of Mamre or the cave bought for the burial of Sarah from Ephrem the Chattean, where the patriarch himself rests with his children, renew after their observation of the places the representation with their mind and see the faithful patriarch with their spirit, the firstling of faith, his circumcision. And they consider also the offshoots of the same root, Isaac, Jacob and so with the recollection of these men they become spectators of the complete history of the patriarchs.[3]

---

[2] Asterius, *hom. Phoc.* 1.2–3 (Allen et al., 168).
[3] Asterius, *hom. Phoc.* 2.1. (Allen et al., 168–69).

CONCLUSION 139

Like statues of ancient heroes, pilgrimage and cultic sites associated with biblical stories become vehicles for contemplating not only the historic figures themselves but also, and more importantly, the virtues of faith that make these figures so memorable. Indeed, though he only refers explicitly to the "complete history of the patriarchs," Asterius, like Augustine, maintains the classical historiographical concern for exemplarity while redefining "complete history" as sacred history.

Asterius's Phocas is not just rhetorically constructed; he is also, in that construction, presented as a rhetor of sorts. Much like Augustine's martyrs, Phocas's commitment to God is demonstrated in the strength of his speech. "The only charge made against this excellent man was that he confessed with a clear voice; even if not questioned, his deeds were manifest, but interrogated, he confessed with joy."[4] Phocas speaks in deed as well as in word. Even his death requires his own persuasive power: "He however admonished them to undertake the execution. . . . With his words he convinced them, and suffered."[5] This is not the rhetor-stateman of Augustine, but it is nevertheless notable that the virtue of this martyr is manifest in his speech, including his ability to persuade his persecutors to follow through with their murderous plan.

I turn next to John Chrysostom's homily *On the Holy Martyrs*. The most striking feature of this sermon—most striking, that is, after our reading of Augustine's martyrdom rhetoric—is John's discussion of the martyrs' voice. It is not accidental, John says, that the martyr shrines are more numerous in the countryside than in the city when the latter is blessed with more numerous preachers:

> Compensating for the poverty of preachers in the wealth of martyrs, God therefore organized a great number of martyrs to be buried among them. Country people don't hear incessant preachers' tongues, but rather a martyr's voice that speaks to them from the tomb and is louder in volume. To teach you that, even when silent, martyrs are louder in volume than we when we speak, when time after time many have preached to many others on the topic of virtue, they have achieved nothing; yet others, though silent, have achieved major successes through the splendour of their life. Consequently the martyrs have effected this to a greater degree, uttering

---

[4] Asterius, *hom. Phoc.* 6.1 (Allen et al., 170).
[5] Asterius, *hom. Phoc.* 8.3 (Allen et al., 171).

voice not with their tongue, but with their deeds—a voice far superior to that which comes from the mouth.[6]

John even gives an example of this martyrial voice through a performance of prosopopoeia recounting what sufferings the martyrs endured for Christ. As one would expect, the intended effect of such eloquence is that the audience would be moved to endure their own present suffering for the sake of a future reward:

> "Therefore you too transfer your eye from the present to the future and you'll catch not even a brief sensation of the tortures." The martyrs say these things and much more and are far more persuasive than we are. If I [John] say that torture is associated with nothing burdensome, I'm not convincing when I say it. After all, there's nothing irksome in offering philosophy like this in theory. But, when martyrs give voice through their actions, no one can contradict them.[7]

This exhortation fits much of what we have seen in Augustine. Yes, the martyrs are *exempla* pointing away from the things of this world to those of the next. But even more striking is the way in which their exemplarity is accomplished rhetorically, either through imagined speech or through deeds that are themselves more persuasive than actual speech. Indeed, one would not be surprised to find these excerpts in a sermon of Augustine himself.

Finally, I take up a sermon by Basil of Caesarea on the martyr Gordius. The paragraphs of this sermon contain a sustained reflection on the relationship between rhetoric and martyr veneration vis-à-vis Prov 29:2, "When the just man is praised, the people will rejoice." Permit me to quote Basil's commentary at length:

> And yet I have been at a loss within myself about what the enigmatic saying of the author of the Book of Proverbs could possibly mean. Does he mean that when an orator or a clever speech-writer composes a speech to stun his audience, deafening his hearers with elegant resonance, the people rejoice, receiving favourably both the breadth of the ideas and the arrangement [of the speech], and the solemnity of the diction and the harmony he has

---

[6] John Chrysostom, *hom. Mart.* 1 (Allen et al., 119).
[7] John Chrysostom, *hom. Mart.* 1 (Allen et al., 119).

wrought? But he certainly wouldn't ever have said that, because nowhere does he use such a figure of speech. Nor would he have encouraged us to show off eulogistically by praising the blessed ones, because he preferred pedestrian diction and plain expression throughout his work. So what do his words mean? [They mean] that people rejoice with spiritual rejoicing at the very remembrance of the exploits of the just, urged on by what they hear to energetic imitation of good persons. I mean that the account of men who have lived a good life produces as it were a light for those who are being kept safe with regard to the road of life. This is why, as soon as we have heard the Spirit recounting the life of Moses, we are immediately energized to emulate the man's virtue, and the gentleness of their way of life obviously becomes a matter of emulation and blessing to each person. I mean that whereas the encomia of other human beings are composed out of the multiplication of words, the truth of the exploits performed by the just is enough to demonstrate the superiority of their virtue. The upshot is that when we set out in detail the lives of those who have been eminent in piety, in the first instance we are glorifying the Master through his servants; we are praising the just through their witness, with which we are familiar; we are making the people rejoice through hearing fine deeds. I mean that the life of Joseph is an encouragement to chastity, and the tales of Samson [are an encouragement] to bravery. Divine teaching, therefore, does not recognize the rule of encomia, but counts the witness of the exploits rather than encomia, on the grounds that it is quite sufficient in order to praise the saints, and enough to profit those striving for virtue.[8]

It would be impossible to overstate the significance of this passage for our study of martyrdom and rhetoric. Basil's words here provide appropriate punctuation to Augustine's own, and therefore this extended quotation indicates the denouement of my study. Basil's confusion over Prov 29:2 derives from a commitment to humility, or at least a rhetorical commitment to that virtue. After all, the point of a martyrial encomium is to honor the martyr, not oneself. One hears echoes of Augustine wrestling with pride in his initial occupation. But like Augustine, Basil knows that rhetoric is useful in the service of the truth. Indeed, his insistence that the skills of encomium are not needed to recount the life of the martyrs itself belies the careful craftsmanship of his training. Further, Basil's argument turns on the idea that the

---

[8] Basil of Caesarea, *hom. Gord.* 1–2 (Allen et al., 58–59).

martyrs are *exempla* of Christian virtue whose lives and deaths, if only told in the simplest, clearest of styles, will not fail to inspire imitation. Moreover, these martyrial *exempla* find their place within the larger sacred history recorded in scripture. Moses, Joseph, and Samson are part of the same historiographical narrative as Gordius and the other Christian martyrs.

All these rhetorical features found in the martyrial preaching of Asterius, John Chrysostom, and Basil would be at home in that of Augustine, suggesting that in this study of his martyr rhetoric we are uncovering not just something characteristic of a single figure but something common in late fourth- and early fifth-century martyr discourse. Only one thing remains unique or, at least, more pronounced in Augustine: his use of forensic rhetoric in the Donatist controversy. This peculiarity does not, however, represent a major deviation by Augustine. Rather, it suggests the deployment of common discursive tools for a particular polemical purpose in a way that only accentuates the shared rhetoric of martyrdom.

Yet this book is about more than rhetorical techniques and polemical contexts. It is about theology too. Augustine crafts his martyrs, rhetorically and as themselves rhetorical, within and at the service of a theological matrix. Augustine knows he is a skilled rhetor; he knows what he is doing when he places the martyrs within a rhetorical mold. But he does not appear to do so cynically. He does so, instead, with a vision of God's providential work in the world, within history, not just the past but also the present as he wrestles, in his eyes, to defend the honor of God's heroes and advance their work, both in this world and in the next. He knows that the martyrs have rhetorical power, and he presents this as precisely why God has used them throughout sacred history to proclaim and establish the city of God on sojourn. This cause separates martyrs from other tragic deaths. This divinely bequeathed role makes good out of the evil of death. This cruciform virtue guarantees that veneration of the martyrs does not supplant worship of God. And it is only through the grace of Christ that the martyrs are able to follow his example and themselves become examples of faithfulness for those who dare not approach Christ's glory on their own.

Bibliography

Primary Sources

Ambrose of Milan

Abr.	*De Abraham* (On Abraham)	OOSA 3
virg.	*De virginibus ad Marcellinam sororem libri tres* (On Virgins)	OOSA 14

Aristotle

rhet.	*Ars rhetorica* (The Art of Rhetoric)	LCL 193

Augustine of Hippo

ciu.	*De ciuitate dei libri uiginti duo* (City of God)	CCSL 47–48 (WSA I.6–7)
conf.	*Confessionum libri tredecim* (Confessions)	O'Donnell (Chadwick)
Cresc.	*Ad Cresconium grammaticum partis Donati* (To Cresconius, a Donatist Grammarian)	CSEL 52 (WSA 1.22)
doct. christ.	*De doctrina christiana* (Teaching Christianity)	CCSL 32 (WSA I.11)
en. Ps.	*Enarrationes in Psalmos* (Expositions on the Psalms)	CCSL 38–40 (WSA III.14–17)
ep.	*Epistulae* (Letters)	CSEL 34, 44, 57, 88 (WSA II)

ep. Io. tr.	*In epistulam Ioannis ad Parthos tractatus decem* (Homilies on the First Epistle of John)	PL 35 (WSA III.13)
c. Faust.	*Contra Faunstum Manicheum libri triginta tribus* (Against Faustus)	CSEL 25.1 (WSA I.20)
c. Gaud.	*Contra Gaudentium* (Against Gaudentius)	CSEL 53 (WSA I.22)
Io. eu. tr.	*In Ioannis evangelium tractatus CXXIV* (Homilies on the Gospel of John)	CCSL 36 (WSA III.12)
c. Iul.	*Contra Iulianum libri sex* (Against Julian)	PL 44 (WSA I.24)
c. Iul. imp.	*Contra Iulianum opus imperfectum* (Unfinished Work against Julian)	CSEL 85.1 (WSA I.25)
c. litt. Pet.	*Contra litteras Petiliani libri tres* (Against the Letters of Petilian)	CSEL 52 (WSA I.21)
mor.	*De moribus ecclesiae catholicae et de moribus Manicheorum libri duo* (On the Catholic and Manichean Ways of Life)	CSEL 90 (WSA I.19)
mus.	*De musica libri sex* (On Music)	CSEL 90 (WSA I.3)
retr.	*Retractiones* (Reconsiderations)	CSEL 36 (WSA I.2)
rhet. (attributed)	*De rhetorica* (On Rhetoric)	PL 32
s.	*Sermones ad populum* (Sermons)	CCL 41; MA 1; PL 38; PLS 2; RB 50–51; SE 56; SPM 1 (WSA III.1–11)
s. Caes.	*Sermo ad Caesariensis ecclesiae plebem* (Sermon to the People of the Church of Caesarinensis)	CSEL 53
s. Dom. mon.	*De sermon Domini in monte* (On the Lord's Sermon on the Mount)	CCSL 35 (WSA I.16)

Cicero

Brut.	*Brutus*	LCL 342
inv.	*De inventione rhetorica* (On Invention)	LCL 386
de orat.	*De oratore* (On the Orator)	LCL 348–49
opt. gen.	*De optimo genere oratorum* (On the Best Kind of Orator)	LCL 386
or.	*Orator ad M. Brutum* (The Orator)	LCL 342
part. or.	*Partitiones oratoriae* (Divisions of Oratory)	LCL 349
rep.	*De republic* (The Republic)	LCL 213
rhet. Her. (attributed)	*Rhetorica ad Herennium* (Rhetoric to Herennius)	LCL 403
top.	*Topica* (Topics)	LCL 386
Tusc.	*Tusculanae disputationes* (Tusculan Disputations)	LCL 141

Cyprian

ep.	*Epistulae* (Letters)	CSEL 3.2
Fort.	*Ad Fortunatam* (To Fortunatus)	CSEL 3.1
laps.	*De lapsis* (On the Fallen)	CSEL 3.1
unit. eccl.	*De unitate ecclesiae* (On the Unity of the Church)	CSEL 3.1

Demetrius

elocut.	*De elocutio* (On Style)	LCL 199

Jerome

| ep. | *Epistulae* (Letters) | CSEL 54–56 |

Optatus of Milevis

| *Parm.* | *Contra Parmenianum Donatistam* (Against Parmenian) | CSEL 26 |

Pauline of Nola

| *carm.* | *Carminae* (Poems) | CSEL 30 |
| *ep.* | *Epistulae* (Letters) | CSEL 29 |

Quintilian

| *inst.* | *Institutio oratoria* (The Orator's Education) | LCL 124–27, 494 |

Sallust

| *Cat.* | *Bellum Catilinae* (The War with Catiline) | LCL 116 |
| *Jug.* | *Bellum Jugurthinum* (The War with Jugurtha) | LCL 116 |

Tertullian

apol.	*Apologeticum* (Apology)	CCSL 1
mart.	*Ad martyras* (To the Martyrs)	CCSL 1
scorp.	*Scorpiace* (Antidote to the Scorpion's Sting)	CCSL 2

Secondary Sources

Allen, Michael. "Universal History 300–1000: Origins and Western Developments." In *Historiography in the Middle Ages*, edited by D. M. Deliyannis, 17–42. Leiden: Brill, 2003.

Allen, Pauline, Boudewijn Dehandschutter, Johan Leemans, and Wendy Mayer. *"Let Us Die That We May Live": Greek Homilies on Christian Martyrs from Asia Minor, Palestine and Syria (c. AD 350–AD 450)*. London: Routledge, 2003.

Allewell, K. *Über das rhetorische Paradeigma. Theorie, Beispelsammlungen, Verwendung in der römischen Literatur der Kaiserzeit*. PhD diss., University of Leipzig, 1913.

Amsler, Mark. *Etymology and Grammatical Discourse in Late Antiquity and the Early Middle Ages*. Amsterdam: John Benjamins Publishing Company, 1989.

Aubin, Jeffery. "Le *De rhetorica* du Pseudo-Augustin: réexamen des objections contre l'authenticité augustinienne." *Revue d'études augustiniennes et patristiques* 59 (2013): 117–34.

Ayres, Lewis. "Augustine on the Rule of Faith: Rhetoric, Christology, and the Foundation of Christian Thinking." *Augustinian Studies* 36 (2005): 33–49.

Ayres, Lewis. "Into the Poem of the Universe: *Exempla*, Conversion, and Church in Augustine's *Confessiones*." *Zeitschrift für Antikes Christentum* 13 (2009): 263–81.

Bastiaensen, A. A. R. "Quelques observations sur la terminologie du martyre chez saint Augustin." In *Signum Pietatis: Festgabe für Cornelius Petrus Mayer OSA zum 60. Geburtstag*, edited by Adolar Zumkeller, 201–16. Würzburg: Augustinus-Verlag, 1989.

Bavel, Tarcisius van. "The Cult of Martyrs in St. Augustine: Theology Versus Popular Religion?" In *Martyrium in Multidisciplinary Perspective*, edited by Mathijs Lamberigts and Peter Van Deun, 351–61. Leuven: Peeters, 1995.

Beard, Mary, John North, and John Price. *Religions of Rome: A History*. Cambridge: Cambridge University Press, 1998.

Benardete, Seth. *The Rhetoric of Morality and Philosophy*: Plato's Gorgias *and* Phaedrus. Chicago: University of Chicago Press, 1991.

Blockley, Roger. "Ammianus Marcellinus's Use of *Exempla*." *Florilegium* 13 (1994): 53–64.

Boeft, Jan den. "Etymologies in Augustine's *De Civitate Dei* X." *Vigiliae Christianae* 33 (1979): 242–59.

Boeft, Jan den. "'*Martyres sunt, sed homines fuerunt*': Augustine on Martyrdom." In *Fructus Centesimus: Mélanges offerts à Gerard J. M. Bartelink à l'occasion de son soixante-cinquième anniversaire*, edited by A. A. R. Bastiaensen, A. Hilhorst, and C. H. Kneepkens, 115–24. Turnhout: Brepols, 1989.

Brent, Allen. "Cyprian's Reconstruction of the Martyr Tradition." *Journal of Ecclesiastical History* 53, no. 2 (2002): 251–63.

Brinton, Alan. "Quintilian, Plato, and the 'Vir Bonus.'" *Philosophy & Rhetoric* 16 (1983): 167–84.

Burns, J. Patout. "Appropriating Augustine Appropriate Cyprian." *Augustinian Studies* 36 (2005): 113–37.

Burns, J. Patout. *Cyprian the Bishop*. London: Routledge, 2002.

Burns, J. Patout, and Robin M. Jensen, *Christianity in Roman Africa: The Development of Its Practices and Beliefs*. Grand Rapids, MI: Eerdmans, 2014.

Burns, Paul C. "Augustine's Use of Sallust in the *City of God*: The Role of the Grammatical Tradition." *Augustinian Studies* 30 (1999): 105–14.

Busch, Peter. "On the Use and Disadvantage of History for the Afterlife." In *Augustine and History*, edited by Christopher T. Daly, John Doody, and Kim Paffenroth, 3–30. Lanham, MD: Lexington Books, 2008.

Calder, William M. "Vir Bonus, Discendi Peritus." *American Journal of Philology* 108 (1987): 160–71.

Cameron, Averil. *Christianity and the Rhetoric of Empire: The Development of Christian Discourse*. Berkeley: University of California Press, 1994.

Cameron, Michael. *Christ Meets Me Everywhere: Augustine's Early Figurative Exegesis*. New York: Oxford, 2012.

Cameron, Michael. "'She Arranges All Things Pleasingly' (Wis. 8:1): The Rhetorical Base of Augustine's Hermeneutic." *Augustinian Studies* 41 (2010): 55–67.

Campenhausen, Hans Freiherr von. *Die Idee des Martyriums in der alten Kirche*. Göttingen: Vandenhoeck & Ruprecht, 1936.

Castelli, Elizabeth. *Martyrdom and Memory: Early Christian Culture Marking*. New York: Columbia University Press, 2004.

Chaplin, Jane D. *Livy's Exemplary History*. Oxford: Oxford University Press, 2000.

Cipriani, Nello. "Rhetoric." In *Augustine through the Ages*, edited by Allen Fitzgerald, 724–26. Grand Rapids, MI: Eerdmans, 1999.

Clavier, Mark. *Eloquent Wisdom: Rhetoric, Cosmology, and Delight in the Theology of Augustine of Hippo*. Turnhout: Brepols, 2014.

Dearn, Alan. "The Polemical Use of the Past in the Catholic/Donatist Schism." PhD diss., University of Oxford, 2003.

DeSoucey, Michaela, Jo-Ellen Pozner, Corey Fields, Kerry Dobransky, and Gary Alan Fine. "Memory and Sacrifice: An Embodied Theory of Martyrdom." *Cultural Sociology* 2 (2008): 99–121.

Dieter, Otto Alvin Loeb, and William Charles Kurth. "The *De Rhetorica* of Aurelius Augustine." *Speech Monographs* 35 (1968): 90–108.

Djuth, Marianne. "Ordering Images: The Rhetorical Imagination and Augustine's Anti-Pelagian Polemic after 418." *Studia Patristica* 43 (2006): 81–88.

Dodaro, Robert. *Christ and the Just Society in the Thought of Augustine*. Cambridge: Cambridge University Press, 2004.

Dodaro, Robert. "Language Matters: Augustine's Use of Literary Decorum in Theological Argument." *Augustinian Studies* 45 (2014): 1–28.

Dodaro, Robert. "Literary Decorum in Scriptural Exegesis: Augustine of Hippo, *Epistula* 138." In *L'esegi di Padri Latini, Dalle origini a Gregorio Magno*, 1:159–74. Rome: Institutum Patristicum Augustinianum, 2000.

Dodaro, Robert. "Political and Theological Virtues in Augustine, Letter 155 to Macedonius." *Augustiniana* 54 (2004): 431–74.

Dodaro, Robert. "*Quid deceat videre* (Cicero, *Orator* 70): Literary Propriety and Doctrinal Orthodoxy in Augustine of Hippo." In *Orthodoxie, christianisme, histoire*, edited by Susanna Elm, Éric Rebillard, and Antonella Romano, 57–58. Rome: École Française de Rome, 2000.

Dodaro, Robert. "The Theologian as Grammarian: Literary Decorum in Augustine's Defense of Orthodox Discourse." *Studia Patristica* 38 (2001): 70–83.

Dupont, Anthony. "Augustine's Anti-Pelagian Interpretation of Two Martyr Sermons. Sermones 299 and 335B on the Unnaturalness of Human Death." In *Martyrdom and Persecution in Late Antique Christianity (100–700 ad). Essays in Honour of Boudewijn Dehandschutter on the Occasion of His Retirement as Professor of Greek and Oriental

Patrology at the Faculty of Theology of the K.U. Leuven, edited by Johann Leemans, 87–102. Leuven: Peeters, 2010.

Dupont, Anthony. "Augustine's Homiletic Definition of Martyrdom: The Centrality of the Martyr's Grace in his Anti-Donatist and Anti-Pelagian Sermones ad Populum." In *Christian Martyrdom in Late Antiquity (300-450 AD): History and Discourse, Tradition and Religious Identity*, edited by Peter Gemeinhardt and Johan Leemans, 155–78. Berlin: DeGruyter, 2012.

Dupont, Anthony. "*Imitatio Christi, Imitatio Stephani*: Augustine's Thinking on Martyrdom Based on His *Sermones* on the Protomartyr Stephen." *Augustiniana* 56 (2006): 29–61.

Dupont, Anthony. "Original Sin in Tertullian and Cyprian: Conceptual Presence and Pre-Augustinian Content?" *Revue d'études augustiniennes et patristique* 63 (2017): 1–29.

Dupont, Anthony. *Preacher of Grace: A Critical Reappraisal of Augustine's Doctrine of Grace in His* Sermones ad Populum *on Liturgical Feasts and during the Donatist Controversy*. Leiden: Brill, 2014.

Eden, Kathy. *Hermeneutics and the Rhetorical Tradition: Chapters in the Ancient Legacy and Its Humanist Reception*. New Haven, CT: Yale University Press, 1997.

Enos, R. L., Roger Thompson, Amy K. Hermanson, Drew M. Loewe, Kristi Schwertfeger Serrano, Lisa Michelle Thomas, Sarah L. Yoder, David Elder, and John W. Burkett, eds. *The Rhetoric of St. Augustine of Hippo*: De doctrina christiana *and the Search for a Distinctly Christian Rhetoric*. Waco, TX: Baylor University Press, 2008.

Fortin, Ernest. "Augustine and the Problem of Christian Rhetoric." In *The Birth of Philosophic Christianity: Studies in Early and Medieval Thought*, edited by J. Brian Benestad, 79–93. Burlington, VT: Ashgate, 2011.

Fortin, Ernest. "Augustine and the Problem of Christian Rhetoric." In *The Rhetoric of St. Augustine*, edited by R. L. Enos et al., 219–34. Waco, TX: Baylor University Press, 2008.

Fournier, Eric. "Amputation Metaphors and the Rhetoric of Exile: Purity and Pollution in Late Antique Christianity." In *Clerical Exile in Late Antiquity*, edited by Julia Hillner, Jacob Enberg, and Jörg Ulrich, 231–49. Frankfurt am Main: Peter Lang, 2016.

Fox, Matthew. *Cicero's Philosophy of History*. Oxford: Oxford University Press, 2007.

Frede, H. J. *Kirchenschriftsteller Verzeichnis und Sigel. 4. Aktualisierte Auflage*, Vetus Latina 1/1. Freiburg: Herder, 1995.

Frend, W. H. C. *The Donatist Church: A Movement of Protest in Roman North Africa*. Oxford: Clarendon, 1952.

Fruchtman, Diane. "Living in a Martyrial World: Living Martyrs and the Creation of Martyrial Consciousness in the Late Antique Latin West." PhD diss., Indiana University, 2014.

Gaddis, Michael. *There Is No Crime for Those Who Have Christ: Religious Violence in the Christian Roman Empire*. Berkeley: University of California Press, 2005.

Garbarino, Collin. "Augustine, Donatists, and Martyrdom." In *An Age of Saints? Power, Conflict and Dissent in Early Medieval Christianity*, edited by Peter Sarris, Matthew Dal Santo, and Phil Booth, 49–61. Leiden: Brill, 2011.

Gaumer, Matthew Alan. *Augustine's Cyprian: Authority in Roman Africa*. Leiden: Brill, 2016.

Gaumer, Matthew Alan. "Dealing with the Donatist Church: Augustine of Hippo's Nuanced Claim to the Authority of Cyprian of Carthage." In *Cyprian of Carthage: Studies in His Life, Language, and Thought*, edited by Henk Bakker, Paul van Geest, and Hans van Loon, 181–202. Leuven: Peeters, 2010.

Gehrke, Jason M. "*Christus Exemplar*: The Politics of Virtue in Lactantius." PhD diss., Marquette University, 2017.

Grig, Lucy. *Making Martyrs in Late Antiquity*. London: Bristol Classical Press, 2004.

Gronewoller, Brian. *Rhetorical Economy in Augustine's Theology*. Oxford Studies in Historical Theology. New York: Oxford University Press, 2021.

Gryson, Roger. *Répertoire general des auteurs ecclésiastiques Latins de l'antiquité et du haut moyen âge*. Freiberg: Herder, 2007.

Harding, Brian. *Augustine and Roman Virtue*. London: Continuum, 2008.

Heath, Malcolm. *Hermogenes, On Issues: Strategies of Argument in Later Greek Rhetoric*. Oxford: Clarendon Press, 1995.

Heath, Malcolm. "The Substructure of *stasis*-Theory from Hermagoras to Hermogenes." *Classical Quarterly* 44 (1994): 114–29.

Heath, Malcolm. "Zeno the Rhetor and the Thirteen *staseis*." *Eranos* 92 (1994): 17–22.

Heath, Malcolm. "στάσις-Theory in Homeric Commentary." *Mnemosyne* 46 (1993): 356–63.

Herdt, Jennifer. "The Theater of the Virtues: Augustine's Critique of Pagan Mimesis." In *Augustine's* City of God: *A Critical Guide*, edited by James Wetzel, 111–29. Cambridge: Cambridge University Press, 2012.

Hermanowicz, Erika. *Possidius of Calama: A Study in the North African Episcopate at the Time of Augustine*. Oxford: Oxford University Press, 2008.

Hermanson, Amy K. "Religion's Rhetoric: Saint Augustine's Union of Christian Wisdom and Sophistic Eloquence." In *The Rhetoric of St. Augustine*, edited by R. L. Enos et al., 311–14. Waco, TX: Baylor University Press, 2008.

Jensen, Robin. "Dining with the Dead: From *Mensa* to the Altar in Christian Late Antiquity." In *Commemorating the Dead: Texts and Artifacts in Context: Studies of Roman, Jewish, and Christian Burials*, edited by Laurie Brink and Deborah Green, 107–43. Berlin: DeGruyter, 2008.

Kennedy, George. *Quintilian*. New York: Twayne, 1969.

Kornhardt, H. *Exemplum. Eine bedeutungsgeschichtiche Studie*. PhD diss., University of Göttingen, 1936.

Kriegbaum, Bernard. *Kirche der Traditoren oder Kirche der Märtyrer? Die Vorgeschichte des Donatismus*. Vienna: Tyrolia, 1986.

La Bonnardière, A.-M. "Les Enarrationes in Psalmos prêchées par saint Augustin à l'occasion de fêtes de martyrs." *Recherches augustiniennes et patristiques* 7 (1971): 73–104.

Lambot, Cyrille. "Les sermons de saint Augustin pour les fetes de martyrs." *Analecta bollandiana* 67 (1949): 249–66.

Lancel, Serge. *Saint Augustine*. Translated by Antonia Nevill. London: SCM Press, 2002.

Lapointe, Guy. *La célébration des martyrs en Afrique d'après les sermons de saint Augustin*. Montreal, 1972.

Lausberg, Heinrich. *Handbook of Literary Rhetoric: A Foundation for Literary Study*. Translated by Matthew T. Bliss, Annemiek Jansen, and David E. Orton. Edited by David E. Orton and R. Dean Anderson. Leiden: Brill, 1998.

Lazewski, Wojciech. "La Sentenza Agostiniana Martyrem Facit Non Poena Sed Causa." PhD diss., Pontificia Universitas Lateranensis, 1987.

Lenski, Noel. "Imperial Legislation and the Donatist Controversy: From Constantine to Honorius." In *The Donatists Schism: Controversy and Context*, edited by Richard Miles, 166–219. Liverpool: Liverpool University Press, 2016.

Leyerle, Blake. "Blood Is Seed." *Journal of Religion* 81 (2001): 26–48.
Lloyd, A. C. "Grammar and Metaphysics in the Stoa." In *Hellenistic Philosophy*, edited by A. A. Long, 58–74. New York: Charles Scribner's Sons, 1974.
Markus, Robert A. "Bonifatius comes Africae." In *Augustinus-Lexikon*, edited by C. P. Mayer, 1: 653–55. Basel: Schwabe, 1986.
Markus, Robert A. *Saeculum: History and Society in the Theology of St. Augustine*. Rev. ed. Cambridge: Cambridge University Press, 1988.
Marrou, Henri-Irenée. *Saint Augustin et la fin de la culture antique*. 4th ed. Paris: Éditions E. de Boccard, 1958.
Martin, Elena. "*Sanctae Famulae Dei*: Towards a Reading of Augustine's Female Martyrs." DPhil thesis, Durham University, 2009.
Mayer, C. P. "'*Attende Stephanum conservum tuum*' (*Serm.* 317, 2, 3). Sinn und Wert der Märtyrerverehrung nach den Stephanuspredigten Augustins." In *Fructus Centesimus: Mélanges offerts à Gereard J. M. Bartelink à l'occasion de son soixante-cinquième anniversaire*, edited by A. A. R. Bastiaensen, A. Hilhorst, and C. H. Kneepkens, 217–37. Turnhout: Brepols, 1989.
McComiskey, Bruce. *Gorgias and the New Sophistic Rhetoric*. Carbondale: Southern Illinois University Press, 2002.
McCoy, Marina. *Plato on the Rhetoric of Philosophers and Sophists*. Cambridge: Cambridge University Press, 2008.
Meador Jr., Prentice A. "Quintilian's 'Vir Bonus.'" *Western Speech* 34 (1970): 162–69.
Mohrmann, Christine. *Études sur le Latin des Chrétiens* I, Storia e Letteratura: Raccolta di Studi e Testi 65. Roma: Edizioni di Storia e Letteratura, 1958.
Moss, Candida. *Ancient Christian Martyrdom: Diverse Practices, Theologies, and Traditions*. New Haven, CT: Yale University Press, 2012.
Moss, Candida. "Martyr Veneration in Late Antique North Africa." In *The Donatist Schism: Controversy and Contexts*, edited by Richard Miles, 56–69. Liverpool: Liverpool University Press, 2016.
Moss, Candida. *The Myth of Persecution: How Early Christians Invented a Story of Martyrdom*. New York: HarperOne, 2013.
Moss, Candida. *The Other Christs: Imitating Jesus in Ancient Christian Ideologies of Martyrdom*. New York: Oxford University Press, 2010.
Murphy, Andrew R. "Augustine and the Rhetoric of Roman Decline." In *Augustine and History*, edited by Christopher T. Daly, John Doody, and Kim Paffenroth, 53–76. Lanham, MD: Lexington Books, 2008.
Murphy, James J. "Saint Augustine and the Debate about a Christian Rhetoric." In *The Rhetoric of St. Augustine*, edited by R. L. Enos et al., 187–204. Waco, TX: Baylor University Press, 2008.
Nadeau, Ray. "Classical Systems of Stases in Greek: Hermagoras to Hermogenes." *Greek, Roman, and Byzantine Studies* 2 (1959): 53–71.
Nuffelen, Peter Van. *Orosius and the Rhetoric of History*. Oxford: Oxford University Press, 2012.
Pellegrino, M. "Chiesa e martirio in Sant'Agostino." In *Ricerche Patristiche* 1, edited by M. Pellegrino, 597–633. Torino: Edizioni di storia e letteratura, 1982.
Pellegrino, M. "Cristo e il martire nel pensiero di Sant'Agostino." In *Ricerche Patristiche* 1, edited by M. Pellegrino, 635–68. Torino: Edizioni di storia e letteratura, 1982.
Petitfils, James. *Mos Christianorum: The Roman Discourse of Exemplarity and the Jewish and Christian Language of Leadership*. Tübingen: Mohr Siebeck, 2016.

Ployd, Adam. "Augustine, Martyrdom, and the Exemplary Rhetoric of History." *Journal of Early Christian Studies* 28 (2020): 423–41.

Ployd, Adam. "Augustine's Martyrs as Ideal Christian Rhetors." *Augustiniana* 71 (2021): 27–43.

Ployd, Adam. "For Their Own Good: Augustine and the Rhetoric of Beneficial Persecution." In *Heirs of Roman Persecution: Studies on a Christian and Para-Christian Discourse in Late Antiquity*, edited by Eric Fournier, 95–111. London: Routledge, 2019.

Ployd, Adam. "*Non poena sed causa*: Augustine's Anti-Donatist Rhetoric of Martyrdom." *Augustinian Studies* 49 (2018): 25–44.

Powell, J. G. F. "Cicero's *De Re Publica* and the Virtues of the Statesman." In *Cicero's Practical Philosophy*, edited by Walter Nicgorski, 14–32. Notre Dame, IN: University of Notre Dame Press, 2012.

Quasten, Johannes. "Die Reform des Martyrerkultes durch Augustinus." *Theologie und Glaube* 25 (1933): 318–31.

Rose, Paula. "Augustine's Reassessment of the Commemoration Meal: *Quod quidem a christianis melioribus non fit*." In *Rituals in Early Christianity: New Perspectives on Tradition and Transformation*, edited by Nienke M. Vos and Albert C. Geljon, 135–52. Leiden: Brill, 2021.

Rose, Paula. "*Refrigerium*." In *Augustinus-Lexikon*, edited by C. P. Mayer, 4:1104–7. Basel: Schwabe, 2018.

Saxer, Victor. *Morts, martyrs, reliques en Afrique chrétienne aux premiers siècles. Les témoignages de Tertullien, Cyprien et Augustin à la lumière l'archéologie africaine.* Théologie historique 55. Paris: Beauchesne, 1980.

Shaw, Brent. "Body/Power/Identity: Passions of the Martyrs." *Journal of Early Christianity* 4 (1996): 269–312.

Shaw, Brent. *Sacred Violence: African Christians and Sectarian Hatred in the Age of Augustine.* Cambridge: Cambridge University Press, 2011.

Shuve, Karl. "Cyprian of Carthage's Writings from the Rebaptism Controversy: Two Revisionary Proposals Reconsidered." *Journal of Theological Studies* 61 (2010): 627–43.

Sutcliffe, Ruth. "To Flee or Not to Flee: Matthew 10:23 and Third Century Flight in Persecution." *Scrinium* 14 (2018): 133–60.

Tilley, Maureen A. *The Bible in Christian North Africa: The Donatist World.* Minneapolis: Fortress Press, 1997.

Tilley, Maureen. *Donatist Martyr Stories: The Church in Conflict in Roman North Africa.* Liverpool: Liverpool University Press, 1996.

Toczko, Rafał. *Crimen Obicere: Forensic Rhetoric and Augustine's Anti-Donatist Correspondence.* Forschungen zur Kirchen- und Dogmengeschichte 120. Göttingen: Vandenhoeck & Ruprecht Verlag, 2020.

Tracy, David. "Charity, Obscurity, Clarity: Augustine's Search for a True Rhetoric." In *The Rhetoric of St. Augustine of Hippo* De doctrina christiana *and the Search for a Distinctly Christian Rhetoric*, edited by R. L. Enos, et al., 267–88. Waco, TX: Baylor University Press, 2008.

Troup, Calvin. *Temporality, Eternity, and Wisdom: The Rhetoric of Augustine's* Confessions. Columbia: University of South Carolina Press, 1999.

Verbraken, Pierre-Patrick. *Études critiques sur les Sermons authentiques de St. Augustin.* Instrumenta Patristica 12. Steenbrugge, 1976.

Walzer, Arthur E. "Quintilian's 'Vir Bonus' and the Stoic Wise Man." *Rhetoric Society Quarterly* 33 (2003): 25–41.

Wetzel, James. *Augustine and the Limits of Virtue*. Cambridge: Cambridge University Press, 1992.
White, David A. *Rhetoric and Reality in Plato's* Phaedrus. Albany: State University of New York Press, 1993.
Winterbottom, Michael. "Quintilian and the *Vir Bonus*." *Journal of Roman Studies* 54 (1964): 90–97.

Subject Index

For the benefit of digital users, indexed terms that span two pages (e.g., 52–53) may, on occasion, appear on only one of those pages.

Adam, 24, 26
adnominatio, 49–54
Agnes, St., 55–56
Ambrose, 16
Amsler, Mark, 52–53
analogy, 93
antithesis, 73–81
argumentation, 4, 5
Arianism, 19
arrangement. See *dispositio*
Asterius of Amasea, 137–39
attacking definitions, 87–88. See also definition, rhetoric of
Aurelius, 16–18
authority of martyrs, 12–13, 21

Basil of Caesarea, 140–42
beatitudes, 90, 94
beauty, 62, 73–78, 80–81
bishops and martyrs, 10–12, 16, 17–18, 23
Blockley, Roger, 35n.5
Boeft, Den, 49–50

Cameron, Averil, 107–8
Carthage, 17–18, 70
Castus and Aemilius, 43
Cicero, 35n.5, 67–69, 96–99, 110, 113–18, 121
City of God (Augustine), 121–22
commemoration. See memory
comparatio, 98, 102, 103, 106
confessors, 10–11
conflict, 70, 73
conjecture, 85–86
Constans, Emperor, 13n.23
Constantine, Emperor, 96
construction of martyrs, 2, 5, 8, 34–35, 38, 48–49, 63, 124, 126–27, 129, 135, 139

context, rhetorical, 4–5, 8–9, 135
Crassus, 114–15
Cratylus (Plato), 52
creation, 78–80
cult of the martyrs
    Ambrose, 16
    and conversion of Augustine, 3–4n.6
    council, Carthage, 17–18
    Cyprian, 10–13
    Donatists, 12–14
    excesses, 14–18, 45, 46–48, 76
    exempla, 45–49
    feasts, 15, 18n.37
    heroism, 43–44
    Monica, 14–16
    North Africa, 9–14, 76
    and paganism, 16
    promotion, Augustine, 18–20
    relics, 19
    rhetorical contexts, 8–9
    van Bavel, 3–4n.6, 14–20
    veneration, 48
culture-making, 68–69
Cyprian
    and Augustine, 12–13, 20, 24–26, 41, 126
    authority of martyrdom, 12–13
    and Christ, 57
    cult, 20
    and Donatists, 12–13
    etymology, 57
    exemplum, 57
    faithfulness, 127–28
    feast day, 46–47
    imitation, 127
    the lapsed, 10–12
    laxism, 11–12
    martyrdom, 10–11, 25, 41, 126, 132–33

156 SUBJECT INDEX

Cyprian (*cont.*)
    original sin, 24–25
    piety, 133
    rhetoric, 126
    rigorism, 12
    statesman, 133

daemon, 72
death, 24, 25–31, 39–40
definition, rhetoric of, 85–88, 91–92
desire, 74–75
Diogenes Laertius, 27
dispositio, 28–31
dissimilarity, 36
Dodaro, Robert, 121, 133–34
Donatism
    church of the martyrs, 83, 84–85, 91, 93–96, 136
    and Constans, 13n.23
    and Cyprian, 12–13
    depiction by Augustine, 101–2
    and forensic rhetoric, 5–6, 83, 85–86, 88, 142
    identity, 13–14
    imperial support, 107–8n.81
    Matt 5:10, 90, 91, 93–95
    non poena sed causa, 90
    parum plena, 89
    persecution, 84–85, 90–91, 93–94, 96, 100, 101–3, 104–7
    proprium, 91
    relatio criminis, 101–2, 103
    and scripture, 91–92, 93–95
    texts, martyrdom, 13–14
    virtue, 90
drunkenness, 23–24, 47–48
Dulcitius, 84–85, 107–8

earthly life, value of, 44
earth to earth, 26–27
education, 37–38, 138
ekphrasis, 97–98
empire, rhetoric of, 107–8
eschatology, 130
etymology, 49–59, 71–72
evil, 24, 26, 27–28, 29–31
example
    Asterius, 137–38

Basil, 141–42
Christ, 39–42
Chrysostom, 140
Cicero, 35n.5, 117
cult of martyrs, 45–49
Cyprian, 57
earthly life, 44–45
and education, 138
emulation, 46, 55–56
and ethics, 35n.5
etymology, 49–59
excesses, 46–48
exempla (rhetoric), 5, 34–38, 59–60, 62–69, 104, 129
and history, 5, 37, 61–69, 72, 136, 138–39
and imitation, 45–48
martyrs, 42–45, 66–67, 69, 135–36
Perpetua and Felicitas, 58–59
persecution, 103–7
persuasion, 129
rhetor, 117, 120
Roman, 64–69, 136
Sallust, 64–65
scripture, 103–7
similarity, 104
spiritualization, 62–63
spiritual vision, 6–7
statesman, 117
Stephen, 57–58
veneration, 48
and virtue, 66–67, 72–73, 129, 137, 141–42
wisdom, 129
witness, 54–59
exhortation, 1

Faustus, 21–24
feasts, martyrs, 14–15, 33–34
Felicitas, 49, 51–52, 53, 58–59
folly of rhetoric, 118–19
forensic rhetoric, 5–6, 83–84, 85–88, 95, 96–99, 142
Fortunius, 90
Fructuosus, 48

Gaius Popilius, 98
glory, 66–67, 68

God
  antithesis, 81
  arrangement of world, 29–30
  and death, 25
  and evil, 29–31
  grace, 43–44
  and history, 78
  Julian, 25
  and martyrs, 19, 142
  providence, 28, 70–71, 78–81
  rhetor, 1–2, 79–80
  salvation, 79–80
  witness, 54
  worship, 48
Gorgias (Plato), 110–11
greater to lesser (*exemplum*), 36, 43
Gronewoller, Brian, 78

Hagar, 105–6
Heath, Malcolm, 85n.5
heroism, 43–44, 67–68, 71–72, 73
historiography, 62–69
history
  antithesis, 78–81
  Asterius, 138–39
  and *City of God*, 65–66, 69
  decline, Roman, 64–67, 70
  and education, 138–39
  and *exempla*, 5, 37, 61–69, 72, 136, 138–39
  figures, 37
  and God, 78
  and heroism, 67–68, 71–72, 73
  and providence, 78–81
  Roman, 63–70, 72
  Sallust, 63–66, 69–70
  and time, 61, 62–69
Horatius, 97–98, 103–4

identity and martyrdom, 12, 13–14
imitation
  and celebration, 45–46
  and drunkenness, 47–48
  emulation, 46
  and *exempla*, 45–48
  feasts, 33
  martyr-rhetors, 127
  and veneration, 22, 34, 34n.4

indifference, 27
inheritance, 92–93
inventio, 28, 49
issue, forensic, 85–88

Jesus Christ
  and Cyprian, 57
  exemplum, 39–42, 57
  humility, 40–41
  judicial mode, 41
  and martyrs, 142
  and Pilate, 40–41
  relationship to martyrs, 6–7, 39n.15, 41–42
  similarity, 41
  and Stephen, 39–40, 57–58
John Chrysostom, 139–40
Julian of Eclanum, 24, 25, 26–28, 30
justice, 116–17, 121–22
Justina, 19

lapsed, 10–12
Lawrence, St., 126, 127, 129
Lenski, Noel, 107–8n.81
Leyerle, Blake, 1n.1
liberal arts, 4n.7
literature, 37–38
locus a causa, 89
love, 123–24

Macarius, 13–14
Maccabean mother, 124–25, 127, 128
Macedonius, 122–23
Manichaeanism, 20–24
Markus, Robert A., 63n.2
marriage, 28
"martyr" (term), 54–59
memory, 16, 17, 61, 63–64, 65. See also history
Mohrmann, Christine, 50
Monica, 14–16
Moss, Candida, 39n.15
motive, 89
Murphy, Andrew R., 64n.11

Nebuchadnezzar, 104–5
non poena sed causa, 83, 84–95, 107–8
North Africa, 9–14, 31, 77

158 SUBJECT INDEX

Numidian Christians, 9

On the Orator's Education
    (Quintilian), 111–12
orator. *See* rhetor
Orestes, 97, 101–2, 103–4

paganism, 16, 22, 23–24, 68
parum plena definition, 88, 89. *See also*
    definition, rhetoric of
pedagogy. *See* education
Pelagianism, 24–31
peoplehood, 122
performance, rhetorical, 130, 131–32
periodization of Augustine's works, 3–4n.6
Perpetua, 9–10, 49, 51–52, 53, 58–59
persecution
    Catholics, 95–96, 100–1, 102, 106–7
    comparatio, 102–3, 106
    correction, 100
    definition, 100–1
    Donatists, 84–85, 90–91, 93–94, 96, 100,
        101–3, 104–7
    efficacy, 1–2
    end of, 69, 70, 73
    exempla, 71, 103–7
    for their own good, 102–3
    Hagar and Sarah, 105–6
    justification, 96–97, 99–105, 106, 107–8
    Matt 5:10, 90–91
    moral state of persecutors, 130–31
    qualitas, 96–103
    relation criminis, 101–2, 103, 106
    rhetorical performance, 125–26
persuasion, 1–2, 109, 117–18, 125–26,
    129, 131–32
Petilian, 12–13
Phaedrus (Plato), 111
philosophy, 111
Phocas, 137–39
piety, 17–18, 66–67, 122–24, 131–32
Plato, 110–11, 120
poena, 89–90
polemicism, 20–32
political theology, Augustine, 121–22
Pontius Pilate, 40–41
Porphyry, 71
proprium, 88–89, 90, 91

prosopopoeia, 126–29
Protasius and Gervasius, 18–19
prudence. *See under* rhetor

Quadratus, 56–57
quality, rhetoric, 85–86, 96–103
Quintilian, 35–38, 76, 86–89, 111–13

rape, 65–66
readmission to the church, 11–12
relatio criminis, 96–97, 98, 101–2, 103, 106
republic, 121–22
rhetor
    audience of Augustine, 126–29
    Augustine, 4, 6, 118–24, 142
    bonus, 111–12, 116, 120–21
    Christian, 118–29
    Cicero, 110, 113–18
    Cyprian, 126
    eloquence, 119–20
    example, 117, 120
    God, 1–2, 79–80
    imitation, 127
    martyrs, 6–7, 109–10, 124–34, 136–37
    moral character, 109–10, 117–21
    order, social, 113–14, 117–18, 131–32
    Plato, 110–11, 120
    prudence/wisdom, 116–17, 119–
        20, 128–29
    Quintilian, 111–13
    statesman, 6–7, 109–10, 113–18,
        120, 121–34
    virtue, 115, 117–18
Rhetoric to Herennius, 51, 75–76
rhetorical turn, 2–3

saevus/saevio, 130–31
Sallust, 64–66
salvation, 79–80
Sarah, 105–6
Saturninus, Lucius Appuleius, 35–36
savagery, 130–33
Scaevola, 66–67
scholarship, Augustine and martyrdom, 3
Scillitan martyrs, 9, 40, 55, 125,
    127, 128–29
Scipio, 67–68
scripture, 91–95, 103–7

SUBJECT INDEX

shrines, martyrs, 14–15
similarity, 35–36, 41
sin, 24–25, 26–27, 29
Socrates, 110–11
spectacle, 74
spiritualization, 62–63, 73
statesman. *See under* rhetor
Stephen, 19–20, 39–40, 48, 57–58
Stoicism, 27, 30, 52–33
suffering, 71, 74, 94–95

temptation, 73
Tertullian, 1–2, 10, 136–37
texts, martyrdom, 9–14
theory, rhetorical, 2–3
time. *See* history
true and false martyrs, 55
Twenty Martyrs, feast day, 33
tyranny, 88–91, 115–16

ugliness, 74–75, 76–77
unity, 13–14
uolet, 92–93
utilitas, 98–99

Varro, 53

veneration, 22–23, 34n.4, 39n.15, 48
victim, blaming the, 97–99
Vincent, 43, 54, 55–56
vir bonus dicendi peritus, 111–12, 120–21
virtue
  beauty, 74–75, 76–77
  Cicero, 115, 116–17
  civic, 122–24
  Donatists, 90
  exempla, 66–67, 72–73, 129, 137, 141–42
  martyrs, 71, 72–97, 133–34
  piety, 66–67, 122–23
  Quintilian, 112–13
  Roman, 62–69
  Sallust, 69–70
  theological, 121, 123–24, 133–34
  See also example; piety; rhetor: moral character
voice, martyrial, 139–40

wisdom. *See* rhetor: prudence
witness, 54–59
word play. *See adnominatio*; etymology
worship of martyrs. *See* veneration

Writings Index

For the benefit of digital users, indexed terms that span two pages (e.g., 52–53) may, on occasion, appear on only one of those pages.

Old Testament
Genesis
   3:19, 26–27
Psalms
   26:4, 74–75
   43:1, 89
   44:22, 21
   64, 77
Proverbs
   29:2, 140

Intertestamental Literature
2 Maccabees
   7, 124
   7:27, 125

New Testament
Matthew
   5:10, 83, 90–92, 93–95
Luke
   21:19, 129
Romans
   8:36, 21
   13:3–4, 17
2 Corinthians
   4:18, 128
   8:9, 125, 128–29
Colossians
   2:30, 125, 128
1 Timothy
   6:7–8, 128–29
   6:17–19, 128–29
1 Peter
   2:13, 40–41
Revelation
   20:4, 130

Greek and Latin Works
Acts of the Scillitan Martyrs
   13–17, 9n.2

Ambrose
De Abraham
   2.10.76, 111n.8
De virginibus ad Marcellinam sororem libri tres
   1.2.5, 66–67n.16
   1.2.8, 66–67n.16
Apuleius
Apologia
   94, 111n.7
Aristotle
Ars rhetorica
   2.23.29, 54n.50
   3.9.8, 75n.31
Asterius
Homilia in sanctum martyrem Phocam
   1.1, 137n.1
   1.2–3, 138n.2
   2.1, 138n.3
   6.1, 139n.4
   8.3, 139n.5
Augustine
De ciuitate dei libri uiginti duo
   2.17, 66n.14
   2.18, 65n.13
   2.21, 122n.42
   4.30, 71n.22, 80n.41
   5.14, 66n.15, 68–69
   10.21, 70, 71–72
   10.32, 71n.23
   11.17, 30n.64
   19, 122
   19.24, 122n.43, 122n.44
   20, 130
   20.9, 130n.64
   22.5, 20n.40
   22.7, 132n.70
Confessionum libri tredecim
   1.16.25–26, 38n.13
   1.17.27, 118n.29

162 WRITINGS INDEX

Confessionum libri tredecim (cont.)
  3.2.2, 74n.26
  3.3.6, 119n.30
  4.2.2, 119n.31
  5.6.10, 119n.32
  6, 10–11
  6.2.2, 14–16
  9, 18–19
  9.7.16, 19n.38
Ad Cresconium grammaticum
    partis Donati
  3.47.51, 84n.3
De doctrina christiana
  1.14.13, 79n.40
  4, 120
  4.1.2, 120n.38
  4.4.6, 119n.35
  4.5.7, 120n.36
  4.27.59, 120n.39
  4.28.61, 120n.40
  4.29.61, 120n.41
Enarrationes in Psalmos
  34.2.1, 84n.3
  34.2.13, 91n.30, 94n.38
  34.2.13, 84n.3
  43.1, 94n.38
  45.1, 91n.30
  64.8, 77n.37
  68.1.9, 84n.3
  118.1.3, 91n.30
Epistulae
  22, 16–18
  22.1.6, 16n.29
  22.3, 17n.31, 17n.32, 17n.33
  22.4, 17n.34, 18n.35
  22.5, 18n.36
  44, 90
  44.2.4, 90n.27, 91n.30, 94n.39
  87.7, 91n.30, 94n.38
  89.2, 84n.3
  93.2, 89n.23
  93.2.8, 91n.30, 94n.38
  108.5, 84n.3
  108.5.14, 91n.30, 94n.38
  155, 121
  185, 99–103, 107–8
  185.2, 84n.3
  185.2.7, 103n.71
  185.2.8, 105n.75, 105n.76
  185.2.9, 89n.23, 91n.30, 106n.77
  185.2.9–11, 94n.40
  185.2.11, 106n.78, 107n.80
  185.3.13, 103n.72
  204, 100n.64
  204.4, 84n.1
Contra duas epistulas Pelagianorum
  4.2.2., 26n.55
Contra Faustum Manicheum libri
    trginta tribus
  5.8, 21n.44
  12.28, 21n.45
  14.1, 22n.46
  20.4, 22n.47
  20.21, 22n.48, 23n.49, 23n.50
Contra Gaudentium
  1.20.23, 91n.30
  1.30.35, 91n.30
  1.36.46, 94n.38
In Ioannis evangelium tractatus CXXIV
  3.21, 75n.30
  11.13, 106n.79
  88.2–3, 91n.30
Contra Iulianum opus imperfectum
  1.50, 25n.54
  1.106, 25n.53
  4.38, 28n.59
  6.27, 27n.56
  6.55, 28n.58
Contra litteras Petiliani libri tres
  2.23.51, 13n.21
  2.71.159, 90n.26
  2.84.186, 100n.61
  2.93.205, 96n.44
De moribus ecclesiae catholicae et de
    moribus Manicheorum libri duo
  1.7.12, 21n.42
  1.9.15, 21n.43
De musica libri sex
  6.11.30, 29n.63
De natura boni contra Manichaeos
  8, 79n.39
De ordine
  2.13.38, 119n.33
Retractiones
  2.48, 100n.62
De rhetorica, 86n.6

WRITINGS INDEX 163

Sermones ad populum
  53A.13, 84n.3
  94A.1, 84n.3
  273.1, 39n.14
  273.2, 44n.24
  273.3–4, 48n.36
  273.6, 56n.56
  274, 56n.57
  275.1, 130n.65
  275.3, 54n.52
  276.1, 42n.20
  277.3, 45n.25
  277A, 84n.3
  277A.1, 81n.42
  280–82, 10n.8
  280.1, 49n.38
  280.2, 133n.72
  282.1, 59n.61
  284.2, 48n.34
  285.2, 89n.23
  285.4, 43n.22
  285.6–7, 84n.3
  299, 24n.51
  299D–F, 9n.3
  299D.4, 125n.50, 125n.51, 126n.52, 128n.61
  299D.6, 127n.56
  299E.2, 40n.17
  299F.1, 56n.55
  299F.2, 55n.54
  299F.3, 45n.26
  299F.4, 46n.29
  300, 124
  300.6, 124n.48, 127n.55
  300.7, 125n.49, 128n.60
  301.2, 131n.66
  302.2, 45n.27
  303.1, 126n.53, 129n.62, 129n.63
  303.2, 127n.57
  305A.1, 46n.30
  306A, 84n.3
  306C.2–3, 57n.58
  307.1, 131n.67
  309.6, 126n.54, 127n.58
  310.2, 131n.69, 132n.71
  310.3, 127n.59, 133n.72
  311.1, 46n.31
  311.5, 47n.32
  313C.2, 58n.59
  313E.5, 41n.18
  314–21, 20n.41
  314.2, 58n.60
  315.8, 42n.19
  316.3, 40n.16
  318.1, 48n.37
  323–24, 20n.41
  325.1, 33n.2
  327, 84n.3
  328.2, 55n.53
  328.4, 84n.3, 90n.24
  328.8, 47n.33
  331.2, 84n.3
  335.2, 89n.23
  335B, 24n.51
  335C.5, 84n.3
  335C.12, 89n.23
  335D, 69, 73
  335D.3, 62n.1
  335G.2, 84n.3
Sermo ad Caesariensis ecclesiae plebem
  7, 94n.38
De sermon Domini in monte
  1.13, 94n.38
Basil of Caesarea
hom.Gord.
  1–2, 141n.8
Cicero
De inventione rhetorica
  1.2, 115–16
  1.2.2, 114n.19
  1.2.2–3, 114n.20
  1.11, 86n.8, 86n.11
  1.21.30, 28n.61
  2.40.116, 92n.32, 93n.35
  2.41.120, 92n.33
  2.41.121, 93n.34
  2.49.144, 88n.15
  2.50.151, 93n.36
  2.72, 98n.53, 98n.54
  2.77, 98n.56
  2.78, 97n.49, 98n.55
  2.83, 97n.52
De oratore
  1.8.30, 115n.21
  1.18, 63n.4
  1.201, 63n.4

WRITINGS INDEX

Partitiones oratoriae
   6.21, 77n.36
Pro Cluentio, 76
Pro Murena, 76
De republic
   2.48, 115n.22
   2.51, 116n.23
   2.67, 116n.24
   2.69, 117n.27
   5.5, 116n.25
   5.8, 117n.26
   6.8, 68n.19
   6.13, 68n.20
Codex Theodosianus
   16.5.38, 96n.46
   16.5.52–55, 100n.64
   16.6.3–5, 96n.46
Cyprian
Epistulae
   55, 11n.14
   64, 24–25
   76.1.2, 91n.28
   76.7.1, 91n.28
   77.2.2, 91n.28
Ad Fortunatum
   11, 66–67n.16
   11–13, 91n.28
   12, 91n.28
De lapsis
   4, 66–67n.16
   13, 66–67n.16
   20, 11n.15
De unitate ecclesiae, 12n.17
   18, 12n.18
   19, 91n.28
Demetrius
De elocutio
   23, 76n.33
Hermogenes
On Issues
   50, 99n.58
   73.2–9, 99n.59
Stas.
   37.8–14, 86n.11
Jerome
Epistulae
   69.8, 111n.9

John Chrysostom
Homilia in martyres
   1, 140n.6, 140n.7
Livy
Praefatio
   10, 64n.9
Optatus of Milevis
Contra Parmenianum Donatistam
   3.3, 96n.48
   appendices 4–7, 96n.43
Passion of Isaac and Maximian
   3, 13n.24
   6, 13n.25
Passio sanctarum Perpetuae et Felicitatis
   1, 10n.6
   3, 9n.5
   4, 10n.6
   6.4, 73n.25
   7–8, 10n.6
Pauline of Nola
Carminae
   19.18–19, 70n.21
   19.283, 66–67n.16
   21.129, 66–67n.16
Epistulae
   49.4, 66–67n.16
Petilian
conl.Carth.
   3.22, 13n.22, 84–85n.4, 95n.41
Plato
Cratylus
   393a, 52n.46
Prudentius
Peristephanon
   1.106–8, 72n.24
   2.505–8, 72n.24
   10.1088–90, 72n.24
Quintilian
Institutio oratoria
   2.5.1, 63n.5
   2.5.19, 63n.5
   2.15.1, 112n.15
   2.15.3, 112n.16
   2.15.33, 112n.17
   2.15.34, 113n.18
   5.10.33, 89n.21

5.10.34–35, 89n.22
5.10.36, 88n.17, 89n.19
5.10.59, 88n.17
5.11.7, 104n.73, 104n.74
5.12.14, 29n.62
7.3.1, 86n.9
7.3.21, 86n.11
7.3.23, 87n.13
7.3.23–24, 87n.13
7.3.24, 87n.12, 87n.13
7.4.8, 97n.50
7.4.9, 99n.57
7.8.1, 93n.37
9.3.32, 76n.35
9.3.66, 51n.44
9.3.82, 76n.34
10.1.34, 63n.6
12.proem.4, 111–12n.11
12.1.1, 112n.12
12.1.3, 112n.13
12.1.23, 112n.13
12.4.1, 63n.6
Rhetorica ad Herennium
  1.2.3, 28n.60
  4.21.29, 51n.43
  4.45.58, 76n.32

Sallust
Bellum Jugurthinum
  4.5–6, 64n.10
  4.7–8, 65n.12
Historiae
  1.11, 65n.13
Seneca the Elder
Controversiae
  1.praef.9, 111n.6
  4.7, 88n.16
Tertullian
Apologeticum
  50, 1n.1, 10n.12
De fuga in persecutione
  4, 10n.10
Ad martyras
  2, 91n.28
De patientia
  13.6, 10n.10
Scorpiace
  5.3, 10n.11
Ad uxorem
  1.3.4, 10n.10
Varro
De lingua latina
  7.4, 53n.48